Collins

AF513301

# Enhanced Science Now

## Revised Edition

*A Science Textbook based on Holistic Learning Theory*

# 6

Name : ..........................................................................................................

Grade : ............................. Section : ........................................................................

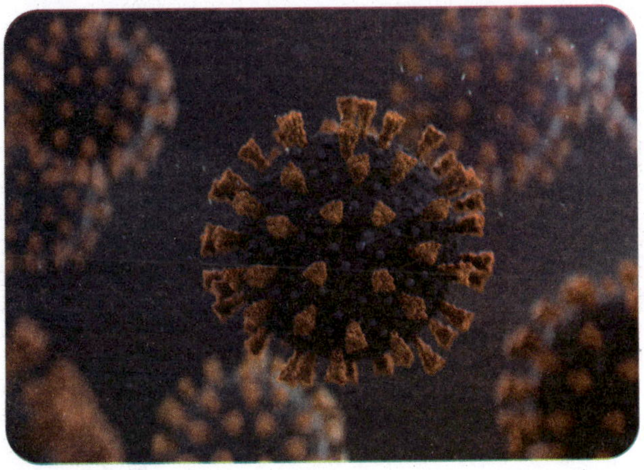

I am a virus that emerged in 2019, causing a global pandemic. My spread led to lockdowns, overwhelmed hospitals and disrupted lives. Humans worldwide wore masks, practised social distancing and developed vaccines. Through collective efforts, my impact lessened and the world worked together to overcome this unprecedented challenge.
What am I? .....................

**Series Editor | Geetha Iyer**

HarperCollins*Publishers*

*Publishing operations in 17 countries and 120+ imprints globally*

William Collins' dream of knowledge for all began with the publication of his first book in 1819. A self-educated mill worker, he not only enriched millions of lives, but also founded a flourishing publishing house. Today, staying true to this spirit, Collins books are packed with inspiration, innovation and practical expertise. They place you at the centre of a world of possibility and give you exactly what you need to explore it.

Published by Collins Learning
An imprint of HarperCollins*Publishers* India
Building No. 10, Tower A, 4th Floor, DLF Cyber City, Gurugram, Haryana 122002, India

First edition: 2025
Reprint: 10 9 8 7 6 5 4 3 2 1
ISBN: 9789365699869

Content developed by **Excelsoft Technologies Pvt Ltd.**
Artwork, typesetting and layout by **AptaraCorp Ltd., Mammoth Studioz Ltd, iBook Services**
Printed and bound in India by Saurabh Printers Pvt. Ltd.

**ACKNOWLEDGEMENTS**

**Title Page:** Yuichiro Chino

**Inside:** Page **5:** grafikazpazurem, Enis Aksoy, bsd studio; **6:** Qvasimodo, Qvasimodo; **7:** kbeis, lvenks, Abscent84, molotovcoketail, Bigmouse108; **8:** nongpimmy, denis_pc; **16:** Linda Holt Ayriss ; **17:** jopelka; **22:** WIN-Initiative, anand purohit, Les Hirondelles Photography, Janos Somodi; **23:** CR Shelare; **24:** lkpro, ArchMan, Napat, Chros; **25:** Photocrea, sandra standbridge, Mogens Trolle; **26-27:** EBFoto, moizhusein, paulrommer, vnlit, Henrik Larsson, sydeen; **37:** Eky Studio, Marques, karamysh, ChrisVanLennepPhoto, Denis Burdin; **39:** Andrzej Kubik, Galyna Andrushko; **41:** Sourabh Bharti; **43:** K. D. Kirchmeier; 56: Federica Grassi; **58:** Irina Cheremisinova; **59:** Paul Starosta, André Muller; **61:** colematt; **63:** ttsz; **64:** Aldona; **66:** Aldona; **67:** ttsz; **73:** skaman306, Aleksandr Zubkov, James Warwick, Brais Seara, ozgurcankaya, aghezzi; **74:** Arundhati Sathe, Максим Крысанов; **75:** chang, Hasan Ashari, VikramRaghuvanshi; **76:** kivoart, Jaromila; **77:** Veena Nair, Everyday better to do everything you love; **79:** ATU Images; **80:** Burke/Triolo Productions; **88:** Jogy Abraham, subodhsathe, ajaykampani, Bhaskar dhapu; **90:** Subas chandra Mahato, kiran nagare, Jogy Abraham; **91:** Hennadii; **97:** ranplett, Jose Luis Pelaez Inc, Saibal, DigiPub, SKashkin, Martin Deja, Jonathan Knowles; ; **99:** ifong, Olga Mishyna, after6pm, tenten10; **100:** Kristina Postnikova; **101:** Dan Kosmayer, Milkovasa; **103:** sa2324, ifong; **104:** iofoto, Laura Adamache; **105:** Mariusz Szczygiel; **109:** Image Source, hidesy; **114:** Pgiam, spooh, Inigo Cia, Zeiss4Me, sambrogio; **115:** Madlen; **117:** narong niamfoi, ssnjaytuturkhi, discpicture; **118:** ttsz; **122:** Brickclay; **126:** bogdan ionescu; **128:** Chadchai Ra-ngubpai, Nick Maslen, Lew Robertson, Jenny Dettrick, kaanates, R.Tsubin; **129:** photo5963, Winai Tepsuttinun, 154062188, urfin, SmileStudio, Suppakij1017; **132:** SmileStudio, Winai Tepsuttinun, Rob Byron; **133:** Udayakumar R; **136:** Ivan Zakalevych; **138:** appleuzr, Faizal A Rahiman; **143:** adventtr; **144:** designer29, Nadezhda Kurbatova, Mariya Parafeynikova, Oleg Vorontsov; **147:** adventtr; **148:** kyoshino, Vladyslav Danilin; **149:** Trinset; **159:** vlabo; ; **160:** ktynzq, magicoven, Bedrin, Ugorenkov Aleksandr, PeJo, Fedorov Oleksiy; **161:** Peter Sobolev; **165:** VectorMine, Nicku; **175:** AlexKol Photography; **178:** Mike Flippo, tiverylucky; **186:** pma2010; **188:** Rehman Asad; **192:** Pan Xunbin; **193:** Jelina Preethi, Nickolay Khoroshkov, Paolo Bona; **198:** THEPALMER; **199:** ekipaj; **202:** Energy Institute - Statistical Review of World Energy (2024); Smil (2017); **208:** Noongraphicstudio, DEV IMAGES; **209:** alxpin; **211:** Iryna Shek, sololos, dore art; **212:** dore art, Iryna Shorokhova, Luke Peterson Photography; **213:** seamartini; **214:** Universal History Archive / Contributor, NASA / Handout; **215:** Space Frontiers / Stringer, Cinefootage Visuals, @Niladri Nath, buradaki; **216:** Historical / Contributor; **217:** innavector; **218:** Universal History Archive / Contributor; **219:** Javier Zayas Photography; **224:** cybrain

**Supplementary Booklet:** Pia Kolle, Icon_Craft_Studio, Olesia Kononenko, Julia_Sudnitskaya, andegro4ka, AleksOrel, angkritth, AlionaManakova, KajaNi, amenic181, triloks, Warchi, Milan_Jovic, sarunyu_foto, eliflamra, sarunyu_foto, AlionaManakova, Iurii Garmash, Moppet, Kameleon007



Browse the complete Collins catalogue at www.collins.in.
For any queries/feedback, please write to us at SCHOOLSUPPORT@harpercollins.co.in.

# Preface

***Enhanced Science Now, Revised Edition*** is a transformative three-book series designed for Classes 6 to 8, aiming to provide students with a holistic and forward-looking learning experience. Embracing the principles of the **National Education Policy (NEP) 2020** and **National Curriculum Framework (NCF) 2023**, this series goes beyond traditional learning approaches to prepare students for the multifaceted challenges of the 21st century.

In this dynamic era, our students face both unprecedented challenges and opportunities that demand a deeper understanding of their role in shaping the world. As educators, we recognize the need to equip them with essential skills, knowledge and a growth mindset to navigate the complexities of modern life successfully.

Our series is founded on the principles of **Holistic Learning Theory**, guiding students to explore their identities, purpose and connection with the community and the environment. Through a strong core content in science, we foster intellectual, emotional, social, artistic, moral and spiritual development, nurturing well-rounded individuals who contribute positively to society.

Innovative features in the series encourage interdisciplinary projects, instill a scientific temper, promote vocational skills and cultivate regional and cultural sensitivities. The series prioritizes **Global Citizenship Education (GCED)** and emphasizes the value of **India's diverse knowledge systems**.

We extend our heartfelt gratitude to all the teachers and educationists who passionately reviewed our books and offered their invaluable feedback. Their contributions have elevated the quality of our content, which will enhance the overall learning experience for students.

Feedback, comments and suggestions from users are always welcome as we continue to strive for excellence in education and better serve the needs of our young learners. Together, let's shape a brighter future for education.

**Authors**

## About the Series Editor

**Dr Geetha Iyer** is the Former Head of Sahyadri School KFI, Pune. She is an author, a naturalist and consultant in the twin fields of education and environment. She is a curriculum specialist with many years of experience in concept development and regularly conducts workshops on all aspects of teaching science.

# Key Features

***Enhanced Science Now Revised Edition*** aligns with the **National Education Policy (NEP) 2020** and the **National Curriculum Framework (NCF) 2023**, promoting holistic education. It focuses on developing intellectual, physical, cognitive, emotional and social skills. With features such as Cognitive Corner, Life Skills, Worksheets and a Supplementary Booklet that contains STEAM Activities, Skills You Need, Happiness Activity Sheets, Vernacular Names, GCED and Assessments, it fosters experiential learning, innovative thinking and creativity. Additionally, the series raises awareness of the Sustainable Development Goals (SDGs) to address global challenges.

Learn more about SDGs at https://www.un.org/sustainabledevelopment/.

**Physical**

- Gross motor skills
- Psychomotor skills

- Projects
- STEAM Activities

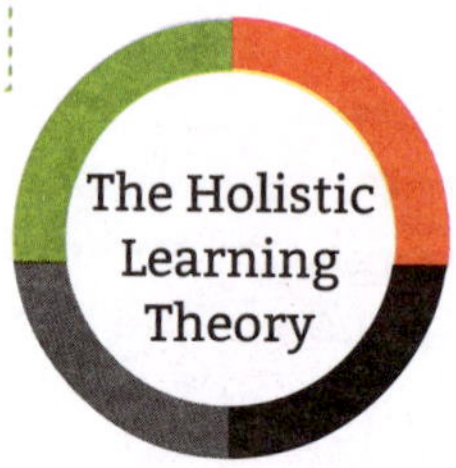


**Intellectual**

Bloom's Taxonomy

- Remembering
- Understanding
- Applying
- Analysing
- Evaluating
- Creating

- Summary
- Exercise

- Cognitive Corner
- Worksheet
- Skills You Need
- STEAM Activities

**Social**

- Coordination
- Working in a team
- Interaction with others
- Social competencies
- Communication with others

- Worksheets
- Vernacular Names
- Life Skills
- STEAM Activities

**Emotional**

- Empathy
- Self-regulation
- Interpersonal (others)
- Intra-personal (self)

- Life Skills
- Happiness Activity Sheets
- GCED

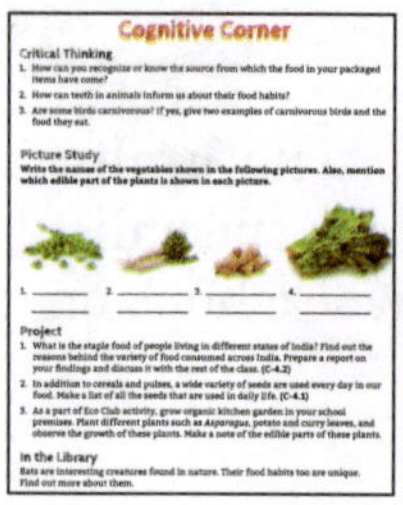

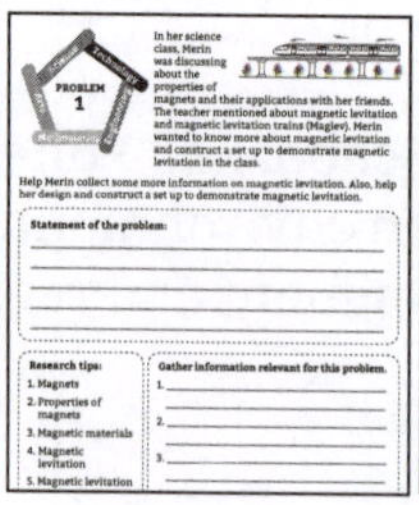

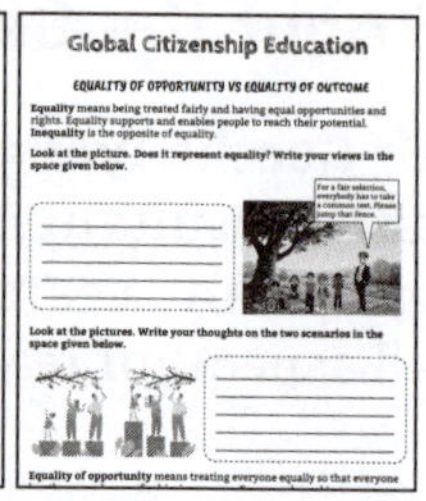


Collins Learning supports the Sustainable Development Goals

# Comprehensive Assessment

The assessment papers employ MCQs tagged with icons to indicate competencies such as Difficulty Levels, Bloom's Taxonomy and Science Learning Skills. Each assessment comes along with a scorecard for self-assessment.

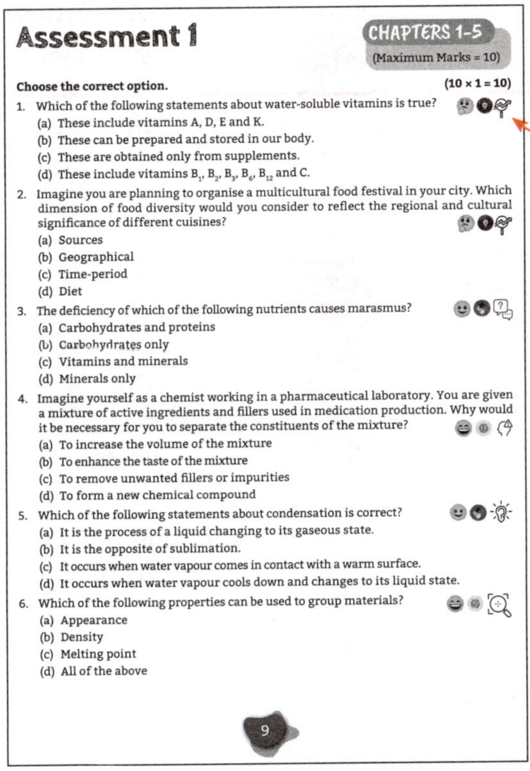

**Assessment 1** CHAPTERS 1-5 (Maximum Marks = 10)

**Choose the correct option.** (10 × 1 = 10)

1. Which of the following statements about water-soluble vitamins is true?
   (a) These include vitamins A, D, E and K.
   (b) These can be prepared and stored in our body.
   (c) These are obtained only from supplements.
   (d) These include vitamins $B_1$, $B_2$, $B_3$, $B_6$, $B_{12}$ and C.
2. Imagine you are planning to organise a multicultural food festival in your city. Which dimension of food diversity would you consider to reflect the regional and cultural significance of different cuisines?
   (a) Sources
   (b) Geographical
   (c) Time-period
   (d) Diet
3. The deficiency of which of the following nutrients causes marasmus?
   (a) Carbohydrates and proteins
   (b) Carbohydrates only
   (c) Vitamins and minerals
   (d) Minerals only
4. Imagine yourself as a chemist working in a pharmaceutical laboratory. You are given a mixture of active ingredients and fillers used in medication production. Why would it be necessary for you to separate the constituents of the mixture?
   (a) To increase the volume of the mixture
   (b) To enhance the taste of the mixture
   (c) To remove unwanted fillers or impurities
   (d) To form a new chemical compound
5. Which of the following statements about condensation is correct?
   (a) It is the process of a liquid changing to its gaseous state.
   (b) It is the opposite of sublimation.
   (c) It occurs when water vapour comes in contact with a warm surface.
   (d) It occurs when water vapour cools down and changes to its liquid state.
6. Which of the following properties can be used to group materials?
   (a) Appearance
   (b) Density
   (c) Melting point
   (d) All of the above

9

Icons

Scorecard

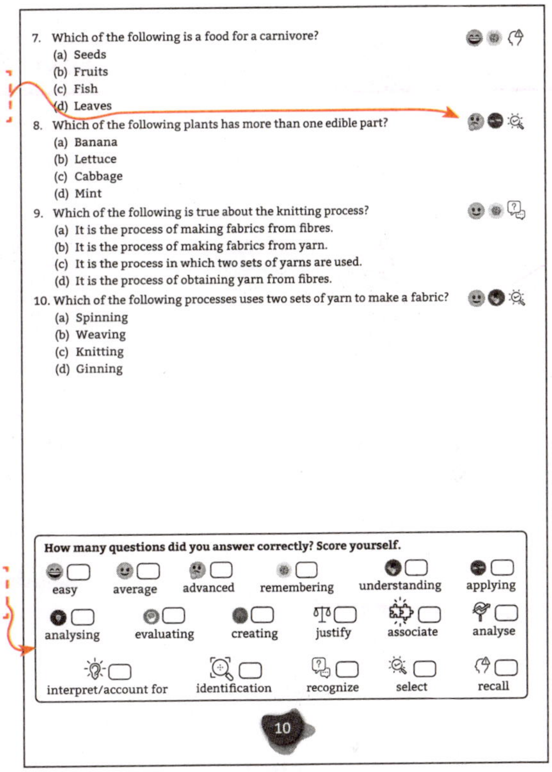

7. Which of the following is a food for a carnivore?
   (a) Seeds
   (b) Fruits
   (c) Fish
   (d) Leaves
8. Which of the following plants has more than one edible part?
   (a) Banana
   (b) Lettuce
   (c) Cabbage
   (d) Mint
9. Which of the following is true about the knitting process?
   (a) It is the process of making fabrics from fibres.
   (b) It is the process of making fabrics from yarn.
   (c) It is the process in which two sets of yarns are used.
   (d) It is the process of obtaining yarn from fibres.
10. Which of the following processes uses two sets of yarn to make a fabric?
   (a) Spinning
   (b) Weaving
   (c) Knitting
   (d) Ginning

**How many questions did you answer correctly? Score yourself.**

easy, average, advanced, remembering, understanding, applying
analysing, evaluating, creating, justify, associate, analyse
interpret/account for, identification, recognize, select, recall

10

# Competencies and Icons in Assessment Papers

## Difficulty levels

easy

average

advanced

## Bloom's Taxonomy

remembering

understanding

applying

analysing

evaluating

creating

## Science Learning Skills

justify

identification

associate

recognize

analyse

select

interpret/ account for

recall

# Contents


Wonders of Science 7

1. Plants Around Us 9

2. Animals Around Us 24

3. Biodiversity 37

4. Life Around Us 57

5. Components of Food 74

6. Materials Around Us 98

7. Methods of Separation 115

8. Measurement of Length and Motion 129

9. Temperature and Its Measurement 144

10. Magnets 160

11. Water and Its States 174

12. Natural Resources 189

13. The Universe 209

# Wonders of Science

Have you ever wondered why the sky is blue, how birds fly or what makes plants grow? Science is the key to unlocking these mysteries. The word science originates from the Latin word "scientia" which means knowledge.

**Science** is an organized way of studying things and finding answers to questions which includes gaining information from experiments and observation. It is not just about learning facts but about being curious and discovering how the world works. From floating leaves, flying balloons to sinking stones, and from magnets attracting iron nails to plants bending towards sunlight, science helps us explore the fascinating reasons behind these everyday wonders.

Why do we see objects appear to move when we are in a moving train? How do magnets pull some objects but not others? Why do we feel hotter in summer and colder in winter? Science guides us in finding answers to these questions and many more. It encourages us to observe, experiment and learn about the forces and phenomena that shape our lives.

Have you ever tasted salty seawater and wondered where the salt in your kitchen comes from? Or watched seeds sprout and asked how weather affects their growth? Science allows us to dive deeper into these questions, helping us understand everything from the preparation of our food to the natural processes that sustain life on Earth.

Blue sky and flying bees and birds

Floating leaves

Moving train

Flying balloons

Hot and cold weather

How do we learn about these amazing phenomena? Through science! Scientists use a process called the **scientific method** to explore the world around us. This method involves six key steps:

1. **Observation:** Science begins with careful observation. You might notice that ice melts faster in some liquids than others. This observation sparks curiosity and leads to a question.
2. **Formulating Questions and Gathering Information:** Science begins with curiosity, prompting questions such as why ice melts faster in salt water than in plain water. To understand this problem better, you gather information about how salt affects the temperature of water.
3. **Making a Hypothesis:** Based on what you have learned, you make a logical guess or prediction about what might happen. For example, you might predict that ice will melt faster in salt water because it makes the water colder.
4. **Conducting Experiments:** To test your prediction, you perform an experiment. You might place ice in both salt water and plain water to see which melts faster.
5. **Analysis:** After conducting the experiment, you analyse the results. You carefully examine the data to see if it supports your hypothesis.
6. **Drawing Conclusions:** After observing the results, you determine whether your prediction was correct. If the ice melts faster in salt water, you have discovered something new!

In your science class, you will use these steps to explore the wonders of our world.

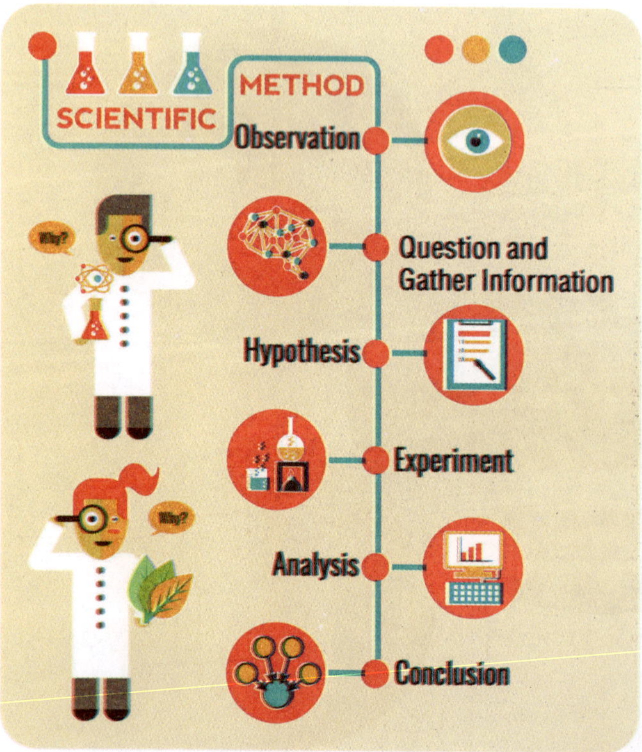


From why ice melts to how plants grow towards light, every experiment is an adventure in discovery. Get ready to ask questions, conduct experiments and uncover the secrets of the world around you. Welcome to the exciting journey of science!

# 1 Plants Around Us

## Curricular Goals

- Explore the living world in scientific terms **(CG-3)**
- Develop sensitivity towards the natural environment **(CG-4)**
- Explore the nature and processes of science through engaging with the evolution of scientific knowledge and conducting scientific inquiry **(CG-6)**
- Communicate own questions, observations and conclusions related to science **(CG-7)**

## Competencies

- Analyse patterns of relationship between living organisms and their environment in terms of dependence on and response to each other **(C-3.3)**
- Observe and describe the diversity among plants in their immediate environment **(C-4.1)**
- Formulate questions using scientific terminology and collect data that is usable as evidence **(C-6.2)**
- Use scientific vocabulary to communicate science accurately in oral and written form, and through visual representation **(C-7.1)**
- Design and build simple models to demonstrate scientific concepts **(C-7.2)**

## Let's Get Started

Plants are an essential part of our natural environment. They provide us with oxygen, food, shelter and numerous other resources.

Observe the given picture of a plant carefully and label its parts.

Plants exist in a wide variety of forms, shapes and sizes. They are categorized into different groups such as trees, herbs, shrubs, climbers and creepers based on their characteristics. The categorization helps us to study and understand the vast diversity of plant life on the Earth.

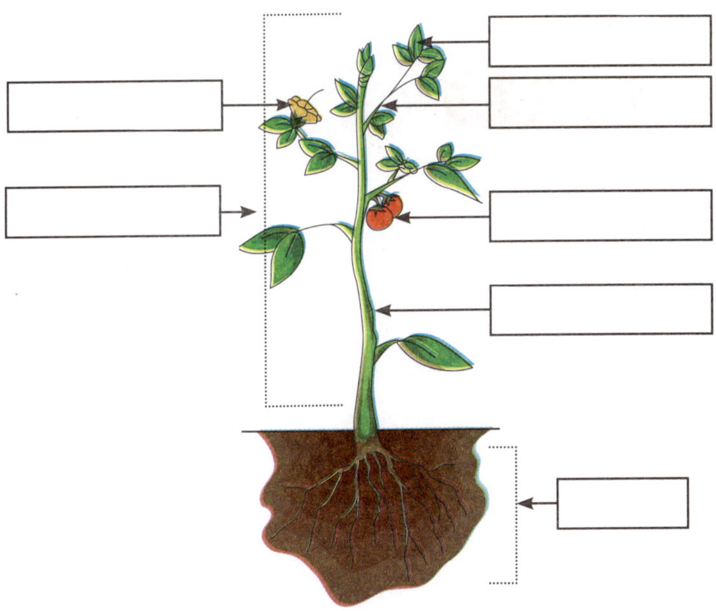

Parts of a plant

# ROOT SYSTEM

a

The parts of the plant found below the ground are called the **root system**. Root is the underground part of a plant. Roots help in holding or anchoring the plant firmly to the soil. They also absorb nutrients and water from the soil to keep the plant alive. Some roots store food in them.

The root, its branches, root hair and root cap together constitute the root system.

## Types of Root System

Root systems are of different types. The two main types of root systems are discussed here.

- **Taproot system:** In this type of root system, there is a **primary root** or **main root**, from which **lateral roots**[1] emerge (Fig. 1.1).

  When a seed germinates, a single root grows downward, developing into the main root and the lateral roots branch out from it.

  Taproots grow deep into the soil. Some examples of plants with taproot system are *Hibiscus* (shoe flower), oleander (rose bay), mango, oak, rose and pumpkins

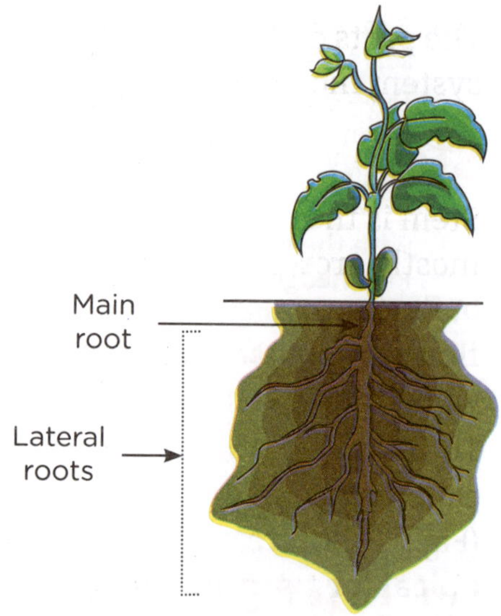


**Fig. 1.1:** The taproot system

**Word Web**

[1]**Lateral roots:** roots that grow from the main root in the soil

- **Fibrous root system:** In this root system, the root that emerges from the seed during germination dies and is replaced by several roots that emerge from a common point from the lowermost tip of the stem (Fig. 1.2).

  There is no main root. The cluster of roots spreads out in the soil, giving support to the plant.

  Fibrous roots do not grow very deep into the soil. As they have the appearance of fibres, this root system is called the fibrous root system.

  A few examples of plants with fibrous root system are maize, wheat, bamboo, sugarcane, coconut and palm trees.

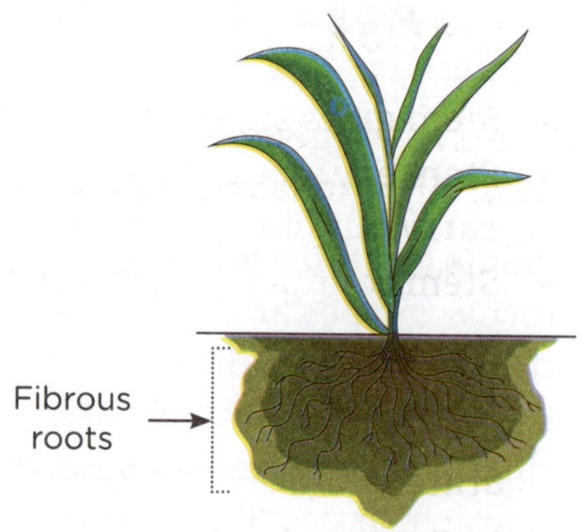


**Fig. 1.2:** The fibrous root system

## Functions of Roots

- Roots anchor the plant by fixing it firmly to the soil.
- Roots help plants to absorb water and nutrients from the soil in order to survive.
- Roots help bind the soil particles together, thereby preventing soil erosion.

## SHOOT SYSTEM

The parts of a plant that are above the ground are called the **shoot system**. The shoot system includes stems, leaves, flowers, fruits, etc.

### Stem

Stem is the part of the plant that is seen above the ground and mostly grows vertically upwards. Stems bear branches, leaves, buds, flowers, fruits and seeds. The stem exposes the leaves, flowers and branches to sunlight. It also supports the plants when the branches become too heavy.

The part of the stem from where the branches and leaves arise is called **node**. The part between two nodes is called the **internode** (Fig. 1.3). There are two types of **buds** seen on stems. They are **apical (or terminal) buds** and **axillary buds**. These two types of buds are necessary for the growth of plants. The stem conducts water from the roots to the leaves and other plant parts and food from the leaves to other parts of the plant.

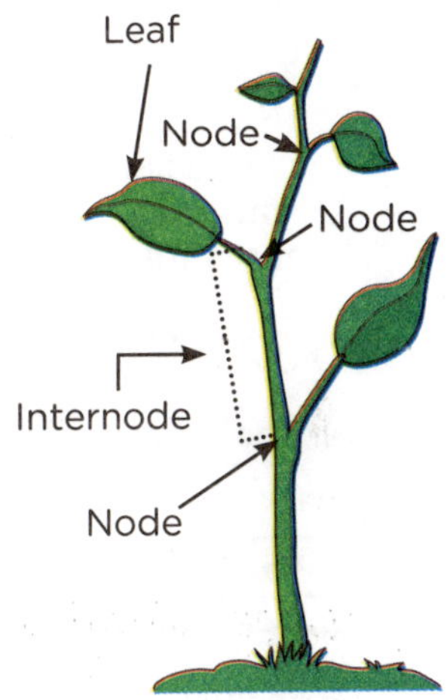

**Fig. 1.3:** Nodes and internode in a stem

## Functions of the Stem

- Stem gives support to the entire plant and its parts.
- Stem exposes the leaves, flowers and branches to sunlight to get nutrients and to carry out photosynthesis and other functions.
- Stem conducts water and food to different parts of the plant.

### Revise and Recall

**State whether the following statements are true (T) or false (F).**

1. Roots help in anchoring the plant firmly to the soil.
2. Fibrous roots grow deep into the soil like taproots.
3. The stem conducts water from the leaves to the roots.
4. The shoot system includes roots and stems.
5. Taproots have a main root with lateral roots branching out.

## Activity 1.1: Grouping of Plants Based on Height and Nature of Stem

**Aim:** To observe and group plants based on their height and nature of their stems

**Materials required:** Notebook and pen, measuring tape or ruler, chart paper and markers

**Procedure:**

1. Go on a nature walk in a garden, park or any area with diverse plant life.
2. Observe various plants and record your findings in your notebooks (plant name, plant height, stem colour and flexibility).
3. To categorize the plant height, measure the plant using a measuring tape or ruler. (Note: Less than 1 metre is short, between 1 to 4 metres is medium, greater than 4 metres is tall.) For plants whose height varies with support, such as climbers, note the climbing extent and label it as 'variable height'. If the plant spreads horizontally or grows along the ground, such as creepers, measure the spread and categorize it as 'spreading or shorter'.
4. Observe the colour of the stem (brown or green). Gently touch and try to bend the stem. Note whether the stem can be easily bent or is stiff.
5. Record your observations in the table given below.

**Observation Table:**

| Plant Name | Height | Stem Colour | Stem Flexibility | Grouping |
|---|---|---|---|---|
| Mint Plant | | Green | Herb | |
| Rose Bush | | | Can be bent | Shrub |
| Mango Tree | | Brown | Stiff | Tree |
| Money Plant | | | | |
| Pumpkin Vine | Shorter | | | |

**Group Discussion:** Discuss the differences observed among herbs, shrubs, trees, climbers and creepers. Discuss how these observations and grouping can be applied in areas such as gardening, agriculture and environmental science.

**Inference:** Based on the data collected, infer the characteristics of herbs, shrubs, trees, climbers and creepers.

- **Herbs:** Short plants that can be bent and branches arising close to the ground.
- **Shrubs:** Medium-height plants with woody or semi-woody stems.
- **Trees:** Tall plants with hard, thick, brown and woody stems.
- **Climbers:** Plants that rely on external support to grow and usually have flexible stems.
- **Creepers:** Plants that spread along the ground, usually have flexible stems that do not support upright growth.

**Conclusion:** Plants can be grouped into herbs, shrubs, trees, climbers and creepers based on their height and stem characteristics.

# LEAVES

Leaves arise from the nodes of stems and branches. The leaves of most plants are green in colour due to the presence of chlorophyll, a pigment which is essential for photosynthesis. However, some plants have leaves of other colours such as red or yellow. The leaves of different plants differ in size and shape.

Look at Figure 1.4, you will see the following structures in a leaf.

**Petiole:** The petiole is the stalk of the leaf. It attaches the leaf to the stem or branch. Leaves in some plants do not have petioles.

**Lamina:** The flat part of the leaf is called leaf blade or lamina.

**Midrib:** The central vein or the main vein of the leaf is called the midrib. It is the extension of the stalk or petiole into the leaf.

**Fig. 1.4:** Parts of a leaf

**Veins:** Veins may be seen as thin lines on the leaf. They are branches of the main vein (midrib).

The arrangement of veins on the lamina of a leaf is called **venation**. Two types of venations are seen in plants.

**Reticulate venation:** The net-like arrangement of veins seen in the leaves of rose and *Hibiscus* plants is called reticulate venation (Fig. 1.4). These leaves have a broad lamina and a petiole.

**Parallel venation:** The parallel arrangement of veins seen in the leaves of maize and wheat plants is called parallel venation (Fig. 1.5). These leaves have a smooth and long lamina.

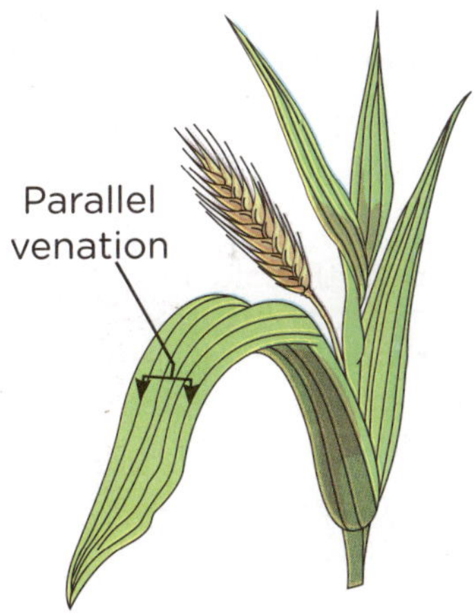


**Fig. 1.5:** Parallel venation

## Functions of Leaves

- Food is prepared in green leaves and stored as starch.

  $$\text{Carbon dioxide} + \text{Water} \xrightarrow[\text{Sunlight}]{\text{Chlorophyll}} \text{Glucose} + \text{Oxygen} + \text{Water}$$

- Plants breathe through stomata present on their leaves.
- Transpiration is another important function of leaves. It is the process by which plants get rid of excess water in the form of water vapour through their stomata.

## FLOWERS

Flowers contain male and female reproductive parts, and hence they are known as the reproductive organ of a plant. When you observe a flower closely, either through the naked eye or using a hand lens, you will be able to observe the following parts in the flower (Fig. 1.6).

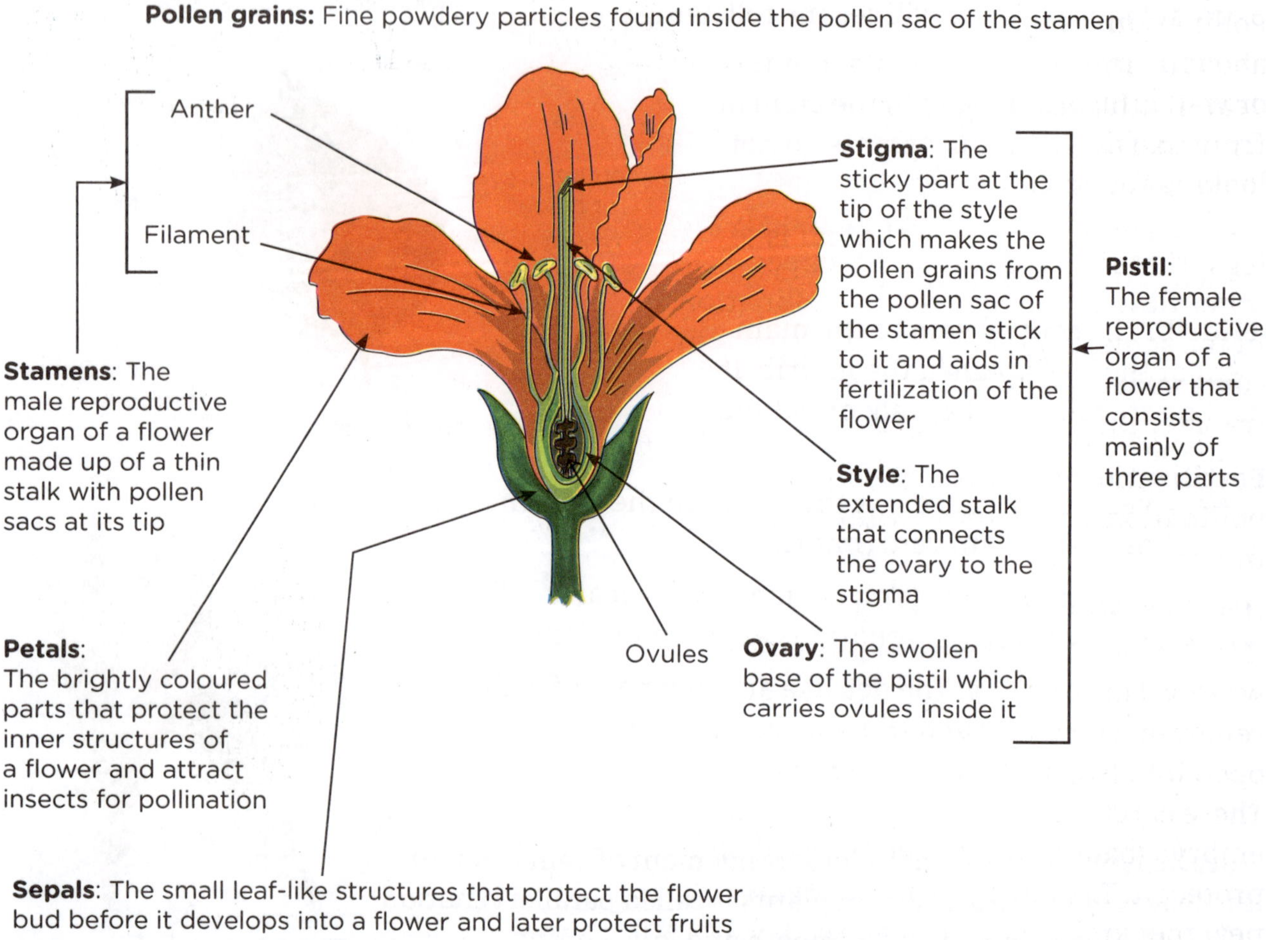


**Fig. 1.6: Structure of a flower**

### Science in Context

In some fruits such as pineapple and strawberry, several flowers (each with an ovary) develop into small fruits. These are clustered or fused together to form a larger fruit.

## Pollination

*The transfer of pollen grains from the anther to the stigma of a flower is called* ***pollination****.* Pollination is mainly brought about by insects (Fig. 1.7), wind or water. Insects always move from one flower to the other looking for nectar. When they sit on flowers, pollens stick to their body and legs. These pollens then get dropped onto other flowers, thereby aiding pollination. In the same way, wind and water currents carry pollens from place to place and transfer them to the stigma of flowers.

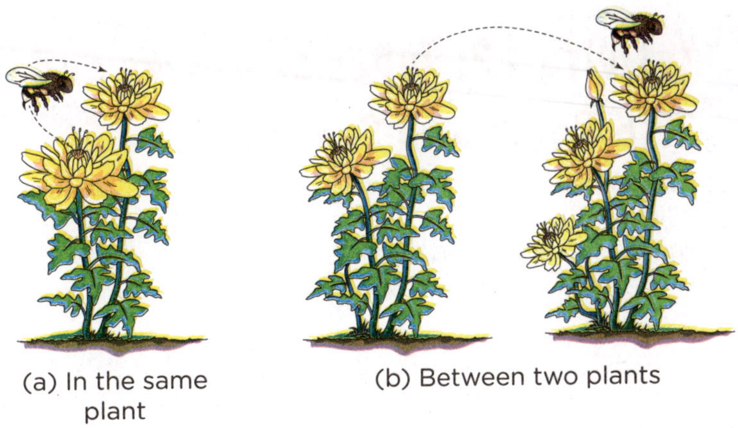


**Fig. 1.7:** Pollination by insects

**Word Web**

[1]**Fertilization:** the process by which the male gamete, located in the pollen grain, fuses with the female gamete, present in the ovule, leading to the development of a seed

**Fertilization**[1] takes place soon after pollination; as a result, ovules change into seeds.

If you observe a bean seed carefully (Fig. 1.8), you will be able to see a seed coat wrapped around it. When this seed coat is removed, you will see that the seed can be split open into two parts, which are the cotyledons. These cotyledons store food for the developing embryo (baby plant) inside the seed and protect it. The embryo will later grow into a new root and a shoot. Not all seeds have two cotyledons or a seed coat that can be separated so easily. A maize seed has only one cotyledon and its seed coat cannot be removed easily.

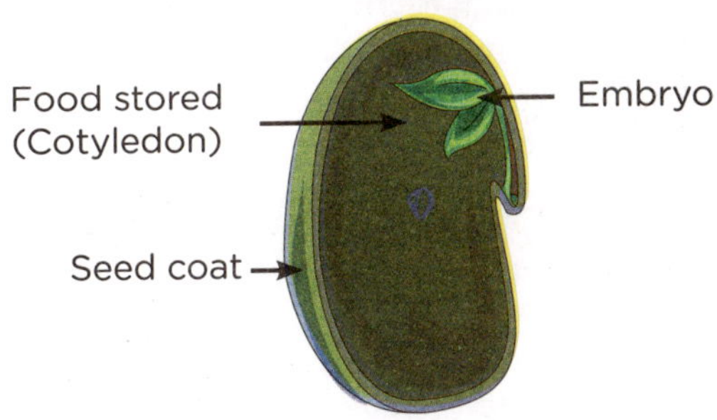


**Fig. 1.8:** Parts of a seed

In flowering plants (Fig. 1.9), the ovaries ripen into matured fruits, which are either dried up or fleshy, containing the seed inside and a pericarp that forms the outer covering of the matured ovary.

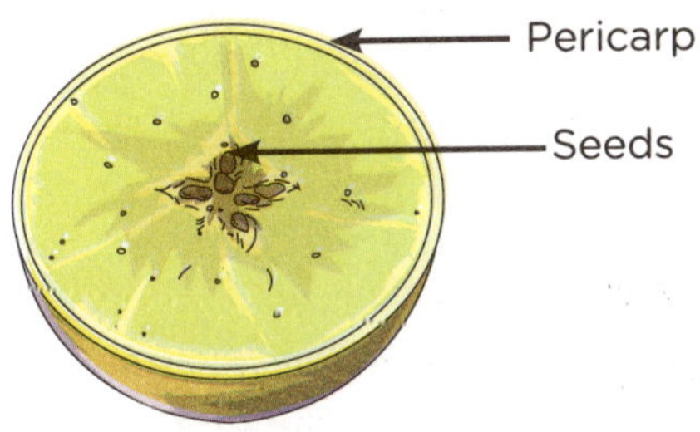


**Fig. 1.9:** Parts of a fruit (matured ovary) in flowering plants

## Activity 1.2: Types of Leaves and Their Relationship with Roots and Seeds

**Aim:** To explore different types of leaves and to link these characteristics with types of roots and seeds

**Materials required:** Notebook and pen, plant samples or access to a garden/park, chart paper, markers and magnifying glasses (optional)

**Procedure:**

1. Go on a nature walk in a garden, park or any area with diverse plant life.
2. Observe various plants and record your findings in your notebook.
3. For each plant, observe and record the leaf arrangement on the stem and branches.
4. Examine the leaf venation pattern and determine if it is reticulate or parallel.
5. Observe the root system if possible, or discuss the typical root type for the plant.
6. Identify the type of seed the plant produces, if known.
7. Use magnifying glasses for a closer look if needed.
8. Record your observations in the table below by writing down the plant names and their characteristics based on what you see in your surroundings.

Imperial Crimson Lily

**Observation Table:**

Few examples are given. You may fill the plant name and the characteristics based on what you see or find in your surroundings.

| Plant Name | Leaf Arrangement | Venation | Root Type | Seed Type |
|---|---|---|---|---|
| Rose | Alternate | Reticulate | Taproot | Dicot |
| Grass | Parallel | | | |
| Mango Tree | | Reticulate | | Dicot |
| Imperial Crimson Lily | Whorled | | Fibrous | Monocot |
| Bean Plant | Opposite | | Taproot | |
| Maize | | Parallel | Fibrous | |

**Group Discussion:** Present your findings. Discuss the differences observed in leaf arrangement and venation patterns. Talk about the correlation between leaf venation, root type and seed type (monocots *vs* dicots).

**Inference:** Based on the data collected, infer the characteristics of monocots and dicots.

- **Monocots:** Parallel venation, fibrous roots, one cotyledon
- **Dicots:** Reticulate venation, taproots, two cotyledons

**Conclusion:** Plants can be classified based on their leaf arrangement, venation patterns, root types and seed types. These characteristics are important in plant identification and understanding plant diversity.

## Activity 1.3: Grouping Plants Based on Production of Flowers, Fruits and Seeds

**Aim:** To group plants based on whether they produce flowers, fruits and seeds

**Materials required:** Notebook and pen, plant samples or access to a garden/park, chart paper and markers, plant identification guide (optional) and magnifying glasses (optional)

**Procedure:**

1. Go on a nature walk in a garden, park or any area with diverse plant life.
2. Observe various plants and record your findings in your notebook.
3. For each plant, check for the presence of flowers, fruits and seeds.
4. Use magnifying glasses for a closer look if needed.
5. Record observations about the presence or absence of these features in the table given below.

Mustard

**Observation Table:**

| Plant Name | Presence of Flowers (Yes/No) | Type of Flower | Presence of Fruits (Yes/No) | Presence of Seeds (Yes/No) |
|---|---|---|---|---|
| Orchids | Yes | Star-like shape, pink in colour and scented | Yes | Yes |
| Mustard | Yes | Cross-shaped, yellow in colour and scented | Yes | Yes |
| Ferns | No | | No | No |
| | | | | |
| | | | | |
| | | | | |

**Group Discussion:** Present your findings. Discuss the differences observed between flowering and non-flowering plants. Talk about the reproductive processes of both types of plants, highlighting how seeds are produced and spread.

**Inference:** Based on the data collected, infer the characteristics of flowering and non-flowering plants.

- **Flowering Plants:** Produce flowers and bear seeds within fruits.
- **Non-flowering Plants:** Do not produce flowers.

**Conclusion:** Plants can be grouped into flowering and non-flowering categories based on their reproductive structures and processes.

## Know the Scientist

**Dr M. S. Swaminathan**

**(7 August 1925–28 September 2023)**

Dr Mankombu Sambasivan Swaminathan was a renowned Indian agronomist and geneticist, celebrated as the "Father of the Green Revolution in India" for his pivotal role in developing high-yielding wheat and rice varieties, which significantly boosted India's food production in the 1960s and 1970s. His efforts greatly enhanced food security and alleviated hunger in the country. In 1987, he received the inaugural World Food Prize and used the prize money to establish the M.S. Swaminathan Research Foundation in Chennai. He was posthumously awarded the Bharat Ratna, India's highest civilian honour, in 2024. Dr Swaminathan was also recognized by the UN for promoting sustainable agricultural practices.

## Revise and Recall

**A. Fill in the blanks.**

1. The part of the leaf that attaches it to the stem is called the __________.
2. The flat part of the leaf is called the __________.
3. The net-like arrangement of veins seen in rose and *Hibiscus* leaves is called __________ venation.
4. The green colour of leaves is due to the presence of the pigment __________.
5. The process by which plants get rid of excess water is called __________.

**B. State whether the following statements are true (T) or false (F).**

1. The petals of a flower are responsible for attracting insects for pollination.
2. The stigma is the sticky part at the tip of the style that helps in pollination.
3. After fertilization, the ovules change into fruits.
4. The cotyledons of a seed store food for the developing embryo.
5. Pollination is the process of transferring pollen grains from the stigma to the anther.

## Keywords

**Nodes:** The part of the stem from where the branches and leaves grow

**Internode:** The portion of the stem between two nodes

**Creepers:** Weak-stemmed plants that grow by spreading horizontally on the ground

**Climbers:** Weak-stemmed plants that grow upright by taking support from nearby objects or other plants

**Reticulate venation:** Veins that are arranged in a net-like pattern in a leaf

**Parallel venation:** Veins that run parallel to one another from the base to the tip of the leaf

**Pollination:** The transfer of pollen grains from the anther to the stigma of a flower

## Summary

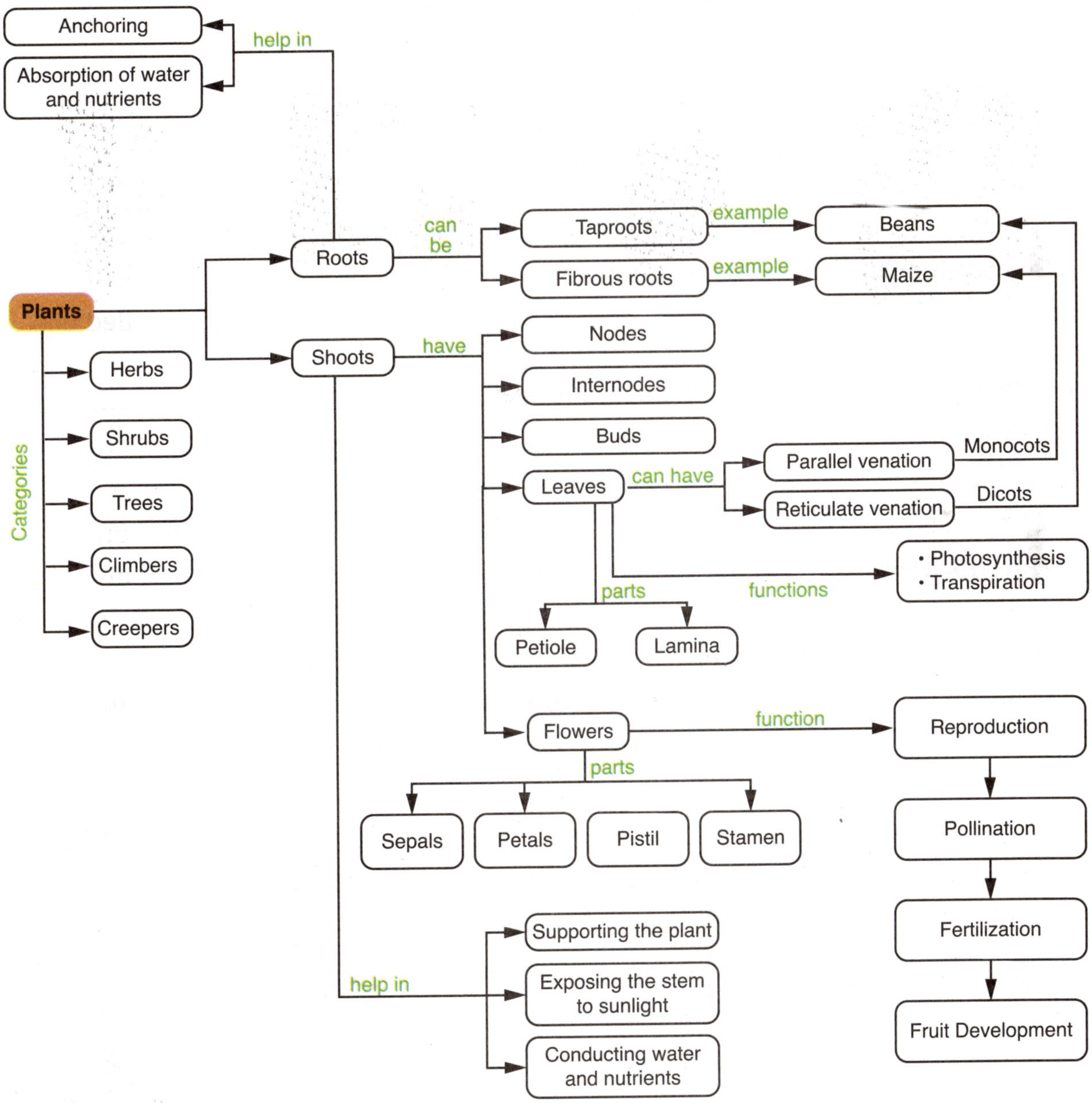

# Exercise

W

ia

**A. Choose the correct option.**

1. Identify the part of the plant that carries both nutrients and water to the entire plant.
   (a) Stem (b) Roots (c) Leaves (d) Flowers
2. Which one of the following is not a function of the roots?
   (a) Roots anchor the plant in the soil.
   (b) Roots draw up water and nutrients from the soil.
   (c) Roots prepare food for the plant.
   (d) Some roots store food for the plant.
3. The main function of the stem is to __________.
   (a) conduct water and food (b) absorb water and nutrients
   (c) prepare food (d) anchor the plant
4. Which of the following is not a characteristic feature of shrubs?
   (a) Short height
   (b) Woody stem
   (c) Multiple branches arising from the base
   (d) Soft, non-woody stems
5. Which of the following is not a part of a flower?
   (a) Style (b) Sepals (c) Ovules (d) Roots

**B. Fill in the blanks.**

ia

1. The stem gets water from the __________. (roots/flowers)
2. The part of the plant that prepares food is the __________. (leaf/root)
3. The portion of the stem between two nodes is the __________. (internode/flower)
4. Plants with __________ venation usually have __________ cotyledons. (parallel/reticulate/one/two)
5. The female reproductive part of a flower is called __________. (pistil/stamen)

**C. State whether the following statements are true (T) or false (F).**

ia

1. All plants have leaves with parallel venation.
2. In a taproot system, there is one main root and several lateral roots.
3. The stem can only conduct water and minerals upward in the plant.
4. Pollination in flowers takes place only by wind or water.
5. Apical buds are responsible for the growth of the plant.

**D. Give one example for each of the following.**

1. A tree ____________________
2. A plant with taproot system ____________________
3. A plant with fibrous root system ____________________
4. A monocot plant ____________________
5. A dicot plant ____________________

**E. Give reasons for the following.**

1. Roots are important for preventing soil erosion.
2. Fibrous roots do not grow very deep into the soil.
3. The stem is important for exposing leaves to sunlight.
4. Some plants and trees have taproots.
5. Pollination is crucial for the formation of seeds in flowering plants.

**F. Answer the following questions briefly.**

1. What is the main function of roots in a plant?
2. How does the fibrous root system differ from the taproot system?
3. Why are stems important for the survival of a plant?
4. What is venation, and how does it differ between maize and rose leaves?
5. What happens to ovules after fertilization in flowering plants?

**G. Answer the following questions.**

1. Describe the functions of roots in plants. Explain how they help in the plant's survival.
2. Explain the process of pollination and its significance in the life cycle of flowering plants.
3. Compare and contrast the structure and function of taproots and fibrous roots. Provide examples of plants for each type.
4. What are the main components of a leaf, and how do they contribute to the process of photosynthesis?
5. Discuss the different parts of a flower and their roles in reproduction. How do flowers attract pollinators?

# Cognitive Corner

## Critical Thinking

1. Imagine you are a bee visiting a garden full of colourful flowers. Why would you frequently visit flowers of different colours? How do your visits help the flowers grow and produce seeds? Does the colour of a flower matter to you as a bee?
2. Scientists have found that plant diversity increased on the Earth with the evolution of insects. Do you think it is true?

## Picture Study

**Write R for reticulate and P for parallel venation in the pictures of leaves given below. Then, identify the plant as monocot or dicot. What type of root system would each have?**

Maize leaves

☐

*Hibiscus* leaf

☐

Rose leaf

☐

Banana leaf

☐

## Project

A greenhouse is a small house or a nursery where plants are grown. The climate inside the greenhouse is controlled to provide the optimum temperature for the growth of plants. The greenhouse is mainly used to grow plants for medicinal research. As a part of the Eco Club activity, make a class trip to a greenhouse and observe the plants growing there. Prepare a report on the information collected. Use the information to design and build models that demonstrate the scientific principles behind greenhouse gardening. **(C-7.2)**

## In the Library

Find out which plant bears the largest flower. Collect some information on the notable characteristics of this plant. **(C-6.2)**

(*Hint*: The flower gives out smell of rotten flesh.)

## In the Laboratory

Take a radish and cut it along its length to get two equal halves. Place the cut portions vertically in a glass with red/blue ink. Take it out after a day and observe after washing. The red/blue spots seen on the radish are special cells that conduct water up the root. Find out more about these cells. **(C-7.2)**

## Life Skills

Growing plants in a garden or in pots not only helps us to understand the value of plants in our lives but also help us to keep in touch with nature. Plants help us in many ways and make our lives more sustainable. Have you ever grown a plant? How do you feel if it grows well? What do you do to ensure it flowers? If you have not grown any plant, try growing one and find out the answers to the above questions. **(C-6.2)**

# Worksheet

Vrikshayurveda, that comes from two Sanskrit words *vriksha* meaning "tree" and *ayurveda* meaning "science of longevity", is the ancient Indian science of plant life. It is a comprehensive treatise on plant life that covers topics such as procuring, preserving and treating seeds before planting; preparing pits for planting saplings; selection of soil; method of watering; nourishments and fertilizers; plant diseases and plant protection from internal and external diseases; and so on. Vrikshayurveda recognizes the fact that our very existence depends upon plants and places a lot of emphasis on planting trees.

Banyan tree

A. Read more about the Vrikshayurveda and write your findings in the space given below.

B. How relevant is Vrikshayurveda in today's time? Elaborate.

C. Make a poster with catchy slogans encouraging people to plant more trees.

# 2 Animals Around Us

## Curricular Goals

- Explore the living world in scientific terms **(CG-3)**
- Communicate own questions, observations and conclusions related to science **(CG-7)**

## Competencies

- Describe the diversity of living organisms observed in the natural surroundings **(C-3.1)**
- Analyse patterns of relationship between living organisms and their environment in terms of dependence on and response to each other **(C-3.3)**
- Use scientific vocabulary to communicate science accurately in oral and written form, and through visual representation **(C-7.1)**

## Let's Get Started

Match the animals with their correct movements.

1.  (a) Hopping

2.  (b) Swimming

3.  (c) Flying

4.  (d) Crawling

Animals are fascinating creatures that live in all sorts of places and eat different kinds of food. Based on this, animals show different types of movement and locomotion.

## WHERE DO ANIMALS LIVE?

Animals can live in many different environments, depending on their needs. Some inhabit dense forests where they find food and shelter among the trees, while others thrive in hot, dry deserts by adapting to scarce water. In the vast oceans, many creatures swim and find their food underwater. While the cold, rugged mountains are home to animals specially adapted to the challenging terrain. In the wide-open grasslands, animals roam freely, hunting or grazing on the abundant vegetation.

## WHY DO ANIMALS MOVE?

Animals move from one place to another for various reasons. One of the main reasons is related to their need for food, shelter, avoiding predators and reproduction.

## Food Habits of Animals

a

Different animals have different food habits. Depending on their food habits, they are grouped into three main types—**herbivores**, **carnivores** and **omnivores**.

### Herbivores

*Animals that eat only plants or plant parts are called* ***herbivores***. Horses, deer and rabbits are a few examples of herbivores. They have four sharp teeth in the front (Fig. 2.1) which they use to cut the plant materials such as grass. Their innermost teeth are large, flat and and ridged to help them crush and grind the plant materials.

Some birds are herbivores. They eat nuts, berries, fruits, seeds, etc. Their beaks are hard enough to break open the seeds, nuts and fruits.

Butterflies (Fig. 2.2) and honeybees feed on nectar of flowers. They have a special mouth part (called **proboscis**) that helps them suck the nectar from flowers without damaging the flowers.

**Fig. 2.1:** Teeth arrangement in herbivores

**Fig. 2.2:** Butterfly sucking the nectar of a flower

## Carnivores

*A carnivore is an organism that primarily eats meat*. Tigers, lions and leopards are a few examples of carnivores. They have sharp, pointed teeth (Fig. 2.3) for tearing the flesh of animals.

Carnivores such as snakes, frogs and chameleons do not tear flesh, they swallow the entire animal.

Frogs (Fig. 2.4) and chameleons have long, sticky tongue to catch insects. When they see an insect nearby, they shoot out their tongue, catch the insect and roll it back into their mouth.

**Fig. 2.3:** Teeth arrangement in carnivores

**Fig. 2.4:** Frog feeding on an insect using its tongue

Some carnivores are described as scavengers and cannibals.
Some plants are also carnivores. For example, pitcher plant captures insects and small animals for food.

## Scavengers

*Animals that eat the remains of dead or decomposing animals are called* ***scavengers***. They help in cleaning the environment by consuming the remains of dead animals which emit foul smell and can be a source of many diseases. Vultures, crows, foxes and hyenas are a few examples of scavengers (Fig. 2.5).

Crow

Hyena

**Fig. 2.5:** Scavengers

## Cannibals

*Animals that feed on individuals of their own kind are called* ***cannibals***. Some spiders (Fig. 2.6) are examples of cannibals.

**Fig. 2.6:** Cannibal: Spider

## Omnivores

*Animals that eat both plants and animals are called* ***omnivores***. Bears, hedgehogs, rats, dogs and crows are a few examples of omnivores.

## Decomposers

*Organisms that feed on the decaying plant and animal matter are called* ***decomposers.*** Organisms such as bacteria and fungi are examples of decomposers. Like scavengers, decomposers also help to keep the environment clean.

### Science in Context

Bacteria and fungi decompose food items by chemically breaking them with the help of enzymes in a way, so that the decomposed food can be absorbed directly. Worms, millipedes and other such soil-dwelling animals feed on decomposing food. Thus, worms and millipedes are called **detritivores**.

## Parasites

*Organisms that live on or inside the body of other living beings for food are called* ***parasites***. The organism they depend on for food are called **hosts**. Most parasites harm their hosts. Mosquitoes, leeches, hookworms and tapeworms are a few examples of parasites (Fig. 2.7).

Mosquito Leech Tapeworm

**Fig. 2.7:** Parasites

## Revise and Recall

**Fill in the blanks.**

1. __________ have large, flat teeth with ridges to help crush and grind plant materials.
2. __________ are animals that eat the flesh of other animals and have sharp, pointed teeth for tearing meat.
3. Animals such as bears and crows that eat both plants and the flesh of other animals are known as __________.
4. Organisms that feed on dead or decaying plant and animal matter, helping to keep the environment clean, are called __________.
5. __________ are organisms that live on or inside the body of another living being for food, often harming their host.

# MOVEMENT IN ANIMALS

Animals are grouped into two categories based on the presence or absence of a backbone (also known as **vertebral column**).

**Science in Context**

Movement in animals can be of two types: movement of body parts, and locomotion, which is the movement from one place to another.

**Invertebrates:** *Animals that do not have a backbone are called* ***invertebrates***, for example, earthworms and insects.

**Vertebrates:** *Animals that have a backbone are called* ***vertebrates***, for example, cat, dog, man, fish and snake.

The way animals move is called their **gait**. The presence or absence of a backbone affects the gait of an animal. Let us study the gait of some animals and the features that help them to move around.

## Movement in Earthworm

Earthworms have neither an internal skeleton nor any limbs. Yet, they can move using their special muscles and hair-like structures called **setae**. If you observe the body of an earthworm, you will see many ring-like structures, called **segments**, on its body. Setae are present in almost all the segments of the earthworm's body and are attached to the muscles on its body wall. Earthworms move by **crawling** (Fig. 2.8). First, the earthworm anchors the rear portion to the ground with the help of its setae and then extends the front part of its body as the muscles in those regions relax. Next, it anchors the front portion to the ground and releases the rear end. The muscles in the rear end contract and are pulled forward. So, by alternate muscle contraction and relaxation, the earthworm slowly moves forward. Earthworms also secrete a slimy substance, which helps them in smooth movement.

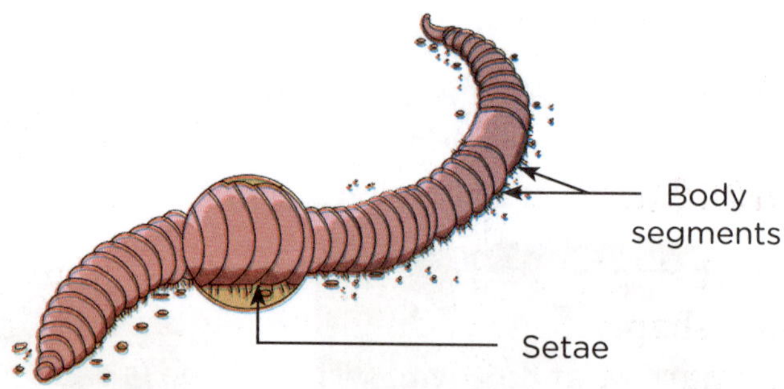


**Fig. 2.8:** Movement in earthworm: Crawling

## Movement in Snail

Snails are known for their slow movement. You may have noticed a hard rounded structure on top of a snail. This is its outer skeleton, called a **shell**, which is primarily made of calcium. The shell helps protect the snail from cold and danger. Snails (Fig. 2.9) move with the help of a thick foot made of strong muscles. Their body consists of a head,

**Fig. 2.9:** Movement in snail: Gliding

tentacles and a long muscular foot. Snails **glide** along the ground using their foot. The muscles of the foot move like a wave. As it moves, it leaves a mucous trail that makes the movement easier and prevents injury.

**Wonder!**

The average speed of a garden snail is 1 millimetre per second. Hence, the saying: *As slow as a snail*!

## Movement in Cockroach

Cockroaches can **walk**, **swim, crawl** and **fly**. A cockroach has no bones, but has an external skeleton that protects its body. A cockroach has six jointed legs and two pairs of wings. Muscles that are attached to the legs and the wings help cockroaches to move. They can walk and climb with the help of their legs and leg muscles (Fig. 2.10). They fly with the help of their wings and wing muscles.

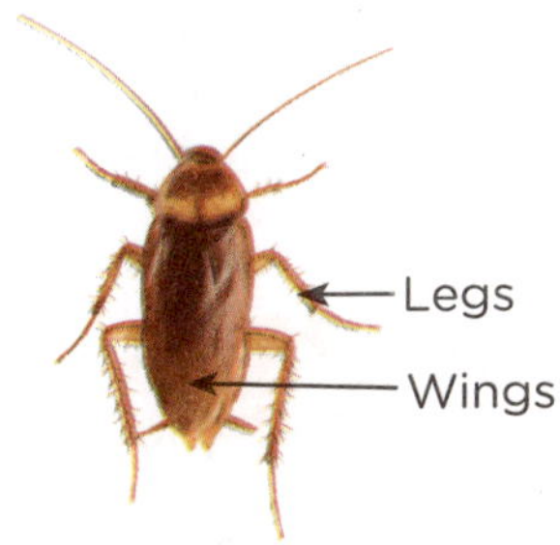


**Fig. 2.10:** Movement in cockroach: Walking

## Movement in Fish

Fish, being vertebrates that live in water, naturally move by swimming. Observe the boat-shaped body of the fish in Figure 2.11. The body of a fish is broad in the middle and narrow at both ends. This shape is called a **streamlined shape** and helps fish to cut through the water easily. Fish have an internal skeleton that is attached to strong muscles. The fins also have skeletal and muscular support.

Most fish have a special structure called a **swim bladder**, which can be filled with air or emptied, allowing the fish to move up and down in the water.

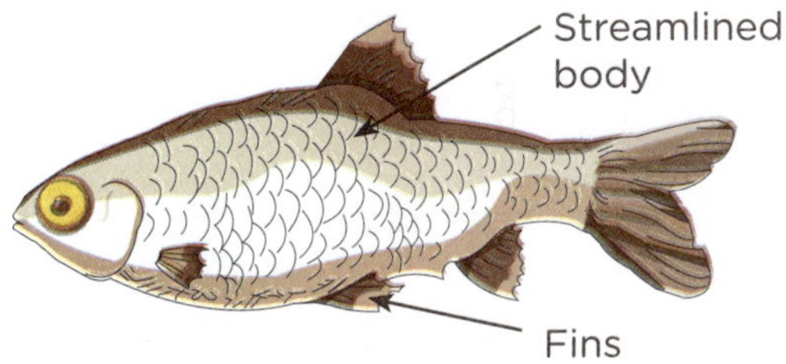


**Fig. 2.11:** Movement in fish: Swimming

## Movement in Bird

Birds can **fly** in the air and **walk**, **run** and **hop** on the ground. Some birds can only walk. Waterfowls such as ducks and pelicans can **swim**. Other type of birds, such as ostriches and kiwis, cannot fly but are good runners.

**Wonder!**

Ostrich is the fastest running bird in the world. It can run up to 70 km/hr.

The birds that can fly have hollow, lightweight bones. Their wings, feathers and specialized muscles attached to the wings help them in flying. The streamlined body shape of birds helps them to move efficiently against the direction of the wind (Fig. 2.12). Birds show two types of flight—flapping and gliding. In flapping flight, birds actively move their wings up and down to generate **thrust**[1] and **lift**[2]. In gliding flight, birds extend their wings and use air currents to stay aloft, moving effortlessly with minimal wing movement.

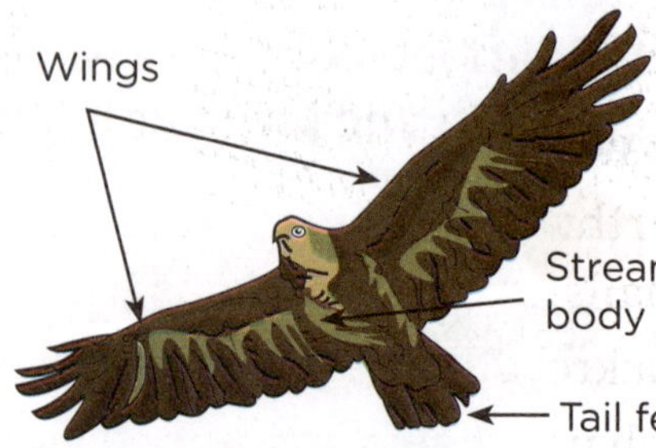

**Fig. 2.12:** Movement in birds: Flight

### Word Web

[1]**Thrust:** push suddenly or violently in a specified direction

[2]**Lift:** raise to a higher position or level

## Movement in Snake

Snakes do not have legs or arms. They move by using their muscles and a long backbone. Snakes are thin and long and have scales all over their body. They have strong muscles attached to their ribs, skin and backbone.

Unlike humans, the ribs are not attached to the chest bone. So, the ribs are free and help in movement. Snakes move by **slithering** or in a zigzag manner (Fig. 2.13). The free ends of ribs act like limbs to grip surfaces, and the contraction and relaxation of muscles help the snake move. Snakes move best on rough surfaces.

**Fig. 2.13:** Movement in snake: Slithering

### Know the Scientist

**Latika Nath**
**(Born on 17 June 1966)**

Latika Nath, born on 17 June 1966, is an Indian wildlife conservationist, author and photographer, known as "The Tiger Princess" for her work in tiger conservation. She is India's first woman wildlife biologist with a doctorate in Tiger Conservation and Management from the University of Oxford. Over the past 25 years, Nath has been involved in numerous conservation projects across India, focusing on research, wildlife photography and raising awareness about habitat preservation. She has travelled globally to photograph various species and works closely with tribal communities to address human–wildlife conflicts.

## Revise and Recall

**State whether the following statements are true (T) or false (F).**

1. Earthworms have an internal skeleton made of bones that helps them move.
2. Snails use their mucous trail to help them move.
3. Cockroaches have bones in their body that assist with their movement.
4. Fish use their streamlined body shape and fins to help them swim effectively in water.
5. Birds that can fly use flapping and gliding movements for movement.

## Activity: Grouping Animals by Movement

**Aim:** To observe and group animals based on their movement and the body parts they use for locomotion

**Materials required:** Pictures of various animals (e.g., fish, birds, insects, mammals), large chart paper and markers

**Procedure:**

1. **Create a Movement Chart:** On a large sheet of chart paper, create a table similar to the one shown below, listing different animals and the body parts they use for movement.

| Name of the Animal | Type of Movement | Body Parts Used for Movement |
|---|---|---|
| Fish | Swimming | Fins |
| Bird | Flying | Wings |
| Snake | Slithering | Body and muscles |
| Kangaroo | Hopping | Legs |
| Elephant | Walking | Legs |

2. **Group and Classify:** Place pictures of different animals under the correct category of movement (e.g., swimming, flying, walking, slithering). Discuss how the body parts of each animal are adapted to their specific type of movement.
3. **Discussion:** Discuss about why certain animals move in particular ways. Find answers to questions such as, "Why do fish have fins instead of legs?" or "How do wings help birds in their movement?" Think of more such questions and search for their answers.

**Conclusion:** This activity will make you understand the relationship between an animal's body structure and the types of movement, and how these adaptations are linked to their survival in different environments.

## Keywords

**Herbivores:** Animals that eat only plants
**Carnivores:** Animals that eat the flesh of other animals
**Omnivores:** Animals that eat both plants and the flesh of other animals
**Scavengers:** Organisms that eat the remains of dead animals
**Cannibals:** Animals that eat the flesh of animals of their own kind
**Decomposers:** Organisms that feed on dead or/and decaying plant and animal matter
**Parasites:** Organisms that live on or inside the body of other living beings for food
**Locomotion:** Movement of the body from one place to another
**Vertebrae:** Individual bones of the backbone
**Slither:** Zigzag movement seen in snakes and other limbless animals

## Summary

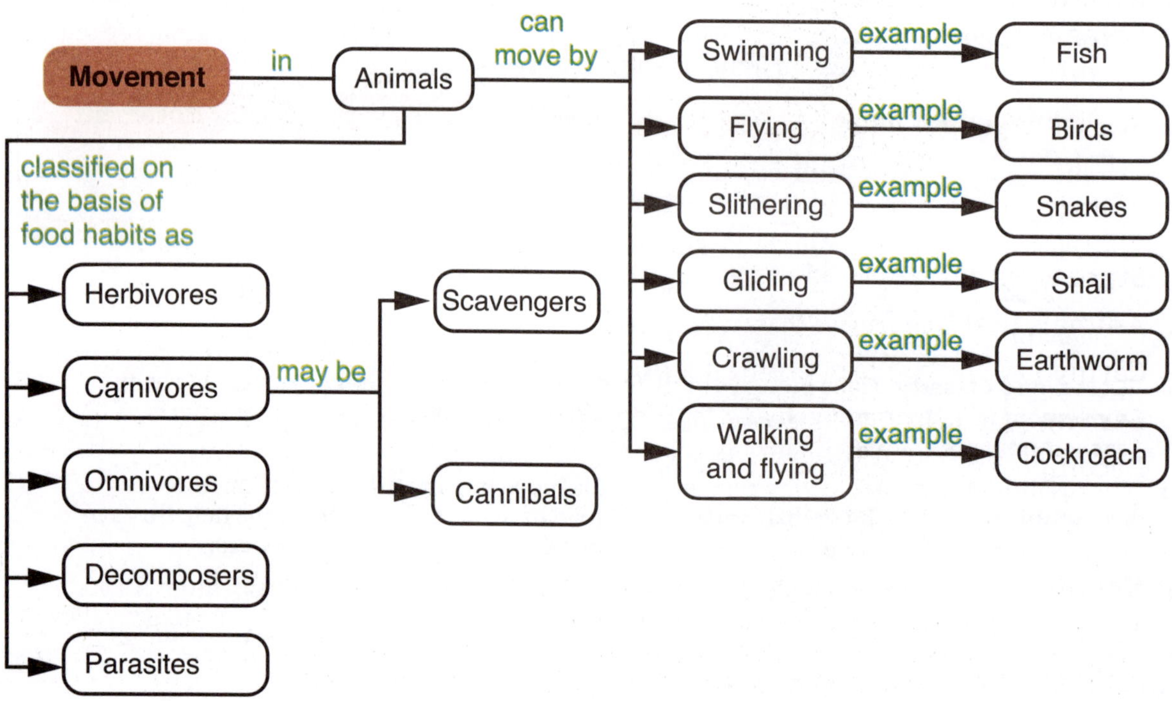

# Exercise

w

ia

**A. Choose the correct option.**

1. Which of the following animals is a herbivore?
   (a) Lion (b) Rabbit (c) Crow (d) Tiger
2. What type of feeding habit do vultures exhibit?
   (a) Herbivores (b) Parasites (c) Scavengers (d) Omnivores
3. What structure helps fish move up and down in water?
   (a) Fins (b) Gills (c) Swim bladder (d) Tail
4. Which type of bird flight is characterized by wings spread and little flapping?
   (a) Gliding (b) Flapping (c) Hovering (d) Diving
5. Which of the following is not present in snakes?
   (a) Scales (b) Backbone (c) Ribs (d) Legs

**B. Fill in the blanks.**

1. Streamlined body is found in ________________. (fish/earthworm)
2. Earthworms have tiny hair-like projections under their body called ________________. (setae/scales)
3. Birds that fly have ________________ bones. (hollow/heavy)
4. Snakes move by ________________ or in a zigzag manner. (gliding/slithering)
5. ________________ are organisms that feed on decaying plant and animal matter. (Carnivores/Decomposers)

**C. State whether the following statements are true (T) or false (F).** ia

1. Animals that live in the ocean are always herbivores.
2. Carnivores have sharp, pointed teeth for tearing flesh.
3. Earthworms move with the help of setae and muscles.
4. Decomposers are harmful to the environment.
5. A snake's ribs are attached to its chest bone.

**D. Name each of the following in one word.** ia

1. Animals that have a backbone ________________
2. Animals that do not have a backbone ________________
3. Body structure that protects a snail from danger ________________
4. The special structure in fish that helps them move up and down in water ________________
5. Number of legs of a cockroach ________________

**E. Give reasons for the following.**

1. Scavengers are important for the environment.
2. Herbivores have flat, ridged teeth.
3. Birds have hollow bones.
4. Earthworms move without limbs.
5. Snakes move best on rough surfaces.

**F. Answer the following questions briefly.**

1. Why do animals move from one place to another?
2. How does the streamlined body of fish help them to move?
3. How do herbivores such as rabbits use their teeth to eat plants?
4. What role do muscles play in the movement of cockroaches?
5. Describe the movement of a snake.
6. How does a bird's body shape help it fly?

**G. Answer the following questions.**

1. Compare and contrast the feeding habits of herbivores, carnivores and omnivores.
2. How do the special adaptations of animals help them survive in their respective environments?
3. Describe the movement of a fish and explain how its body structure aids in this movement.
4. Discuss the different ways birds move and the features that enable them to do so.
5. Explain the importance of decomposers.

# Cognitive Corner

## Critical Thinking

1. Compare the adaptations of fish and birds for movement in their respective environments. How do the structures in their bodies contribute to their ability to move efficiently in water and air?
2. How do the movement strategies of scavengers and predators, such as hyenas and lions, contribute to their survival in their ecosystems? Consider their feeding habits and how their movement helps them find food.
3. How do the locomotion mechanisms of earthworms and snakes reflect their body structures? Explain how their movement methods are adapted to their environments and physical forms.
4. What are the features in birds that help them in flight? Which of these features are not likely to be seen in flightless birds?

## Picture Study

Draw and examine the teeth of a herbivore and a carnivore. Discuss how the structure of these teeth helps the animal in its feeding habits.

## Project

1. Conduct a research on scavengers and decomposers. Then observe scavengers or decomposers in your environment with the help of your teacher and a write a report on the benefits they give to the ecosystem. **(C-7.1)**
2. Observe the movement of a fish in a fish tank or watch a video of a fish swimming in a fish tank. Which fin helps it to change its direction? Which fins help it to move forward? Write a diary entry based on your findings. **(C-7.1)**

## In the Library

Find out about the different body movements animals use to communicate.
Collect information about the animals given below. **(C-7.1)**

- Ants
- Honeybees
- Dogs

## Life Skills

1. Animals adapt to their environments to survive, such as how a fish's streamlined body helps it swim efficiently in water. Think about a time when you faced a challenge in your environment (e.g., school, home or social setting). How did you adapt to the situation, and what skills did you use to overcome the challenge? **(C-7.1)**
2. How can you practise environmental responsibility in your daily life? Provide examples of actions you can take to help keep your community clean and healthy. **(C-6.1)**

# Worksheet

Animal movement is essential for their survival and well-being. Whether they are herbivores, carnivores or omnivores, animals move to find food, secure shelter, avoid predators and reproduce. These movements help maintain healthy populations and ensure that each organism continues to fulfill its role in the ecosystem. Understanding these behaviours provides insight into the complex relationships between animals and their environments, highlighting the importance of preserving their habitats and maintaining environmental balance.

1. Why is it important to preserve the homes of herbivores?

______________________________________________

______________________________________________

______________________________________________

2. How does the balance in the food chain contribute to stability in the environment?

______________________________________________

______________________________________________

______________________________________________

3. How does climate change impact the movement patterns of animals?

______________________________________________

______________________________________________

______________________________________________

4. How do water quality and river health affect fish movement and survival?

______________________________________________

______________________________________________

______________________________________________

5. Reflect on how different types of food and movement patterns among animals influence their environment. Write a short paragraph on the interconnectedness of animal health, environmental sustainability and human activities.

______________________________________________

______________________________________________

______________________________________________

# 3 Biodiversity

## Curricular Goals

- Explore the living world in scientific terms **(CG-3)**
- Explore the nature and processes of science through engaging with the evolution of scientific knowledge and conducting scientific inquiry **(CG-6)**
- Communicate own questions, observations and conclusions related to science **(CG-7)**

## Competencies

- Describe the diversity of living organisms observed in the natural surroundings **(C-3.1)**
- Analyse patterns of relationship between living organisms and their environment in terms of dependence on and response to each other **(C-3.3)**
- Formulate questions using scientific terminology, and collect data that is usable as evidence **(C-6.2)**
- Represent real world events and relationships through diagrams **(C-7.3)**

## Let's Get Started

Look at the pictures given below. Choose the appropriate name for the places from the choices given in the box and write them in the space given below each picture.

| Polar region | Forest | Desert | Ocean | Mountains |
|---|---|---|---|---|

_______________

_______________

_______________

_______________

_______________

*The place where an organism lives naturally is called its* ***habitat***. It provides the organism with suitable conditions to live and reproduce. Plants and animals often share the same habitat.

## ECOSYSTEM

An **ecosystem** is a relationship between living organisms such as plants, animals and microbes, and non-living factors such as air, water and soil found in a specific area. An ecosystem can be as small as a pond or as large as a forest. In an ecosystem, energy flows through food chains, and nutrients are recycled, maintaining balance and supporting the survival of life forms.

## BIODIVERSITY

**Biodiversity** is a word used to describe the organisms and their habitats of a given area, whether small like a grassland, large like an ocean or the entire planet. It includes all kinds of plants, animals and microorganisms, as well as the differences within each species. High biodiversity is important because it helps ecosystems stay healthy, recover from changes and provide us with resources such as clean water and air.

## HABITAT

a

A **habitat** is the specific place where plants, animals or other organisms live. It is like their home, where they find food, water, shelter and the right conditions to survive.
A habitat consists of both biotic (living) and abiotic (non-living) components. The biotic components are the living organisms, and the abiotic components include non-living things such as air, water, light and soil.
Habitats can be terrestrial (forests or deserts) or aquatic (ponds, rivers or oceans).

## Terrestrial Habitats

*Habitats on land are called* ***terrestrial habitats***. Accordingly, the animals that live on land are called terrestrial animals. Some terrestrial habitats are discussed below.

### Grasslands

This region is dominated by grass, small trees and shrubs (Fig. 3.1). Grasslands get moderate rain and are usually windy and dry. Some animals that can be found in a grassland are zebra, giraffe, deer, tiger and lion.

**Fig. 3.1:** Grassland

### Mountains

Mountains are habitats found at higher altitudes. They are usually extremely cold and windy (Fig. 3.2).

**Fig. 3.2:** Mountain

Depending on the altitude, these regions sometimes experience snowfall as the temperature decreases. Some animals that can be found in a mountain habitat are yak, sheep, mountain goat, etc.

### Forests

Forests (Fig. 3.3) are habitats characterized by the presence of a large number of plants, trees and animals, supporting diverse forms of life. In forests, animals form various relationships to survive such as the predator–prey relationship between lions and deer. These habitats experience a range of climates, from warm and humid to cold and harsh, which influence the types of plants and animals that thrive there. Common trees include oaks, pines and evergreens, while animals such as elephants, deer, wolves, birds and insects inhabit these regions. Forests also serve as a vital home for countless species of plants, such as orchids, mosses and ferns, creating rich ecosystems that support both flora and fauna.

**Fig. 3.3:** Forest

### Deserts

Deserts are sandy regions with scanty rainfall. Most deserts get less than 10 inches of rainfall each year and are very hot and dry. Some deserts that are hot during the day may become cold at night. Some deserts are always cold such as the Gobi desert in Asia. The largest hot desert in the world is the Sahara in Africa, which experiences temperatures of up to 122 degrees Fahrenheit (50 degrees Celsius) during the day.

**Fig. 3.4:** Desert

Plant life in the deserts includes cacti and some thorny plants. Animals usually found in the deserts (Fig. 3.4) are camels, kangaroo rats, rattlesnakes, etc.

### Polar Regions

Polar regions are covered in snow and remain cold for most of the year. During winter, the temperatures can go as low as –37 °C.

Animals commonly found in the polar regions (Fig. 3.5) are polar bears, penguins, seals and walruses.

**Fig. 3.5:** Polar region

## AQUATIC HABITATS

**Fig. 3.6:** Aquatic habitat

Aquatic habitats refer to environments in water where a wide variety of plants and animals live. These habitats include areas such as rivers, lakes, ponds, coasts, oceans and **estuaries**[1]. Many organisms thrive in these habitats, including different species of fish, frogs, turtles, crabs, octopuses, starfish and whales. Aquatic plants such as lotus, water lilies, seaweeds and mangroves also grow here, contributing to the rich biodiversity. Some ocean ecosystems, such as **coral reefs**, support vibrant communities of creatures such as corals, sponges, lobsters and dolphins, providing a home for numerous species.

**Word Web**

[1]**Estuary:** a coastal region where a river or stream containing freshwater meets the salty water of the sea or an ocean

## Revise and Recall

**State whether the following statements are true (T) or false (F).**

1. A habitat consists of both biotic (living) and abiotic (non-living) components.
2. Mountains are habitats found at lower altitudes.
3. The dominant vegetation in grasslands includes tall trees and dense underbrush.
4. The Gobi Desert is the hottest desert.
5. Estuaries and coral reefs are examples of desert habitats.

## Case Study: Silent Valley Movement

The Silent Valley Movement in Kerala was a significant environmental campaign during the 1970s and 1980s aimed at protecting the Silent Valley, a pristine rainforest in the Western Ghats. The movement began when the Kerala State Electricity Board proposed a hydroelectric project that threatened the valley's rich biodiversity. Environmentalists, scientists and local communities rallied to save the valley, highlighting the ecological importance of its unique flora and fauna. The campaign gained widespread support, eventually leading to the project's cancellation. In 1984, Silent Valley was declared a national park, preserving its natural beauty for future generations.

**Critical Thinking**

Compare the objectives and strategies of the Silent Valley Movement with those of environmental movements in India, such as the Chipko Movement or Save Dehing Patkai. What lessons can be learned from these movements to address today's environmental challenges?

**Project Idea**

Research and create a presentation on the Narmada Bachao Andolan. Discuss how public awareness and participation in environmental conservation have evolved over time in India.

# ADAPTATIONS

a

As you have learnt, the sea and the desert are two extremely different habitats having very different kinds of plants and animals. When you compare the organisms in the desert and the sea, such as the camel and the shark, how do you think their body structures help them to survive in their habitats?

*The features and habits developed in plants and animals that enable them to survive in their surroundings are called* ***adaptations****.*

An example of adaptation shown by animals is **camouflage**. By camouflaging, most animals blend in with their habitats. Most animals escape from their predators or catch their prey by camouflaging. For example, tigers have black stripes on yellow–orange skin with a lighter underside that helps them to remain hidden among tall dry grasses (Fig. 3.7). Several insects appear very similar to leaves or twigs to hide from their predators. Polar bears have white furs to blend in with the snow.

**Fig. 3.7:** A camouflaging tiger

Different animals and plants show different adaptations to survive in their habitats. Let us discuss some of these in the following sections.

## Adaptations for Tropical Rainforests

Tropical rainforests (Fig. 3.8) have dense vegetation with high rainfall. Plants in the lower level get very less sunlight. There is intense competition for food and other resources among animals.

**Plants:** Plants that grow in forests (and grasslands) are called **mesophytes**. Several herbs, shrubs and trees such as ebony, mahogany, rosewood, rubber and cinchona grow well in rainforests.

- Many plants grow very tall to avail maximum sunlight, for example, ebony and rosewood. Vines such as lianas climb up the trees to reach the sunlight.
- Certain plants that grow near the ground have broad leaves to absorb as much sunlight as possible.

**Fig. 3.8:** A rainforest

- Many plants have pointed leaves called **drip tips**. It allows water to run off the leaves quickly without damaging or rotting the leaves.

**Animals:** Rainforests are inhabited by animals and birds such as sloth bears, flying frogs, gorillas, jaguars, toucans, macaws and monkeys.

- Sloth bears move very slowly and use camouflage to hide from predators.
- The flying frogs escape predators by gliding in the air with the help of their fully webbed front and hind feet and a flap of loose skin that stretches between their limbs.
- To avoid competition for food with other animals, toucans have long, large bills allowing them to reach and cut fruit from branches that are too weak to support their weight. Macaws have strong, hard beaks to crack hard nuts. Monkeys have tails that act as an extra limb, allowing them to hang from branches and jump from tree to tree in search of food.

## Adaptations for Temperate Forests

Temperate forests have varying climate over a year. Plants and animals living in this forest need to adapt and survive in different seasons.

**Plants:** Coniferous trees such as maples, oaks and beeches abundantly grow in temperate forests.

- To survive in wide range of climate, most plants have broad leaves and prepare food mainly in summer season. As autumn sets in, these plants begin shedding their leaves. This allows them to store water or moisture to survive the cold, as they remain dormant or inactive during winter.
- Plants also have a thick bark to protect themselves from the cold winter.

**Animals:** A variety of animals from small squirrels to large mammals are found in a temperate forests.

- Squirrels and chipmunks gather nuts and seeds during summer and store these in hollow logs or holes in the ground for winter.
- Bears, woodchucks and raccoons eat as much as possible in summer. These animals then hibernate during the winter. This way, these animals survive the colder weather and overcome food scarcity.
- Many birds migrate to warmer climates.

## Adaptations for Boreal Forests

Boreal forests have a cold, harsh climate, usually with heavy snowfall. So, the variety of plants and animals is much less than those found in other habitats.

**Plants:** Many varieties of plants such as coniferous trees (pines and firs), mosses, lichens and black spruce are found in boreal forests (Fig. 3.9).

- Coniferous trees have a cone-like shape. This shape allows snow to fall off easily and thus avoid damage to the plant.
- These trees have needle-like leaves to avoid loss of moisture and retain more water. The shape also helps in avoiding damage by strong winds.

**Animals:** Porcupines, elks, bobcats, grizzly bears, red foxes and snowshoe hares are abundant in the boreal forests.

- These animals have thick fur in order to stay insulated from the cold.
- They have also evolved large feet or hooves in order to walk easily through the thick snow.
- Animals hibernate during coldest months.

An elk

**Fig. 3.9:** Boreal forest

A red fox

### Case Study: Human-Wildlife Conflict

The wildlife in India faces increasing threats from human–animal conflicts, particularly with elephants and tigers. In 2023, Assam reported severe conflicts with over 500 human deaths annually due to elephants encroaching on human habitats, while Odisha experienced significant conflicts due to habitat destruction from mining and infrastructure. Tigers in the Terai region of Uttar Pradesh are also affected, leading to tension and calls for lethal measures. Recent mitigation efforts include community-based solutions and advanced technologies such as solar fences and Artificial Intelligence (AI)-based warning systems. For example, Assam's introduction of solar-powered fences and Odisha's establishment of elephant reserves and community volunteers are key initiatives. These strategies align with ongoing campaigns, such as expanding elephant corridors and using drones for monitoring, to balance conservation with human safety.

**Critical Thinking**

How can conservation strategies be adapted to address both immediate and long-term human–animal conflicts in regions such as Assam and Uttar Pradesh?

What role can technology and community engagement play in developing effective solutions to such conflicts?

**Project Idea**

Design a conflict mitigation plan incorporating lessons from recent campaigns, such as AI-based warning systems and community-led initiatives. How can these methods be applied to enhance conservation efforts in specific conflict zones such as Assam or Uttar Pradesh?

## ADAPTATIONS FOR GRASSLANDS

Some adaptations shown by plants and animals living in grasslands (Fig. 3.10) are given below:

**Plants:** The region is predominantly covered with varieties of grasses, some shrubs and moderately sized trees. These plants and trees have some common adaptations:

- **Roots:** Grasses have long and strong roots to support them in windy conditions and to penetrate the soil to find water. Hence, these grasses are able to survive even in the dry season. Grasses may die in the driest season, but will start to bud and grow again when conditions are favourable.
- **Stem:** Grasses have thin and flexible stalks so that they do not break in strong winds.
- **Leaves:** The leaves of shrubs and trees are reduced to smaller sizes to reduce loss of water.

**Fig. 3.10:** Grassland

**Animals:** Several animals such as tigers, lions, foxes, cheetahs, deer, zebras and giraffes live in this habitat. These animals can be categorized into predators (for example, lions and foxes) and prey (for example, deer and zebras). Some common adaptations in the animals that live in grasslands are listed below:

- **Predators:** They have eyes on the front of their head to provide a focused vision. Lions and cheetahs have sharp, **retractable**[1] claws.
- **Prey:** They have eyes on either side of their head, which help them to look in multiple directions for danger. They have strong hind legs that help them run faster to escape from their predators.
- Some animals camouflage themselves as they have similar colour or even shape to match their surroundings. This is an adaptation to hide from the predators or even sometimes to attack a prey.
- Animals (e.g., the antelope) adapt to dry conditions in a grassland when water is scarce by eating at night when the leaves have the most water in them or by eating early in the morning when there is dew on the leaves.
- The black rhinoceros chews **succulent**[2] leaves that have excess water in them.
- Elephants make 'wells' by digging into the Earth. Other animals also use this water.
- Animals burrow into the soil beneath the grass or hide in tufts of grass. These behavioural adaptations are important for survival in grasslands.

**Word Web**

[1]**Retractable:** that can be pulled back inside

[2]**Succulent:** thick and fleshy

## Adaptations for Deserts

Some adaptations shown by plants and animals living in deserts (Fig. 3.11) are given below:

**Plants:** Plants adapted to live in desert conditions are called **xerophytes**. Different kinds of cacti inhabit deserts.

Some common adaptations seen among plants of this region are as follows:

- **Roots:** The sandy soil cannot hold water, so the water is stored at a very low level below the ground. The plants growing in these regions have very long roots, which can penetrate deep into the soil in search of water.
- **Stems:** Many cacti have green succulent stems that store water and carry out photosynthesis. A thick waxy layer helps to retain water.

**Fig. 3.11:** Plants and animals in a desert

- **Leaves:** To reduce the loss of water due to transpiration, the leaves of cacti are reduced to spines. This also prevents predators from feeding on them. The process of photosynthesis is taken up by the fleshy stems.

**Animals:** Deserts are home to reptiles, insects and small mammals. Animals such as camels, rats, snakes live in these habitat. Some common adaptations are as follows:

- They have thick skins with fewer pores.
- They hardly sweat and excrete less urine in order to retain water in their body.
- Desert animals are adapted to be active during early mornings and late evenings when the temperature is moderate, and they rest during the day when it is the hottest.
- These animals have less fur and very little body fat, which allows them to lose heat through their skin surface.
- Some adaptations specific to few animals are given below:
    - **Camels:** Camels have long legs to stay away from the heat of the sand. They can drink a large amount of water at a time and can stay without water for long periods of time. They have a hump on their back to store fat. Other animals are adapted to drink very little water or get it from the food they eat.
    - **Rats and snakes:** They burrow under the sand during daytime to stay away from the heat. They restrict their movement during the day and hunt for prey during the night.

## Adaptations for Mountains

Some adaptations shown by plants and animals living in mountains (Fig. 3.12) are given below:

**Fig. 3.12:** Plants and animals in mountains

**Plants:** The foothills of mountains contain plenty of trees. As we go up the mountains, plants are adapted to the harsh climate. Several trees such as the pine and fir grow in this region.

Towards the top of the mountain, coniferous trees are prevalent as they are much better at dealing with the cold weather. At very high altitudes, such as those on the mountaintops, the surface is covered with snow and ice, so only very few plants can survive.

Some common adaptations of such plants are as follows:

- Trees grow tall to trap sunlight.
- Leaves are small and needle shaped.
- Conical shape of the trees with sloping branches allows the snow to slide down easily.

**Animals:** Animals such as yaks, mountain sheep, mountain goats, snow leopards and llamas are adapted to the mountainous habitats as they are **sure-footed**, that is, they can walk with ease on unsteady paths of the mountains. They have thick woolly furs to survive the cold weather.

Some common adaptations of animals living in mountains are listed below:

- They have thick fur covering their body to protect them from cold weather.
- Some animals such as the yak and mountain goat have long hair all over their body to protect them from the cold weather.
- Strong hooves of mountain sheep, goats and yaks help them to walk on the slopes of the mountains.
- During the winter season, the animals living in these habitats move less and conserve their energy by hibernating or migrating down from the mountains.

## Adaptations for Polar Regions

Some adaptations shown by plants and animals living in polar regions (Fig. 3.13) are given below:

**Fig. 3.13:** Polar region

**Plants:** Plants such as cotton grass, bearberry, arctic willows and arctic poppy are adapted to withstand extreme cold and grow in the polar regions.

- Since plants need to breathe for their survival, they have adapted by producing needle-like leaves to let the snow that falls on them to slide off easily. These leaves are waxy to avoid the sticking of snow on them.
- The conical shape of the trees prevents snow from getting accumulated on them.
- These plants grow for a very short season and then wither away.

**Animals:** Some common adaptations are discussed below:

- Animals that have thick fur survive well in the polar habitats. Animals living in this habitat need to compete for food, protect themselves from predators and breed. Polar bears, arctic foxes and penguins have body structures that help them survive in these habitats.
- Polar bears have two thick layers of fur on their body and a layer of fat under their skin.
- They are well insulated and move slowly and rest often to avoid getting overheated.

**Science in Context**

Fish in the polar regions have anti-freeze molecules in their body, which prevent water in their tissues from freezing in extreme cold climate.

- Birds that live in these habitats cannot cope during extreme climatic conditions and migrate to other countries. They return when the climate is moderate or suitable for them to live there.
- Penguins have a thick skin and a lot of fat to protect their body from the cold. You may have seen pictures of penguins huddled together. This is to keep themselves warm. Their bodies are streamlined and they have webbed feet, making them good swimmers.
- Other animals such as reindeers, foxes, seals and whales are also adapted to survive in these regions as their bodies are adapted to the polar habitat.

## Adaptations for Aquatic Habitat

Plants and animals that live in water develop special adaptive features to help them grow and survive. The more time they spend in water, the more adapted the organisms are to survive in the aquatic habitat.

**Plants:** Aquatic plants are called **hydrophytes**. They may be fully submerged, partially submerged or floating on the surface. Hydrophytes can be classified into several types.

- Some plants remain underwater while some **float** in water. For example, duckweed does not have well-developed roots. It floats on water in a pond.
- Some plants are **submerged**, such as *Hydrilla*. They have soft stems.
- Some plants, such as cattails and bulrushes, grow in shallow water, with their roots submerged but stems and leaves above the water surface. These are **emergent** plants.
- Some plants such as lotus and water lily are **fixed** as the flowers and leaves float on water but their stems remain fixed by means of roots to the soil at the bottom of the pond.

Here are some adaptations shown by aquatic plants.

- Plants that live in water are adapted to have special tissues that help them to take in dissolved gas from the water.
- Floating plants typically have short or poorly developed roots. This adaptation allows them to avoid damage from water currents and helps them remain buoyant. They cannot reach the nutrients in the mud at the bottom, so they rely on nutrients in the water to grow. Most of their leaves are above the water, which allows them to take in carbon dioxide from the air.
- Submerged plants typically have flexible stems that can bend with water currents, preventing breakage and allowing them to withstand the movement of water. Rooted submerged plants can get a lot of their nutrients from the mud at the bottom of the water. They can also use their stems and leaves to absorb nutrients from the water.

- Flowers stick out above the surface of the water, which helps the plant in pollination.
- The waxy coating on the leaves and stem prevents the plant from rotting.

**Animals:** Here are some adaptations seen in aquatic animals (Fig. 3.14).

- A smooth and streamlined body of fish helps reduce friction as they move through the water. Animals that do not have a streamlined body such as octopuses and squids are adapted to live in deeper waters and move by jet propulsion using their body parts.

**Fig. 3.14:** Animals in an aquatic habitat

- Aquatic animals have various breathing organs that help them adapt to life in water. Most fish use gills to extract oxygen from water. However, some aquatic animals, such as dolphins and whales, breathe using lungs. Unlike humans, they do not have noses for breathing; instead, they have blowholes on top of their heads, which they use to inhale and exhale air. To breathe, these animals must come to the water surface, and they are adapted to hold their breath for long periods while underwater.
- Webbed feet and flippers help aquatic animals to paddle easily.
- Slow-moving animals, such as sea stars or starfish, have adapted to protect themselves from predators by producing chemical substances in their skin.

## Case Study: Project Tiger in India

Project Tiger, initiated in 1973, is a crucial conservation initiative aimed at protecting Bengal tigers from poaching, habitat destruction and human encroachment. Starting with nine reserves, the project has expanded to 53 reserves covering over 75,000 square kilometers. Key achievements include a significant increase in tiger populations—from 1411 in 2006 to 2967 in 2018—and enhanced community involvement in conservation. However, challenges remain, such as human–wildlife conflict, poaching and habitat fragmentation. Recent wildlife-saving campaigns in India, like the Save Aarey Forest movement, highlight the ongoing struggle to balance conservation with development, reflecting a broader commitment to protecting biodiversity across the country.

**Critical Thinking**

How can the lessons learned from Project Tiger be applied to address challenges faced by other recent wildlife conservation efforts in India such as the Save Aarey Forest movement?

**Project Idea**

Design a conservation plan that integrates successful strategies from Project Tiger with those used in recent campaigns such as Save Aarey Forest. Consider how to effectively balance wildlife protection with human development needs, and propose methods for enhancing community involvement and mitigating conflicts.

## Activity: Exploring Animal Adaptations

**Aim:** To explore how animals' physical features are adapted to their environments

**Materials required:** Pictures, videos or documentaries of animals in different environments (deserts, forests, water, mountains) and notebooks for observations

**Procedure:**

1. **Observation and Grouping:** Observe pictures of animals from different environments. Note the features that make these animals suited to their habitats such as fur, body shape and type of limbs.
2. **Group by Habitat and Adaptation:** Group the animals based on their habitats (e.g., desert, aquatic, forest, mountain). Then list the adaptations that help each group of animals survive in their respective environments.

| Habitat | Animal | Adaptation |
|---|---|---|
| Desert | Camel | |
| Forest | Monkey | |
| Aquatic | Dolphin | |
| Mountain | Snow Leopard | |

3. **Create a Poster:** Create a poster showcasing the different groups of animals and their unique adaptations. Draw or paste pictures and write a brief description of adaptation shown by each animal.

**Conclusion:** This activity will help you to appreciate the diversity of animal life and how physical adaptations are crucial for survival in different ecosystems. By grouping animals based on their environment and adaptations, you will gain a deeper understanding of the interconnectedness of life on Earth.

### Know the Scientist

**Madhav Gadgil**

**(Born on 24 May 1942)**

Madhav Gadgil is a renowned Indian ecologist known for his work in ecology, environmental policy and biodiversity conservation. He played a pivotal role in formulating India's National Biodiversity Strategy and Action Plan and chaired the Western Ghats Ecology Expert Panel, which provided conservation guidelines for the Western Ghats. Gadgil has authored many influential scientific papers and books on environmental conservation and has received prestigious awards, including the Padma Shri (1981) and Padma Bhushan (2006), for his contributions.

## Keywords

**Camouflage:** The ability to blend with the colour or characterisitics of one's immediate environment to prevent detection by enemies

**Prey:** An animal hunted or captured by another animal for food

**Predator:** Animals that kill and eat other animals for their survival

**Mesophytes:** Plants that grow well in forests and grasslands

**Xerophytes:** Plants that grow well in deserts

**Hydrophytes:** Plants that grow only in water

**Submerged plant:** A plant growing beneath the surface of water

## Summary

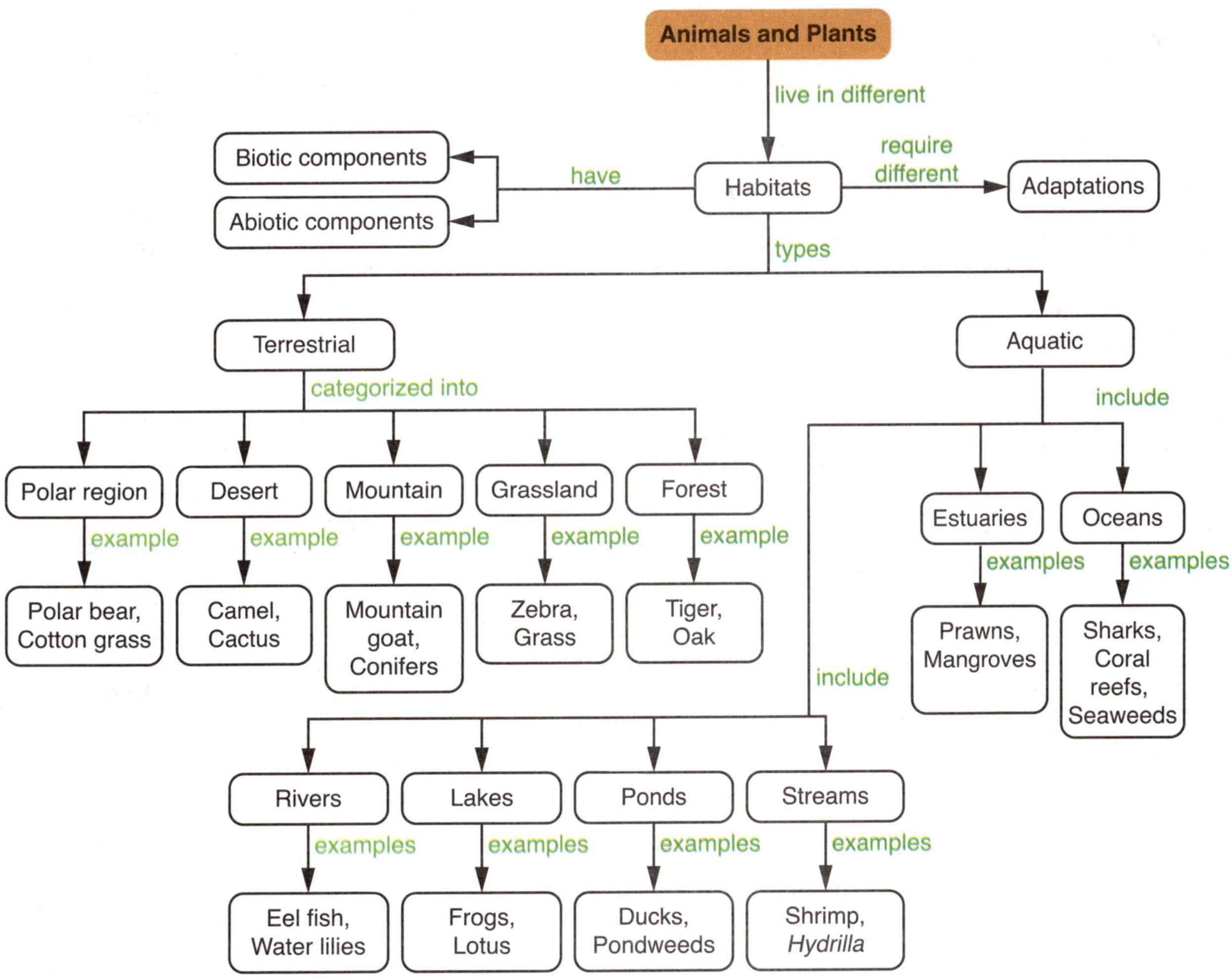

# Exercise

w

ia

**A. Choose the correct option.**

1. A camel has long legs to ______________.
   (a) walk fast on the sand (b) walk slowly on the sand
   (c) keep its body away from the heat (d) run on the sand
2. The thick and waxy stem in a cactus plant helps in ______________.
   (a) storing water (b) absorbing water
   (c) excreting water (d) reducing loss of water
3. Animals living in mountainous regions have ______________.
   (a) strong beaks (b) long legs
   (c) thick fur (d) humps
4. The trees that grow in mountainous regions have ______________.
   (a) cone-shaped and short branches
   (b) curved-shaped and sloping branches
   (c) curved-shaped and long branches
   (d) cone-shaped and sloping branches
5. The needle-like leaves of mountain trees help in ______________.
   (a) absorption of water
   (b) sliding off the snow
   (c) making the trees look attractive
   (d) absorbing sunlight

**B. Fill in the blanks.**

ia

1. The function of spines in desert plants is to ______________. (reduce water loss/attract insects)
2. Animals living in mountainous regions are adapted to live in ______________ climate. (warm/cold)
3. The habitat of frogs is ______________. (pond/trees)
4. Desert snakes and rats come out mostly during the ______________. (day/night)
5. Fish absorb oxygen from water using their ______________. (nostrils/gills)

**C. Give two examples for each of the following.**

1. Animals that live in grasslands __________ __________
2. Types of habitats __________ __________
3. Adaptations of a camel for a desert habitat __________ __________
4. Types of terrestrial habitats __________ __________
5. Adaptations of aquatic plants __________ __________

**D. Give reasons for the following.**

1. In rainforests, the tree leaves have special tips.
2. Grasses have thin and flexible stalks.
3. Roots of desert plants are very long.
4. Plants in polar regions have waxy leaves.
5. Plants in polar regions have waxy, needle-like leaves.

**E. Answer the following questions briefly.**

1. What is a habitat?
2. Name the major habitats found on the Earth.
3. Name a plant and an animal found in an aquatic habitat.
4. What are the main types of forests found on the Earth?
5. What are grasslands? What kind of plants and animals are found there?
6. What is adaptation? List two adaptations that the plants growing in forests show.

**F. Answer the following questions.**

1. Explain how an ecosystem functions and describe the role of biodiversity in maintaining the balance of an ecosystem. Use examples to illustrate your answer.
2. Compare and contrast terrestrial and aquatic habitats. Discuss the biotic and abiotic components of each and explain how these components support the organisms living in these habitats.
3. What are the adaptations seen in animals living in the polar regions to withstand the extreme climatic conditions?
4. What are the features seen in predators and prey that helps them adapt to their way of life?
5. Compare and contrast the adaptations of plants and animals in grasslands and deserts. How do these adaptations reflect the different environmental conditions of these two habitats?
6. Discuss the adaptations of plants and animals in mountain regions. How do these adaptations enable them to survive in the cold and harsh conditions of mountainous environments?

# Cognitive Corner

## Critical Thinking

1. What are the potential consequences of prioritizing short-term comfort and economic growth over the preservation of forests?
2. Suppose you have bought some fish from a store to add to your aquarium at home. What steps would you take to acclimatize the fish to the new environment?

## Project

1. As a part of Eco Club activity, visit a nearby zoo and make a list of the plants and animals living there. Identify the ones that are not in their natural habitat. Find out how the zoo is helping them adapt to the environment they are kept in. Present your report to the class, and discuss if it is a good practice to keep animals and plants away from their natural habitat. **(C-3.1)**
2. Select an animal and its habitat. Research how the animal's physical and behavioural traits help it survive in its specific environment. Create a presentation or a model showcasing the animal's adaptations.

   Compare adaptations across different environments to identify common strategies animals use to survive in extreme conditions. **(C-9.1)**

## In the Laboratory (C-6.2)

Take two healthy and well-watered plants with many leaves (mesophytes) and label them as A and B. Examples: *Geranium, Duranta* and *Impatiens.*

Take two healthy and well-watered succulents (xerophytes) that can grow in dry conditions and label them as C and D. Examples: *Bryophyllum, Kalanchoe, Sedum* and *Portulaca.*

Cover the soil in all the pots with plastic sheets. Gently cover one twig each of all the four plants with clean and transparent polythene bags without damaging the leaves (as shown in the given picture). Tie the mouth of polythene bags near the base of each twig using a string.

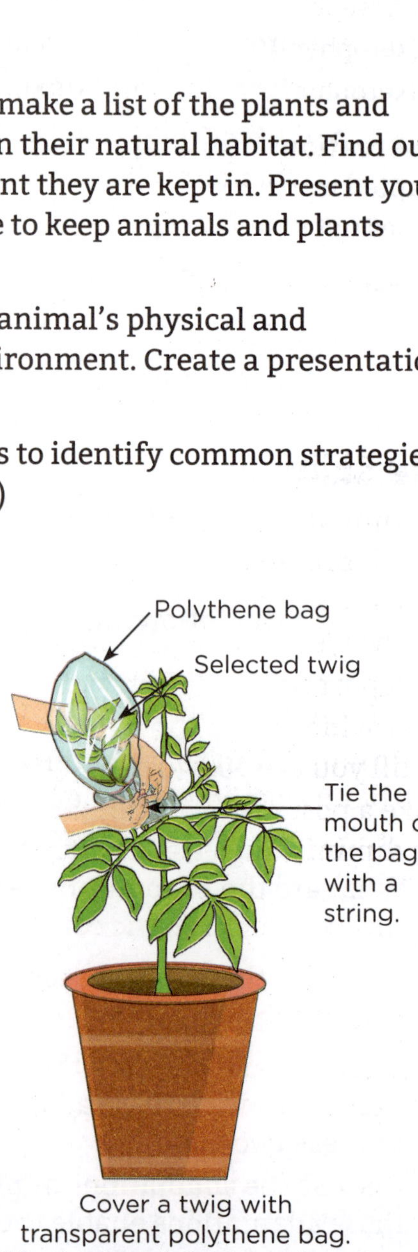


Cover a twig with transparent polythene bag. (Do this for all the four plants.)

Keep the two plant set-ups (A and C) in a place where they can receive maximum sunlight for 30 minutes. Keep the other two plant set-ups (B and D) in a place where they receive minimum/no sunlight for 30 minutes. Observe the inner surface of all the polythene bags (A and C; B and D) after 30 minutes and fill in the observation table given below.

| Plants | Experimental set-ups | Water droplets in polythene bags (More/Less/No) |
|---|---|---|
| A (mesophyte) | Kept in sunlight | |
| B (mesophyte) | Kept in shade/darkness | |
| C (xerophyte) | Kept in sunlight | |
| D (xerophyte) | Kept in shade/darkness | |

**Observation:** Transpiration takes place in the leaves of mesophytic plants (plants that are adapted to grow in areas that receive moderate rainfall) in the presence of sunlight, while it does not take place in xerophytic plants even in the presence of sunlight.

Inference: ______________________________

______________________________

______________________________

## Life Skills

All animals, small or large, play an important role in their habitats. We must do our part to protect these animals and the habitats they depend on for their survival.
Here are a few suggestions:

- Always dispose of waste in the proper place.
- Report poaching or cruelty to animals to nearby authorities.
- Provide an abandoned pup/kitten/chick at least a temporary shelter in your home till you are able to take it to a proper animal shelter.

Make a poster explaining some ways in which we can save the existing habitats that are diminishing each day due to human activities. **(C-7.3)**

# Worksheet

## Ocean Facts!

- Three-fourths of Earth's surface is covered by oceans
- Nearly 2,00,000 species live in oceans
- More than 3 billion people depend on ocean biodiversity for their livelihoods.
- Oceans buffer the impact of global warming by absorbing about 30% of carbon dioxide released by various human activities

What can you do to contribute towards saving or preserving the ocean and the many lives depending on it? Create slogans or taglines that can be used to spread awareness about **World Oceans Day**.

**Checklist for writing a slogan or a tagline:**

- A slogan or a tagline is a short sentence or phrase that is easy to remember and is used to spread an idea.
- Make the message stand out
- Call for action
- Make it catchy with rhythm or rhyme
- Keep it short

1.

2.

3.

4.

# 4 Life Around Us

## Curricular Goals

- Explore the living world in scientific terms **(CG-3)**
- Communicate own questions, observations and conclusions related to science **(CG-7)**

## Competencies

- Distinguish the characteristics of living beings from non-living things **(C-3.2)**
- Analyse patterns of relationship between living beings and their environment in terms of dependence on and response to each other **(C-3.3)**
- Design and build simple models to demonstrate scientific concepts **(C-7.2)**
- Represent real world events and relationships through diagrams **(C-7.3)**

## Let's Get Started

Observe the given picture carefully. In the space given below, write any five living beings and five non-living things that you can see in the picture.

Living beings ____________________

Non-living things ____________________

# CHARACTERISTICS OF LIVING BEINGS

We see plants, animals, insects, chairs, books, cars, soil, sky, water and people around us. Are all these living? No, some of these are living, while some are non-living.

Human beings, animals, plants and microorganisms are living beings.

Living beings have some characteristics that make them different from non-living things. Let us study these characteristics.

- **Living beings need food:** All living beings need food for their survival and growth. Food helps the body to grow and provides energy to carry out different activities. Plants produce their own food by a process called **photosynthesis**. Therefore, plants are called **autotrophs**. Human beings and animals depend on plants and other animals for their food (Fig. 4.1). Therefore, they are called **heterotrophs**.

**Fig. 4.1:** Sheep eating grass

- **Living beings grow:** Just as you can no longer fit into clothes from four years ago because you have grown, plants and animals also experience growth over time. Growth is a fundamental characteristic of all living beings. Whether it is a baby maturing into an adult (Fig. 4.2), a seedling becoming a full-grown plant (Fig. 4.3) or a tree getting taller, growth plays a crucial role in life. This process occurs as living beings take in nutrients and energy from their surroundings, which fuel their development and increase their size. Just like you need food to grow, all living beings rely on nutrition to survive and sustain their growth.

**Fig. 4.2:** A baby grows into an adult.

**Fig. 4.3:** An adult plant grows from a seedling.

- **Living beings move:** Living beings move from one place to another in search of food, water, shelter and safety. For example, people may travel to a nearby market to buy food (Fig. 4.4). Even plants, although they remain rooted in one spot, can exhibit movement. For example, climbing plants such as peas and cucumbers use vine-like structures called tendrils to grasp and wrap around objects for support. Some flowers open and close in regular patterns.

**Fig. 4.4:** A woman at a market to buy food.

Insectivorous plants, such as **bladderwort**, uses small, bladder-like traps to catch prey (Fig. 4.5). These bladders have hinged flaps and sensory hairs that detect when an insect touches them. Once triggered, the bladder rapidly opens, creating a vacuum that pulls in the prey. Inside the bladder, the trapped insect is digested, and the plant absorbs the nutrients.

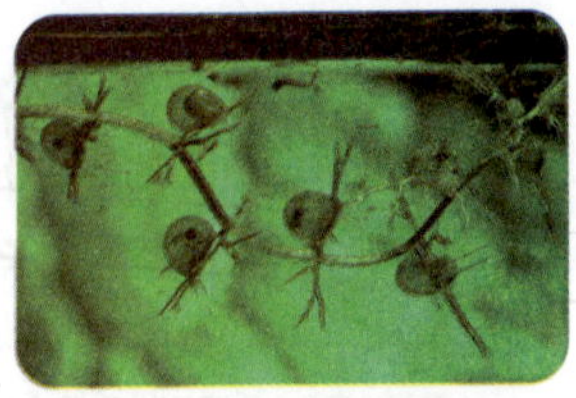

**Fig. 4.5:** Bladderwort containing caught mosquito larvae.

- **Living beings respire:** Living beings breathe in oxygen and breathe out carbon dioxide (Fig. 4.6). The oxygen that enters the body during breathing helps in breaking down the food consumed to produce energy. This process is called **respiration**. Plants breathe through tiny pores called **stomata** (singular: stoma) that are present mostly on the underside of leaves (Fig. 4.7).

**Fig. 4.6:** A dog breathes through its nose

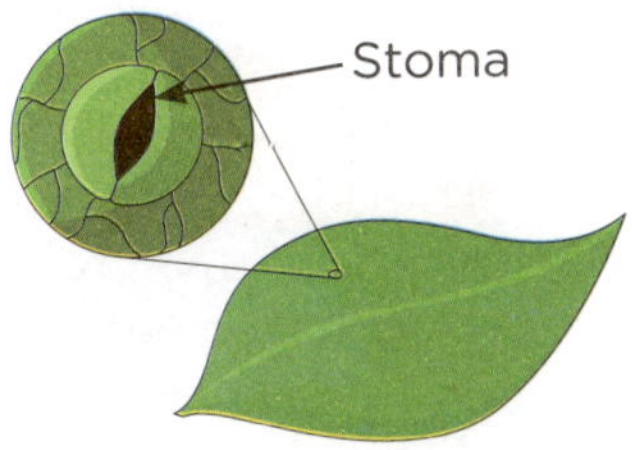


**Fig. 4.7:** Underside of a leaf showing a stoma

### Science in Context

Earthworms breathe through their skin.

- **Living beings respond to stimuli:** Anything in the environment that can cause a change in behaviour or affect an organism is known as **stimulus**. It can be internal (like hunger) or external (like light, sound or touch).
  For example:
  **Stimulus:** A strong odour.
  **Response:** A person might turn their head away or cover their nose to avoid it.
  Every living being responds to stimuli in some way.
  For example, the touch-me-not plant (*Mimosa pudica*) quickly closes its leaves when touched (Fig. 4.8), and the night-blooming jasmine (*Cestrum nocturnum*) only flowers at night. Animals also react to various stimuli such as heat, cold, sharp objects and smell. For example, a dog might seek shade or water on a hot day to cool down (Fig. 4.9) or a cat will swiftly pull its paw back if it steps on something sharp, like a thorn.

**Fig. 4.8:** Folded leaves of *Mimosa pudica* plant when touched

**Fig. 4.9:** A dog in water on a hot day

### Science in Context

- Firefly eggs flash their light in response to a gentle tapping or vibrations.
- The largest organ of excretion in humans is the skin.

- **Living beings excrete:** All living beings remove waste products from their body through the process of excretion. Animals remove or excrete wastes in the form of urine, sweat and carbon dioxide. Plants excrete wastes in the form of secretions such as gum and resins. They also excrete excess water as water vapour through a process called **transpiration**.
- **Living beings reproduce:** All plants and animals reproduce their own kind. Plants reproduce through seeds, spores and other plant parts. Animals reproduce in different ways. For example, many of them lay eggs while some others give birth to young ones (Fig. 4.10).

A hen lays an egg — A chick comes out of the egg — Mother with her child

**Fig. 4.10:** Living organisms can reproduce

**Wonder!**

A baby blue whale is born after an entire year of development inside its mother's womb.

- **Structural organization:** Another key characteristic of living beings is their structural organization. As shown in Figure 4.11, living beings have a complex and organized structure, from the smallest unit, the cell, to the entire being, the organism.

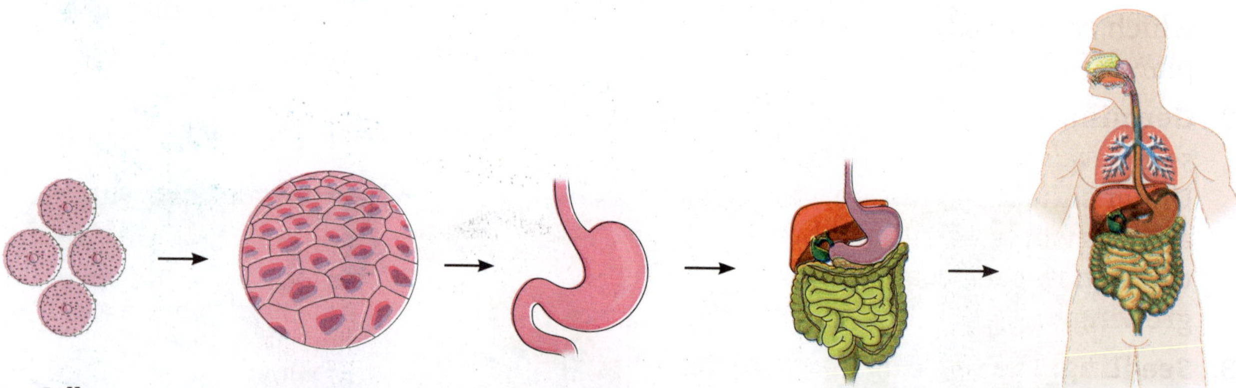

Cells → Tissue → Organ → Organ system → Organism

**Fig. 4.11:** Structural organization in living organisms

Some organisms are made up of only one cell. These single-celled organisms are called **unicellular** organisms, for example, *Amoeba, Euglena, Paramoecium*, yeast and other types of bacteria. On the other hand, some organisms are made up of many cells and are called **multicellular** organisms, for example, spiders, jellyfish, crabs, dogs, trees and human beings. This intricate organization, whether in simple unicellular or complex multicellular forms, defines what we call living organisms.

- **Lifespan and death:** Living organisms are born, grow into adults, grow old and finally die. This entire proces is called the **life cycle** of an organism.

## Revise and Recall

**Match the following.**

| | |
|---|---|
| 1. Unicellular | (a) Green plants |
| 2. Multicellular | (b) *Amoeba* |
| 3. Stomata | (c) Plants and animals |
| 4. Autotrophs | (d) Animals |
| 5. Heterotrophs | (e) Gaseous exchange in leaves |

## LIFE CYCLE OF A PLANT

Understanding the life cycle of a plant helps us appreciate the stages from seed to maturity. The life cycle of a plant (Fig. 4.12) includes several key stages that are mentioned below.

1. **Seed**: The process begins with a seed, which contains the embryo of a new plant.
2. **Germination**: *The process by which a seed develops is called **germination**.* Under suitable conditions, the seed absorbs water, swells and breaks through its seed coat to begin growing.
3. **Seedling**: The seedling grows roots, stems and leaves. The leaves then start to perform photosynthesis.

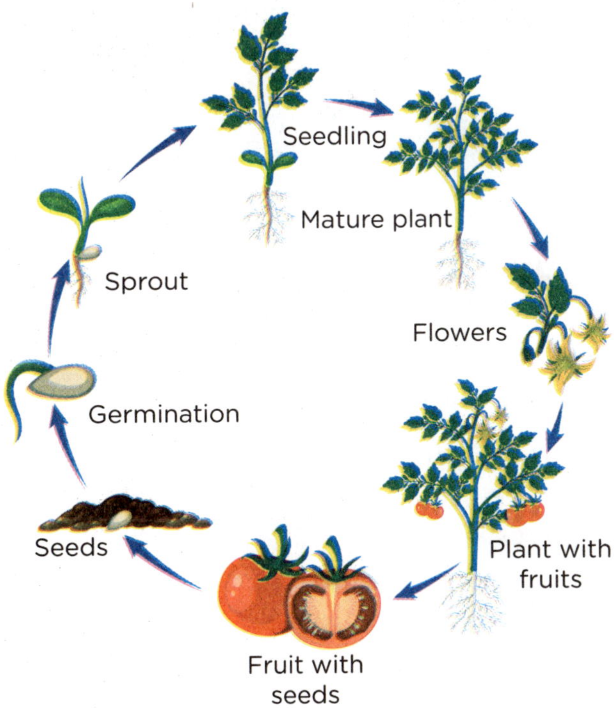


**Fig. 4.12:** Life cycle of a tomato plant

4. **Mature Plant**: The plant grows to maturity and starts producing flowers, if it is a flowering plant. Non-flowering plants, such as ferns and mosses, also reach maturity and reproduce. However, they reproduce using spores or other specialized structures.
5. **Flowering and Fruiting**: Flowers develop, and pollination occurs, leading to fruit formation.
6. **Seed Production**: The fruit matures and produces seeds, which are dispersed to start a new cycle.

**Know the Scientist**

**Dr Chandrima Shaha**
**(Born on 14 October 1952)**

Dr Chandrima Shaha is a prominent cell biologist renowned for her research on cell death and cell survival mechanisms, which has significant implications for disease treatment. She has served as the President of the Indian National Science Academy (INSA) and has received numerous awards, including the Shanti Swarup Bhatnagar Prize.

### Activity 4.1: Investigation

Explore the life cycles of plants that reproduce without seeds, such as through vegetative propagation, spore formation and budding. Using a potato or ginger, observe how new shoots and roots develop from an existing part of the plant. Note how *Bryophyllum* leaves produce small plantlets. Record your observations over several weeks and compare the growth processes of these plants to those that reproduce from seeds. (*Hint*: Note the initial condition of the plant parts and track new shoot and root development over time, including measurements and growth patterns. Also, make drawings of the plants at different stages of growth to observe the changes over time.)

**Questions for reflection:**

1. What are the differences in growth rates and reproductive methods between seed-bearing plants and those that reproduce vegetatively or through spores?
2. How do different reproductive methods help plants in surviving and spreading across in different environments?

## Conditions Essential for Germination of a Seed

Seeds require specific conditions to germinate effectively. The essential conditions are listed below.

- **Water**: Seeds need water to soften the seed coat and activate growth processes.
- **Air**: Seeds require oxygen for cellular respiration and growth.
- **Temperature**: Optimal temperatures vary but are generally necessary for **enzyme**[1] activation and seed **metabolism**[2].
- **Light**: Some seeds require light, while others germinate better in darkness.

**Word Web**

[1]**Enzyme:** proteins that are produced by living organisms that help to speed up certain metabolic reactions in the body

[2]**Metabolism:** the process by which living organisms' bodies convert food into energy and use it to build and repair tissues

Germination (Fig. 4.13) begins when the seed absorbs water, causing the seed coat to swell. The embryo inside the seed then begins to grow, developing into a seedling with roots, a stem and leaves. Germination requires specific conditions such as the right amount of water, oxygen and the appropriate temperature. Once these conditions are met, the seed can successfully germinate and start the journey of becoming a mature plant.

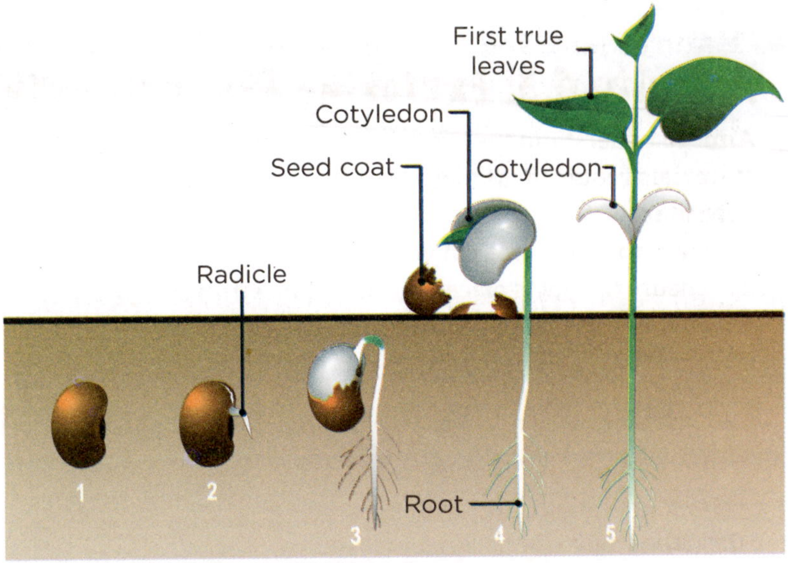


**Fig. 4.13:** Germination of a bean seed

## Activity 4.2: Experiment on Seed Germination

**Aim**: Investigate how different conditions affect seed germination

**Materials required**: Four pots, kidney beans, garden soil and water

**Procedure**:

1. Prepare Pots:
   - **Pot A**: No water, placed in direct sunlight
   - **Pot B**: Waterlogged soil, placed in direct sunlight
   - **Pot C**: Moist soil, placed in darkness
   - **Pot D**: Moist soil, placed in direct sunlight
2. Plant one or two seeds in each pot.
3. Record your observations in the table given below.

**Observation Table:**

| Pot | Air | Sunlight | Water | Prediction (Will the seeds germinate?) | Observation | Possible Reason |
|---|---|---|---|---|---|---|
| A | Yes | Yes | No | | | |
| B | Yes | Yes | Excessive | | | |
| C | Yes | No | | | | |
| D | Yes | Yes | | | | |

**Questions**: Is sunlight necessary for germination? Which pots show germination? What conditions favour seed germination?

**Conclusion**: Seeds require the right amount of water and air for germination. Excessive water or lack of sunlight can inhibit germination, while proper moisture and air support successful seed growth.

## Activity 4.3: Exploring Plant Growth

**Aim**: To understand the life cycle of a plant

**Materials required**: Kidney beans, pots, soil and water

**Procedure**:

1. Plant the seeds in a pot with soil.
2. Ensure the pot is placed in a location with appropriate sunlight and water it regularly.
3. Monitor the plant over three months (that is, 13 weeks) and record observations in given table.

**Observation Table**:

| Date | Plant growth stage | Sketch |
|---|---|---|
| Day 3 | | |
| Day 15 | | |
| Day 30 | | |
| Day 45 | | |
| Day 60 | | |
| Day 90 | | |

**Questions**:

1. How long does it take for changes to occur?
2. After how many days does the first flower appear?
3. What happens to the plant after the fruits are formed?
4. Can you see a new generation of seeds?

**Conclusion**: A seed grows into a mature plant that produces flowers. Flowers develop into fruits (pods) containing seeds. The plant eventually dies, completing its life cycle. The seeds from the fruit will grow into new plants, continuing the cycle.

## Growth and Movement in Plants

Plants grow and move in response to environmental stimuli such as light and gravity.

**Growth Direction**:

- **Roots**: Grow generally downward, responding to gravity.
- **Shoots**: Grow generally upward, seeking light.

**Movement**:

- **Gravitropism**: Roots grow downward in response to gravity (Fig. 4.14).
- **Phototropism**: Shoots grow towards light (Fig. 4.15).

**Fig. 4.14:** Gravitropism

**Fig. 4.15:** Phototropism

## Activity 4.4: Growth of Roots and Shoots

**Aim**: Observe how plants grow under different light conditions

**Materials**: Bean or gram seeds, glass beakers, moist cloth and three cardboard boxes

**Procedure**:

1. **Setup**: Use the cardboard boxes to create the conditions given below. Place one beaker in each cardboard box.
   - **Beaker A**: Seedlings are exposed to sunlight from all directions.
   - **Beaker B**: Seedlings placed upside down exposed to sunlight from all directions.

     (*Hint*: Plant the seedling as usual. Then invert the container, ensuring the roots are at the top and the stem is exposed, hanging down towards the ground.)
   - **Beaker C**: Seedlings exposed to sunlight from one direction.
2. Record your observations in the table given below.

**Observation Table:**

| Beaker | Sunlight Direction | Direction of Plant | Shoot Growth | Root Growth |
|---|---|---|---|---|
| A | All directions | Upright | | |
| B | All directions | Upside down | | |
| C | One direction | Upright | | |

**Questions**:

1. What is the direction of growth for roots and shoots?
2. Do predictions match observations?

**Conclusion**: Shoots grow toward light, while roots grow downward. Plants respond to environmental stimuli to optimize growth and survival.

## Revise and Recall

**Fill in the blanks.**

1. The process by which a seed develops into a mature plant and eventually produces seeds is known as the __________ of a plant.
2. In the life cycle of a flowering plant, the __________ develops into fruit, which contains seeds.
3. During __________, the seed absorbs water and begins to swell, eventually breaking through the seed coat.
4. The growth and movement of plant shoots towards light is called __________.
5. The __________ of a plant involves stages such as germination, growth, flowering and seed production.

# LIFE CYCLE OF ANIMALS

Understanding the life cycles of animals provides us with insights into their growth, development and the ecological roles they play. Just like plants, animals undergo significant changes throughout their lives. These changes can vary widely among different species and are essential for their survival and reproduction.

## Life Cycle of a Mosquito

Mosquitoes are common insects known for their role as **vectors**[1] of diseases such as malaria, dengue fever and chikungunya. Understanding their life cycle helps in managing mosquito populations and preventing the spread of these diseases.

**Word Web**

[1]**Vectors:** an insect or an animal that carries and transmits pathogens (disease-causing germs such as viruses or bacteria) from one host to another, spreading diseases

**Stages in the Life Cycle of a Mosquito (Fig. 4.16):**

1. **Egg Stage**: The female mosquito lays eggs on or near still water, such as ponds or puddles. The eggs float on the water in clusters or rafts.
2. **Larva Stage**: After a few days, the eggs hatch into larvae, which are also called **wrigglers**. These worm-like larvae live in the water, eat tiny bits of food and come up to the surface to breathe.
3. **Pupa Stage**: The larvae change into pupae, which are comma-shaped and float on the water. Pupae do not eat but move to the surface for air while their bodies change into adult mosquitoes.
4. **Adult Stage**: After a few days, the adult mosquito emerges from the pupa. It rests on the water surface to dry its wings before flying away. Adult mosquitoes live for about 10 to 15 days.

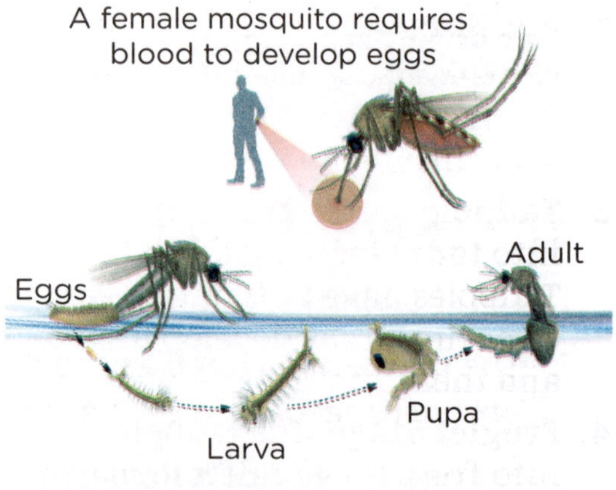


**Fig. 4.16:** Life cycle of a mosquito

**Wonder!**

Female mosquitoes need blood to lay eggs, which is why they bite humans and animals. This essential feeding behaviuor provides them with the nutrients required for egg production. However, this bite is not just a harmless act—it is the critical moment when they transmit diseases. This makes mosquitoes one of the most dangerous creatures on the planet.

## Activity 4.5: Exploring Life Stages of a Mosquito

**Aim:** Understand and observe the stages in the life cycle of a mosquito through virtual experiences

**Materials required:** Access to a computer or tablet with Internet connectivity

**Procedure:**

1. Take a virtual tour of a mosquito breeding environment through an online platform that simulates stagnant water sources and the mosquito life cycle.
2. Observe the different stages of the mosquito life cycle, including eggs, larvae, pupae and adult mosquitoes, through interactive videos.
3. Brainstorm the impact of environmental conditions on mosquito development.
4. Discuss measures to prevent mosquito breeding, such as removing standing water and using insect repellents.

**Conclusion:** Understanding the mosquito life cycle helps in implementing effective control measures to reduce the spread of mosquito-borne diseases. For example, eliminating breeding sites and using larvicides can significantly cut down mosquito populations.

# Life Cycle of a Frog

Frogs undergo a fascinating transformation from eggs to adults through a process called **metamorphosis**. Their life cycle includes both aquatic and terrestrial stages, reflecting their adaptations to different environments.

**Stages in the Life Cycle of a Frog (Fig. 4.17):**

1. **Egg Stage**: A female frog lays **eggs** in water, often in clusters. The eggs, called **spawn**, are covered in a jelly-like substance to keep them safe.
2. **Embryo Stage**: After a few days, the eggs develop into **embryos**. These embryos grow inside the egg and soon become tadpoles.
3. **Tadpole Stage**: The embryos hatch into **tadpoles**, which live in water. Tadpoles have tails but no legs. Over time, they develop hind legs and then front legs.
4. **Froglet Stage**: The tadpoles turn into **froglets**. Froglets look like small frogs but still have tails. They start spending time on land but need to go back to water sometimes.
5. **Adult Frog Stage:** The froglet becomes an **adult frog**. The tail disappears and the frog can live both in water and on land. Adult frogs are able to lay eggs, starting the life cycle again.

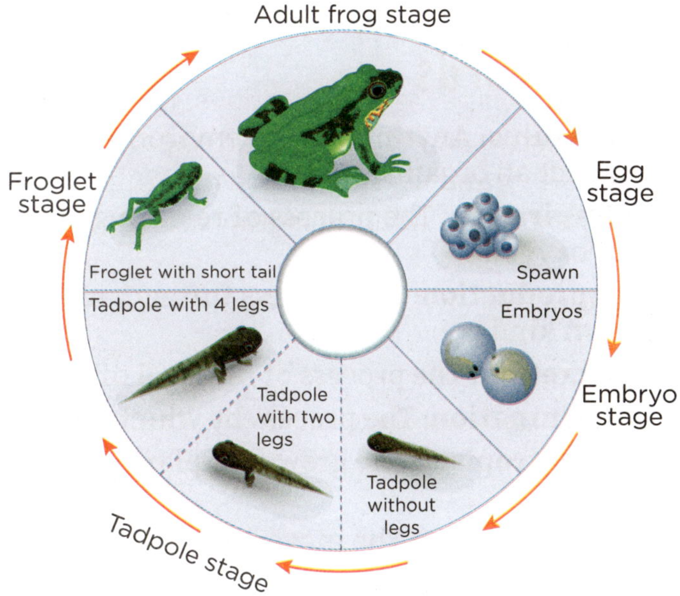


**Fig. 4.17:** Life cycle of a frog

## Activity 4.6: Observing Life Stages of a Frog

**Aim:** Identify and understand the stages in the frog life cycle

**Materials required:** Pond water samples, magnifying glass and safety equipment

**Note:** Perform this activity under an adult supervision.

**Procedure:**

1. Observe the pond water for frog eggs (spawn).
2. Record changes in the eggs and follow their development into tadpoles.
3. Note the transformation from tadpole to froglet and then to adult frog.
4. Discuss the ecological roles of frogs and their habitat changes throughout their life cycle.

**Conclusion:** Learning about how frogs grow helps us understand their development.

## Revise and Recall

**State whether the following statements are true (T) or false (F).**

1. Mosquito larvae, also known as wrigglers, are commonly found in stagnant water.
2. The pupa stage of a mosquito is comma-shaped and floats on the water.
3. In the life cycle of a frog, the tadpole stage is characterized by the presence of legs and the absence of a tail.
4. Frogs lay their eggs in clusters of jelly-like substances known as spawn in water bodies.
5. Adult mosquitoes typically live for 10 to 15 days and may transmit diseases like malaria and dengue fever.

## Keywords

**Stimulus:** Anything in the environment that can cause a change in behaviour or affect an organism

**Respiration:** The process of releasing energy from digested food with the help of oxygen

**Reproduction:** The process through which living organisms produce their own kind

**Excretion:** The process of removal of waste products from the body

**Germination:** The process by which a seed develops into a new plant

**Gravitropism:** The growth of plant root system towards soil under the effect of gravity

**Phototropism:** The movement of plants shoot system towards light

# Summary

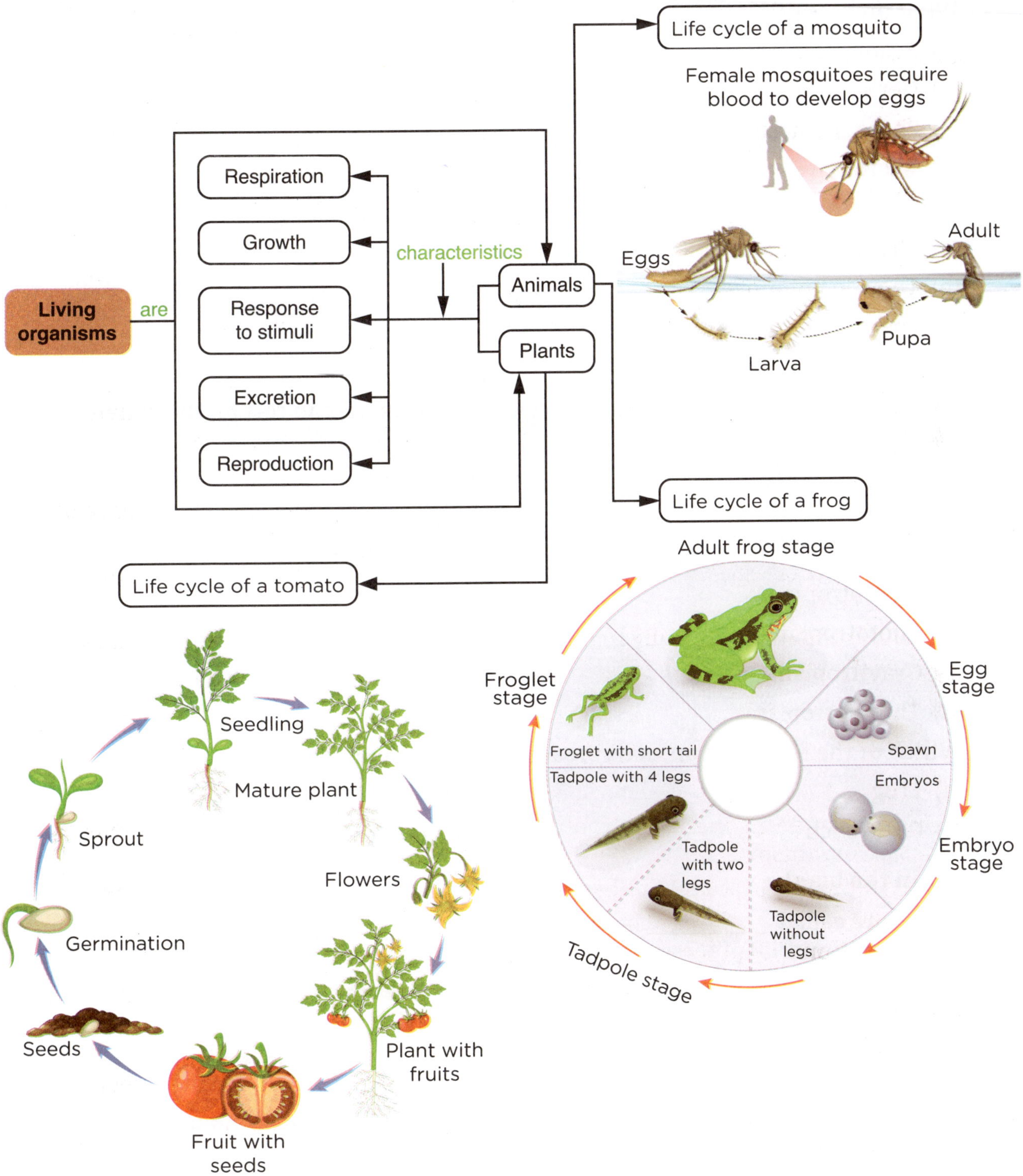
Living organisms
are
Respiration
Growth
Response to stimuli
Excretion
Reproduction
characteristics
Animals
Plants
Life cycle of a mosquito
Female mosquitoes require blood to develop eggs
Eggs
Larva
Pupa
Adult
Life cycle of a frog
Adult frog stage
Egg stage
Spawn
Embryos
Embryo stage
Tadpole without legs
Tadpole with two legs
Tadpole with 4 legs
Tadpole stage
Froglet with short tail
Froglet stage
Life cycle of a tomato
Seedling
Mature plant
Flowers
Plant with fruits
Fruit with seeds
Seeds
Germination
Sprout

# Exercise

W

**A. Choose the correct option.**

ia

1. What process do plants use to make their own food?
   (a) Respiration
   (b) Germination
   (c) Photosynthesis
   (d) Excretion
2. Which of the following is a characteristic of living beings?
   (a) They need food.
   (b) They do not move.
   (c) They do not respond to stimuli.
   (d) They do not grow.
3. In which stage of the mosquito life cycle does the mosquito rest on the water surface to dry its wings?
   (a) Egg (b) Larva
   (c) Pupa (d) Adult
4. What is the term used for a plant's growth in response to light?
   (a) Hydrotropism
   (b) Phototropism
   (c) Gravitropism
   (d) Thigmotropism
5. Which of the following animals breathe through their skin?
   (a) Frog (b) Dog
   (c) Cockroach (d) Mosquito

**B. Fill in the blanks.**

ia

1. Plants are called __________ because they produce their own food through photosynthesis.
2. The __________ stage in the frog's life cycle involves the tadpole turning into a froglet.
3. __________ is the process by which living beings remove waste products from their bodies.
4. In the mosquito life cycle, the __________ stage is characterized by the mosquito larvae floating in the water.
5. The process of a seed developing into a new plant is called __________.

**C. State whether the following statements are true (T) or false (F).**

1. Plants do not move from place to place but can still show movement.
2. Mosquito pupae feed on organic matter in the water.
3. Frogs are capable of living in both terrestrial and aquatic environments.
4. All living beings have a lifespan and eventually die.
5. In the frog life cycle, the embryo stage occurs before the tadpole stage.

**D. Give reasons for the following.**

1. Some animals are made up of a single cell.
2. *Mimosa pudica* closes its leaves when touched.
3. Living organisms reproduce.
4. Respiration is essential for living organisms.
5. Mosquitoes need still water to lay their eggs.

**E. Answer the following questions briefly.**

1. How do living organisms differ from non-living things?
2. How do ducks reproduce?
3. How do plants respond to changes in their surrounding?
4. Why do we need food?
5. Define the term 'life cycle'.

**F. Answer the following questions.**

1. Discuss the characteristics of living organisms that differentiate them from non-living things. Provide examples to support your explanation.
2. Describe the process of seed germination and the conditions necessary for a seed to germinate successfully. Include the different stages of growth from a seed to a mature plant.
3. Explain the life cycle of a mosquito in detail, describing each stage from the egg to the adult mosquito. How does understanding this life cycle help in controlling mosquito populations?
4. What are the stages in the life cycle of a frog, and how do these stages reflect the frog's ability to live in both aquatic and terrestrial environments? Include details about the transformation from tadpole to adult frog.
5. How do plants respond to environmental stimuli like light and gravity? Explain how these movements help plants survive and grow.

# Cognitive Corner

## Critical Thinking

1. Is respiration different from breathing?
2. Are fingernails and hair living parts of our body? Give reasons for your answer.
3. We know that living organisms can move. Clouds can move too. Are they living? Why or why not?

## Picture Study

**Identify the characteristics of living organisms depicted in these pictures.**

1. ________________

2. ________________

## Projects

1. Create a model of the life cycle of a mosquito using craft materials. **(C-7.2)**
2. Make a chart showing the stages of seed germination and plant growth. **(C-7.1)**
3. Conduct a simple experiment to observe the growth of a seedling under different light conditions. Document your findings. **(C-6.2)**

## In the Library

Plants also respond to stimuli. Find out the names of at least four plants and how they respond to stimuli by referring to the Internet. Create a report with diagrams to showcase your findings. **(C-7.2)**

## Life Skills

1. Research the impact of deforestation on the life cycles of frogs and present your findings. Collaborate with your friends and take the initiative to assign specific roles to each member to ensure effective contribution and successful completion of the project. **(C-6.1)**
2. Design a poster to educate others on how to prevent mosquito breeding in your community. **(C-5.1)**

# Worksheet

Life on Earth is sustained by the sun's heat and light, with plants uniquely capable of converting sunlight into food. This energy transfer forms the foundation of various life forms that rely on plants directly or indirectly through the food chain. Forests exemplify harmonious coexistence, providing a diverse habitat where plant and animal life interact, with wild animals depending on plants or other animals for their survival.

Forest

A. By means of arrows, show the way in which food reach from the plants to the higher animals.

Grass

Bird's eggs

Fox

Crocodile

Hippopotamus

B. How does the preservation of forests and biodiversity (SDG 15) contribute to sustaining life on Earth?

C. In the context of SDG 15, how can promoting sustainable land use and responsible forestry practices help ensure the availability of essential resources such as water and oxygen?

D. Discuss the role of SDG 15 in addressing the impact of human activities on the environment, particularly in preventing deforestation and protecting natural habitats for wildlife, thus promoting ecological balance and preserving Earth's life-sustaining capabilities.

# 5 Components of Food

### Curricular Goals

- Understand the components of health, hygiene and well-being **(CG-4)**

### Competencies

- Undertake a nutrition-based analysis of food components with special reference to Indian culinary practices and modern understanding of nutrition and explain the effect of nutrition on health **(C-4.1)**
- Examine different dimensions of diversity of food – sources, nutrients, climatic conditions, diets **(C-4.2)**

## Let's Get Started

Observe the given pictures and answer the following questions.

Meal A

Meal B

1. Which meal is based on processed foods and fast-food culture?

_______________

2. Which meal is healthier for our body and why?

_______________

_______________

3. Can you specify which ingredients in this meal come from plant sources and which come from animal sources? List them separately.

_______________

_______________

The food we eat contains substances called **nutrients** that our body requires to grow and stay healthy. In this chapter, we will learn about the various nutrients found in our food, their importance and the disorders caused by the lack/excess of nutrients in the body.

# FOOD

Food is an essential part of our lives, providing us with the energy and nutrients we need to grow, stay healthy and perform daily activities. The types of food (Fig. 5.1) we eat can vary greatly depending on factors such as culture, personal preference, availability and **culinary**[1] practices.

**Fig. 5.1:** Visual representation of food available across the world

**Word Web**

[1]**Culinary**: related to cooking

**Wonder!**

**Indigenous** food refers to the traditional food that are native to a particular region or culture, often derived from local plants and animals passed down through generations. This reflects the cultural heritage and ecological conditions of their origin. Due to globalization and migration, indigenous food items are now found worldwide. Additionally, the advancements in agricultural practices has contributed to the spread of this food. As people share their culinary traditions across borders, this has become integrated into diverse cuisines globally.

## Culinary Practices

Our food habits and culinary practices have evolved over time. Many factors, such as technological advancements and cultural exchanges, have influenced these changes. Table 5.1 gives a few examples of how cooking practices have changed over time.

**Fig. 5.2:** *Chulha*

**Fig. 5.3:** Gas stove

**Table 5.1:** Culinary Practices

| Cooking Method | Traditional | Modern |
|---|---|---|
| **Cooking Stove** | ***Chulha*** (Fig. 5.2)<br>• A traditional clay stove using wood or cow dung cakes as fuel.<br>• Common in rural households. | **Gas Stove** (Fig. 5.3)<br>• A modern cooking appliance using gas as fuel.<br>• Faster and more efficient. |
| **Grinding Spices/Grains** | ***Sil-Batta*:** A manual stone grinder used for grinding spices and grains. | **Electric Grinder:** A modern electric device that grinds spices and grains quickly and easily. |

1. *What are "chula" and "sil batta" called in your native language?*
2. *What other changes in culinary practices have you come across? Give any two examples from your observations.*

## Activity 5.1: Record Your Meals

**Aim:** Understand your eating habits by recording the food items you consume over a week

**Materials required:** Notebook, pen or pencil

**Procedure:**

1. For one week, write down everything you eat for breakfast, lunch, dinner and snacks.
2. Use the table below as an example to record your meals. Specify each type of food and drink consumed.

| Day | Breakfast | Lunch | Dinner | Snacks |
|---|---|---|---|---|
| Monday | Bread, butter, milk | Rice with chicken curry | Chapati, potato curry, cucumber salad | Biscuits, orange |
| Tuesday | Idlis with coconut chutney | Vegetable biryani with cucumber raita | Rice, mackerel fish curry | Milk and biscuits |
| Wednesday | Pongal with coconut chutney | Curd rice with mango pickle | Rawa dosa with tomato chutney | Roasted chickpeas |

**Observation and Analysis:**

1. After a week, review your table and note any patterns. Do you eat the same food items regularly? Are there variations in your meals?
2. Discuss with your classmates to see if their food choices are similar or different from yours.
3. How diverse is the range of food you consume each day?

**Discussion:**

1. What do your observations tell you about your eating habits?
2. What similarities and differences do you notice?
3. Why are food choices different between you and some of your classmates?
4. What are the reasons for food consumed by you and some of your classmates similar?
5. Do you include a variety of vegetables, fruits, proteins and grains in your diet?
6. How balanced are your meals in terms of carbohydrates, proteins and fats?

## Activity 5.2

Analyse the two dishes shown here and make a chart on healthy food choice. (*Hint*: To analyse, identify the dishes, gather nutritional information, compare the ingredients and then evaluate health benefits.)

- Based on the nutrient content, which dish do you think is a healthier choice?
- Think of ways to modify the less healthy dish to make it a more nutritious option.

## Activity 5.3: Interview an Elder

**Aim:** Learn about changes in food habits and cooking practices by interviewing elderly people

**Materials required:** Prepared list of questions, notebook, pen or pencil

**Procedure:**

1. Prepare a list of questions to ask elderly family members or neighbours about their food habits and cooking practices when they were younger. (Be polite and respectful while talking to elders.) Some sample questions include:
   a. What kind of food did you eat when you were younger? Is the food you eat now different from earlier times? Why?
   b. What were the main cooking methods back then, and how have modern methods affected cooking nowadays?
   c. Have you noticed any changes in the way food is prepared today?
   d. What do you think caused these changes?
   e. How did you preserve food in the past, and what methods do you use now?
2. Conduct the interview and record their responses.

**Discussion:**

1. What differences did you find between the past and present cooking practices?
2. Why do you think these changes occurred?
3. How have technological advancements affected the way we cook today?

**Conclusion:** Cooking practices have evolved due to various factors such as technology and lifestyle changes. By understanding these changes, we can appreciate the convenience of modern cooking while also recognizing the importance of traditional methods.

# NUTRIENT REQUIREMENT

The major nutrients required by our body are carbohydrates, proteins, fats, vitamins and minerals. In addition to these, we need roughage or dietary fibres and water. When a food item has a particular nutrient in higher quantities, it is said to be rich in that nutrient compared to other nutrients present in that food item. For example, potato is a carbohydrate-rich food.

## Carbohydrates

Our body requires energy to do work and other activities. Carbohydrates (Fig. 5.4) are the main source of energy and are a major part of the staple diet of people all over the world. Cereals (rice, wheat, maize, millets), tubers such as potatoes and tapioca are the major sources of carbohydrates. Starch and sugars are the forms of carbohydrates present in the food we eat. Rice, wheat and potatoes are some sources of starch. The table sugar we use, fruits and honey are some sources of sugar.

**Fig. 5.4:** Sources of carbohydrates

## Activity 5.4: Experimental Investigation

**Aim:** To investigate the presence of starch in various food items

**Materials required:** 2 grams of rice flour, a test tube, water, 10 mℓ of iodine solution, tray, tissue paper, apple and potato slices (cut the apple and potato into slices just before you begin the investigation)

**Procedure:**

**Test 1**

1. Take 2 grams of rice flour in a test tube; add 5 mℓ of water in the test tube and make a solution.
2. In the test tube, add 2 or 3 drops of iodine solution.

**Observation:** The colour of the iodine solution changes from yellow–brown to blue–black.

**Inference:** Iodine changes colour from yellow–brown to blue–black only in the presence of starch.

**Conclusion:** Rice flour has starch.

**Test 2**

1. Place a slice of potato on a tissue paper placed on a tray.
2. Add 2–3 drops of iodine solution on the slice.

Observe the change and explain the reason for the change observed.

**Test 3**

Repeat Test 2, but use apple slices in place of potato slices.

Before you begin the test with apple slices, predict the result. See whether your prediction comes true.

**Observation:** The starch present in the potato slice changes the colour of iodine to blue–black, but the iodine dropped on the slice of apple remains yellow–brown.

**Conclusion:** The change of colour confirms the presence of starch in potatoes. Starch is not present in apples.

The apples turned brown on the cut surfaces. Why?

# Fats

Fats also provide energy to our body. For the same amount of food consumed, fats give more energy than carbohydrates. We get fats from both plant and animal sources (Fig. 5.5). Fats are required for the proper development and functioning of the brain and nervous system. Fats are also required to develop immunity in children. However, too much fat in the diet can lead to obesity.

Some sources of fats are egg yolk, edible oils, ghee, butter and meat. Fats can be categorized into saturated fats and unsaturated fats. Saturated fats such as butter are usually solid at room temperature, whereas unsaturated fats such as groundnut oil, sunflower oil, olive oil, gingelly (sesame) and mustard oil (examples of vegetable oil) are usually liquid at room temperature.

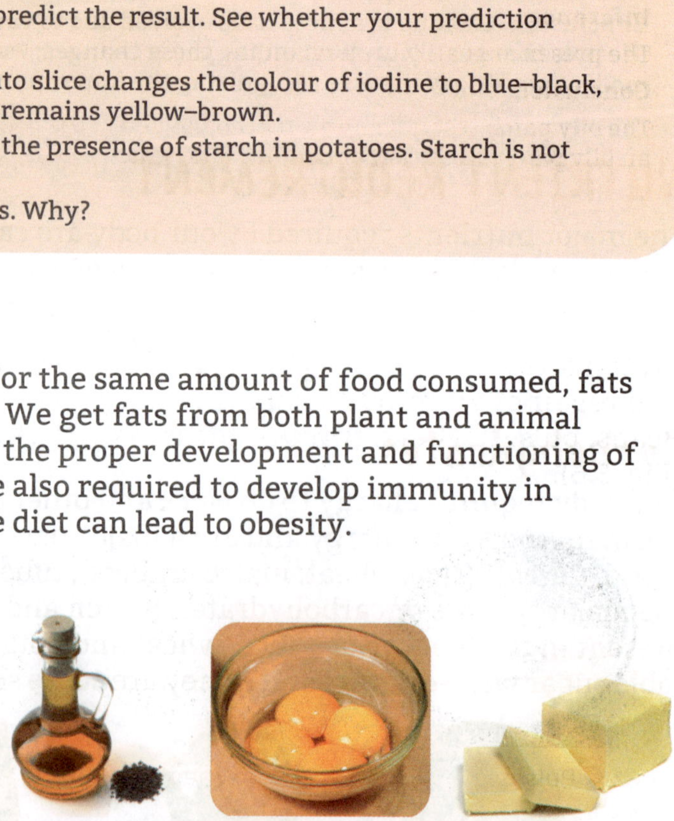


**Fig. 5.5:** Sources of fats

## Activity 5.5: Experimental Investigation

**Aim:** To investigate the presence of fats in various food items

**Materials required:** Food samples (e.g., peanuts, cheese, butter, potato chips), brown paper or plain white paper, paper towel, spatula or spoon, water (optional), light source (e.g., a lamp or sunlight)

**Procedure:**

1. Take small pieces of the food samples you want to test and place each sample on separate pieces of brown or plain white paper.
2. Fold the paper over the food sample and press it firmly with your fingers. Be careful not to tear the paper.
   If the food sample is dry, such as nuts, powder it first and then press it between the paper.
   If the food sample is oily, such as butter, press gently to avoid tearing the paper.
   If the food sample contains water, allow the paper to dry completely.

**Observation:** After pressing, unfold the paper and observe if any oily patches appear on the paper.

Hold the paper up to a light source. Check if the light shines faintly through the oily patch.

If the paper develops an oily patch and allows light to pass through faintly, the food item contains fats. If there is no oily patch, the food item likely does not contain fats.

**Inference:**

The presence of an oily patch on the paper indicates that the food item contains fats.

**Conclusion:**

The oily patch test is a simple method to detect the presence of fats in food items. Food that leave an oily patch on the paper contain fats, which are important for energy storage in the body.

## Proteins

Proteins are the building blocks of any living body. They are required for the growth and repair of worn-out tissues. We get proteins from both plant and animal sources. Beans, pulses, wheat, sprouts, meat, fish, milk and cheese are protein-rich food (Fig. 5.6).

Pulses

Wheat

Sprouts

Fish

**Fig. 5.6:** Sources of proteins

## Activity 5.6: Experimental Investigation

**Aim:** To investigate the presence of proteins in various food items

**Materials required:** Test tubes, water, 5–10 groundnuts, copper sulphate solution, droppers, caustic soda, test tube stand, mortar and pestle

*Precaution: Caustic soda is highly corrosive and can cause severe burns or injury, so it must be handled with protective gear and care. Do this activity only under the guidance of your teacher.*

**Procedure:**

1. With the help of a mortar and pestle, make a paste of the groundnuts.
2. Transfer about one teaspoon of this groundnut paste into a test tube containing 5 $m\ell$ water and shake it well.
3. With the help of a dropper, add two drops of copper sulphate solution to the test tube.
4. With another dropper transfer 10 drops of caustic soda solution into the test tube.
5. Leave the test tube in the test tube stand for five minutes.

**Observation:** The colour of the solution in the test tube changes to violet.

**Conclusion:** The change in colour to violet indicates the presence of proteins.

## Revise and Recall

**Match the following.**

| | |
|---|---|
| 1. Carbohydrates | (a) Butter |
| 2. Unsaturated fat | (b) Sprouts |
| 3. Proteins | (c) Vegetable oil |
| 4. Saturated fat | (d) Wheat |

# Vitamins

Vitamins (Fig. 5.7) play a very important role in the growth and development of the human body. There are about 13 vitamins that have been recognized to be present in plant and animal sources. Vitamins help us to develop immunity against many disorders. There are two types of vitamins—fat soluble and water soluble.

Carrots Spinach Oranges Eggs Meat

**Fig. 5.7:** Sources of vitamins

**Fat-soluble vitamins** (A, D, E and K) are absorbed with dietary fat and stored in the body's fat tissues and liver. They play crucial roles. Vitamin A supports vision and skin health, Vitamin D aids in calcium absorption and bone health, Vitamin E acts as an antioxidant and Vitamin K is essential for blood clotting. These vitamins are released from storage as needed by the body.

**Water-soluble vitamins** are vitamins $B_1$, $B_2$, $B_3$, $B_6$, $B_{12}$ and C. These vitamins cannot be prepared or stored in our body. We get these from the different types of food items that we eat. Therefore, it is important that we include food items that are rich in these vitamins in our meals. Key examples include Vitamins C and B complex which support immune function, energy production and overall health.

Table 5.2 shows the different kinds of vitamins and their sources.

**Table 5.2:** Vitamin-rich foods

| | |
|---|---|
| **Vitamin A** | Orange, ripe yellow fruits, leafy vegetables, carrot, pumpkin, squash, spinach, liver, soy milk and milk |
| **Vitamin B complex ($B_1$, $B_2$, $B_3$, $B_6$, $B_{12}$)** | Oatmeal, unpolished rice, milk products, broccoli, leafy vegetables, fish, unpolished cereals, eggs, meat (lamb and liver of chicken are high in Vitamin $B_{12}$) and fish |
| **Vitamin C** | Many fruits especially citrus fruits such as orange and lemon and vegetables such as cauliflower and cabbage |
| **Vitamin D** | Fish, egg, liver and mushroom |
| **Vitamin E** | Vegetable oils, nuts and seeds, wheatgerm, yam, mango, kiwi and green leafy vegetables such as beetroot leaves |
| **Vitamin K** | Green leafy vegetables such as spinach and fenugreek leaves, fruits such as pomegranate, figs, berries and avocado and other food items such as tomatoes, egg and liver of chicken and goose |

## Benefits of Vitamins

Vitamins are crucial for maintaining overall health as they support various bodily functions, including energy production, immune defense and cellular repair. Each vitamin has a specific role in regulating processes that keep the body functioning optimally. Some benefits are given below.

- **Vitamin A** supports vision, skin health, and immune function.
- **Vitamin $B_1$ (Thiamine)** aids in energy metabolism and nerve function.
- **vitamin $B_2$ (Riboflavin)** helps with energy production and maintains healthy skin.
- **Vitamin $B_3$ (Niacin)** supports energy production and benefits skin and digestive health.

### Science in Context

With advancements in science and technology, dietary supplements are designed and developed to provide adequate amounts of nutrients that may be missing in our diets.

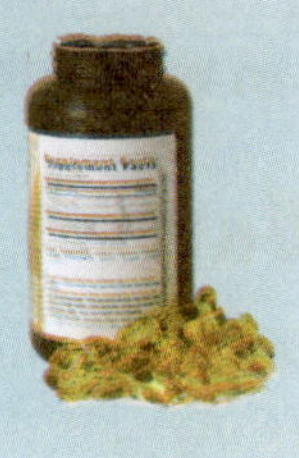

- **Vitamin $B_6$ (Pyridoxine)** is important for protein metabolism and brain health.
- **Vitamin $B_{12}$ (Cobalamin)** is essential for red blood cell formation and proper neurological function.
- **Vitamin C** boosts immune function, aids in collagen production and acts as an antioxidant.
- **Vitamin D** enhances calcium absorption, promotes bone health and supports the immune system.
- **Vitamin E** acts as an antioxidant, protecting cells from oxidative damage
- **Vitamin K** is crucial for blood clotting and maintaining healthy bones.

## Minerals

Minerals are required for making our bones strong, building muscles and proper functioning of the body. There are two types of minerals—major minerals and trace minerals. They are grouped based on the requirement of the body. **Major minerals** are required in high quantity by the body, for example, calcium, chlorine, magnesium, phosphorus, potassium, sodium and sulphur. **Trace minerals** are needed by the body in very less amount, for example, iron, zinc, cobalt, copper and iodine. The sources of minerals are milk products, green leafy vegetables, meat, fruits, seeds and pulses (Fig. 5.8).

**Fig. 5.8:** Sources of minerals

## Dietary Fibre

Dietary fibre is also known as **roughage**. This is provided by various plant products such as fruits, leafy vegetables and whole grains. Roughage helps in easy bowel movement ensuring removal of the undigested food, thereby preventing constipation. Roughage is of two types, soluble and insoluble, depending on their solubility in water.

**Soluble fibre** gives us a feeling of fullness after eating. It is found in varying amounts in all plant-based foods. Food sources that have soluble fibre are peas, soya bean, oats, berries, apples, oranges, cucumbers, etc.

**Insoluble fibre** is found in food sources such as whole wheat/whole grains, tomato, cabbage and green leafy vegetables. It adds bulk to our diet and helps in easy passage of food through the digestive system. It also helps in getting rid of undigested food and waste from the body.

## Water

Water makes up most part of all the food items that we consume. Water is added in almost all the food we prepare or cook. Water is required for all body functions and to maintain our body temperature.

Many chemical reactions happen due to water; the minerals present in water help in contraction of muscles and transmission of nerve impulses. Nutrients are transported by water to all parts of the body. Loss of water in the form of sweat and urine helps to remove toxins from our body.

Drinking 6–8 glasses (2–3 litres) of water daily keeps the body healthy.

### Know the Scientist

**Dr Kamala Sohonie**

**(18 June 1911–28 June 1998)**

Dr Kamala Sohonie was a trailblazing Indian biochemist and the first Indian woman to earn a Ph.D. in science. She made significant contributions to biochemistry and nutrition, particularly in understanding the role of vitamins, especially Vitamin C in human health. Her research clarified the relationship between diet and health and led to the introduction of '**Neera**,' a health drink derived from palm extract, which greatly improved the health of malnourished tribal adolescents and pregnant women. For her impactful work, she was honoured with the **Rashtrapati Award**.

## BALANCED DIET

a

It is important that the food we consume every day provides us all the required nutrients in appropriate amounts (Fig. 5.9). *A diet that provides all essential nutrients such as carbohydrates, proteins, fats, vitamins and minerals, in the right proportions to support overall health, improve bodily functions and maintain fitness, is known as a* ***balanced diet***. The composition of a balanced diet varies based on the age, physical activity and health of people.

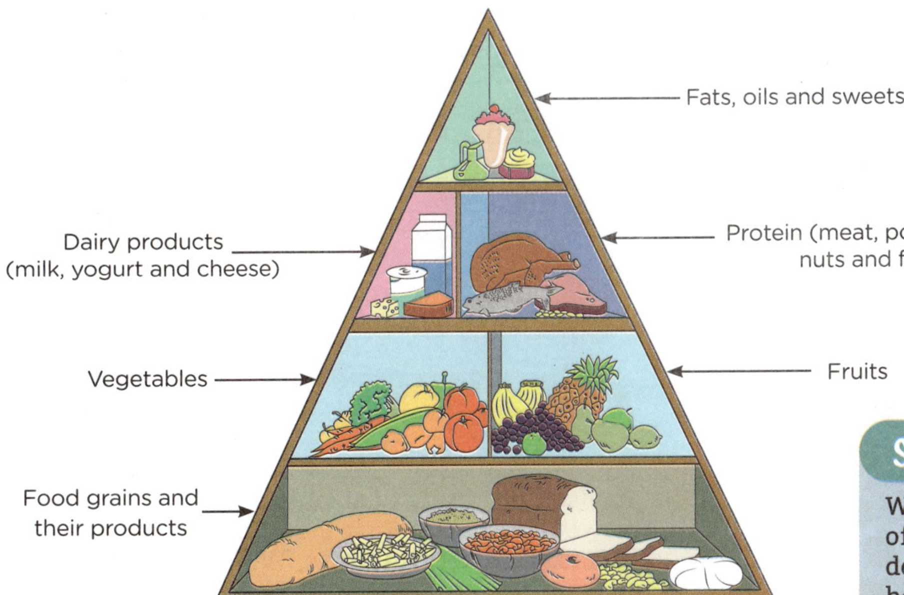


**Fig. 5.9:** Food pyramid for a healthy and balanced diet

### Science in Context

We need to eat a number of serves from each group depending on our age and how active we are.

## Counting Calories

Counting **calories**[1] is the practice of tracking the number of calories consumed through food and beverages to manage weight, ensure balanced nutrition or achieve specific dietary goals.

### Word Web

[1]**Calories:** units used to measure the energy value of food

The calorie intake requirement for a person depends on various factors, including age, sex, weight, height, physical activity level and overall health goals. The daily calorie needs are generally estimated based on an individual's Basal Metabolic Rate (BMR) and Physical Activity Level (PAL). BMR represents the number of calories needed to maintain basic bodily functions at rest, while PAL considers the additional calories needed for physical activity.

Table 5.3 shows the estimated calorie intake requirements for different adult groups.

### Science in Context

People who are trying to lose weight often choose low-calorie food and avoid items such as crisps and chocolate that do not align with a balanced diet. To maintain a healthy eating pattern, it is advisable to minimize the consumption of crisps and chocolates due to their high calorie content and excessive salt, sugar and fat levels.

**Table 5.3:** Estimated calorie intake requirements per day

| Gender | Sedentary adults | Moderately active adults (engaging in light physical activity or exercise) | Active adults (engaging in regular exercise or physical labour) |
|---|---|---|---|
| Female | 1800 to 2200 calories | 2000 to 2400 calories | 2200 to 2800 calories |
| Male | 2200 to 2320 calories | 2400 to 2800 calories | 2800 to 3000 calories |

Consuming too few calories can lead to malnutrition and energy deficiency, while excess calorie intake can result in weight gain and related health issues. Understanding and managing calorie intake in the context of a balanced diet ensures that the body receives the necessary energy to perform daily activities, support bodily functions and maintain overall health and well-being.

### Activity 5.7

Find out the calorie content in different food items. Then, create a balanced diet chart for yourself considering the calorie intake requirement per day.

## Science in Context

Apart from the diet, a supplement for vitamin D is present in sunlight. When sunlight falls on the skin, it causes reactions to produce vitamin D. This is the reason why vitamin D is called sunshine vitamin.

Sodium chloride, potassium, calcium and magnesium are responsible for easy movement of muscles and body parts. The imbalance of these nutrients can affect your thinking, movement and vision. When the amount of minerals is not sufficient in the body, you suffer from muscle cramps.

Sunlight: a source of vitamin D

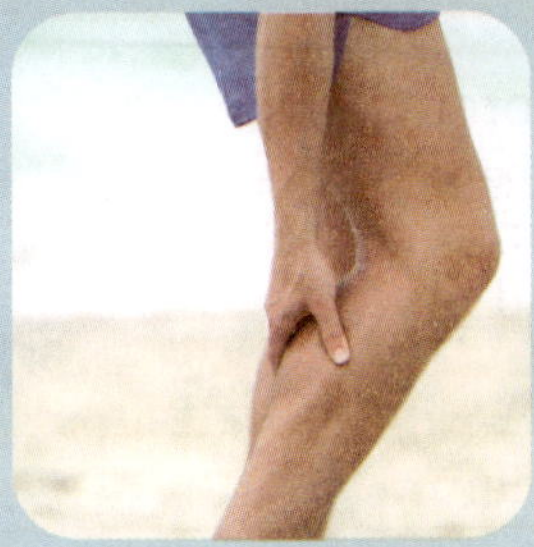

Muscle cramp

# NUTRIENT-RELATED DISORDERS

As discussed earlier, our diet should have all the essential nutrients in the required proportions. Lack or excess of nutrients in the body can cause disorders.

## Deficiency Disorders

If the nutrient intake by the body is not sufficient, it creates deficiency of that particular nutrient. If this condition of insufficient consumption of food containing nutrients continues for a long time, it leads to nutrient deficiency. *The disorders caused due to nutrient deficiency in the diet are called **deficiency disorders*** (Fig. 5.10).

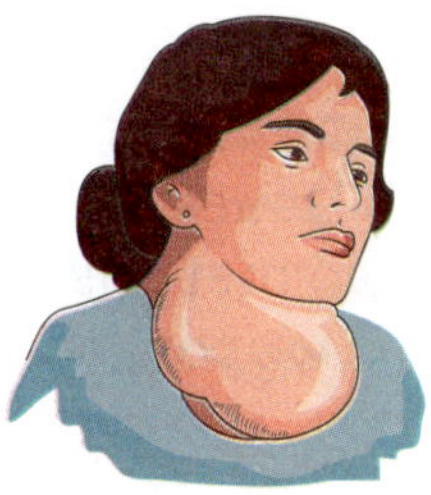

A person suffering from simple goitre

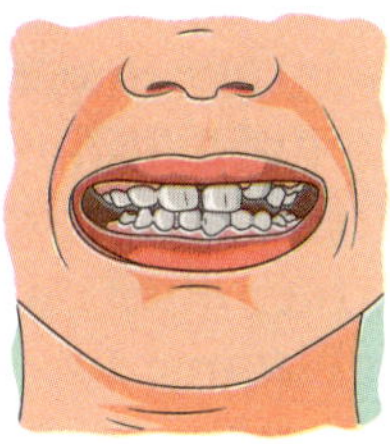

A person suffering from scurvy

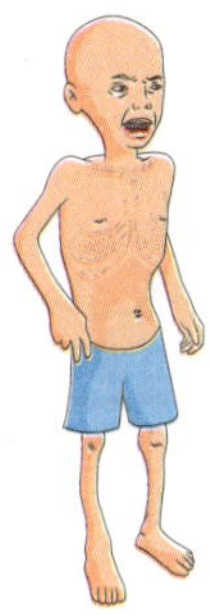

A child suffering from marasmus

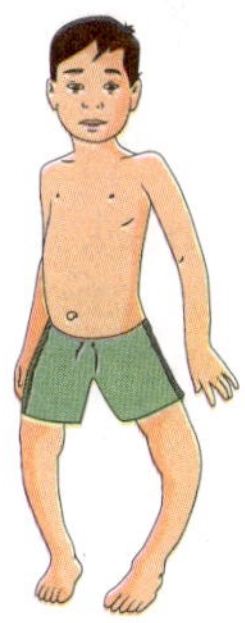

A child suffering from rickets

**Fig. 5.10:** Deficiency disorders

Table 5.4 lists the disorders caused due to the deficiency of carbohydrates, proteins, minerals and vitamins.

**Table 5.4:** Deficiency disorders

| Nutrients | Deficiency Disorder | Symptoms |
|---|---|---|
| Proteins | Kwashiorkor | Thin limbs, bloated belly due to swelling of liver, sleeplessness, slow growth |
| Carbohydrates, fats and proteins | Marasmus | Severe muscle wasting, stunted growth |
| **Minerals** | **Deficiency Disorder** | **Symptoms** |
| Calcium | Bone and teeth decay | Weak bones and tooth decay |
| Iodine | Simple Goitre | Swollen glands in the neck, sluggishness |
| Iron | Anaemia | Weakness, paleness |
| **Vitamins** | **Deficiency Disorder** | **Symptoms** |
| Vitamin A (Retinol) | Inability to see in poor light and skin problems | Vision becomes poor in darkness, sometimes leading to night blindness, and dry skin |
| Vitamin $B_1$ (Thiamine) | Beriberi | Weak muscles, very little energy and poor growth in children |
| Vitamin $B_2$ (Riboflavin) | Ariboflavinosis and Photophobia | Cracked lips, inflammation of the lining of mouth and tongue, mouth ulcers, cracks at the corners of the mouth and a sore throat, dry and scaling skin, eyes become sensitive to bright sunlight |
| Vitamin $B_3$ (Niacin) | Pellagra | Diarrhoea, drying of skin and irritability |
| Vitamin $B_{12}$ (Cobalamin) | Anaemia | Lack of appetite, pale skin, low stamina |
| Vitamin C (Ascorbic acid) | Scurvy | Bleeding gums, wounds take a long time to heal |
| Vitamin D, minerals: calcium and phosphorus | Rickets in children; Osteomalacia in adults | Rickets: Bones become soft and deformed Osteomalacia: Bone pain and prone to fracture |
| Vitamin K | Bleeding disorder | Uncontrolled bleeding from wounds, delayed blood clotting |

## Excessive Intake of Nutrients

When the intake of nutrients is more than what is required by the body, it may cause a condition called **obesity**, especially when the excess energy is not utilized by the means of exercise. Obesity leads to various health problems such as disorders of the heart.

### Case Study: Addressing Micronutrient Malnutrition in India

Despite significant economic progress and advances in healthcare, India faces a severe challenge with micronutrient malnutrition. Over 70% of the population consumes less than 50% of the Recommended Daily Allowance (RDA) for vital micronutrients, leading to high rates of vitamin and mineral deficiencies. These deficiencies contribute to significant health issues, including *anaemia*, vitamin A deficiency and iodine deficiency. Government initiatives, such as the 10th Five Year Plan, set ambitious goals to combat these deficiencies, but inadequate implementation and poor monitoring have hindered progress. The Indian Micronutrient Investment Plan (2007–2011) aims to prioritize this issue, but effective strategies and robust monitoring are essential to achieve the desired outcomes.

**Critical Thinking**

How can the effectiveness of government programs to combat micronutrient malnutrition be improved? What role can local communities play in ensuring their success?

**Project Idea**

Research the availability and consumption of micronutrient-rich foods in your community. Develop a plan or campaign to raise awareness and increase access to these essential nutrients, particularly targeting vulnerable populations such as pregnant women and young children.

# DIVERSITY OF FOOD

India is a land of diverse cultures, traditions and climates. This diversity is reflected in the variety of food consumed across its many states. The types of food traditionally consumed in different regions are closely linked to the crops grown there, the climate and cultural practices.

## Choice of Food

The choice of food in different regions of India is not random. It is influenced by various factors such as:

- **Climate:** The local climate plays a crucial role in determining which foods are grown and consumed. For instance, coastal regions with a humid climate may focus on seafood and tropical fruits, while arid regions with a dry climate might rely on drought-resistant grains and legumes.
- **Cultivation:** The type of crops that grow well in a region due to the soil and climate heavily influence the local cuisine.
- **Taste Preferences:** Over time, people in different regions develop preferences for certain flavours, spices and cooking methods.
- **Culture:** Cultural practices, festivals and traditions often dictate the food prepared and consumed in a region.
- **Traditions:** Many traditional dishes have been passed down through generations and are deeply rooted in the history and heritage of the region.

**Fig. 5.11:** Diversity of food in India
*(Can you name the food items and the region where it is from?)*

## Activity 5.8: Investigation

Find out the types of food traditionally consumed and the crops grown in various states of India. Refer to books in a library. Search the Internet. Interact with your friends, family and neighbours to collect information. Add more in the table given below.

Analyse the data provided in the table to identify similarities and differences in traditional foods and beverages across various states in India. Discuss how the locally grown crops in each state influence the regional cuisine.

**Traditional Food Items in Various States of India**

| State | Locally Grown Crops | Traditional Food Items Eaten | Beverages |
|---|---|---|---|
| **Assam** | Rice, tea, mustard | Rice, fish tenga (sour fish curry), *khar* (alkaline curry), *pitha* (rice cakes) | Black tea, rice beer (*Apong*) |
| **Gujarat** | Millet, cotton, groundnut, wheat | *Dhokla*, *thepla*, *khakhra*, *khandvi*, *undhiyu* (mixed vegetable), *fafda* | *Chaas* (buttermilk), tea |
| **Jharkhand** | Rice, maize, pulses, millets, oilseeds | *Dhuska* (deep-fried rice pancakes), *litti chokha*, bamboo shoot curry | *Handia* (rice beer), black tea |
| **Karnataka** | Rice, ragi, urad, coconut | Idli, dosa, *sambhar*, coconut chutney, *ragi mudde*, *palya*, *rasam* | Buttermilk, coffee, tea |
| **Kashmir** | Rice, saffron, apple, walnuts, maize | *Rogan josh* (lamb curry), *yakhni* (yogurt-based curry), *dum aloo* (potato curry) | *Kahwa* (spiced tea), noon chai |
| **Kerala** | Rice, coconut, spices | *Puttu* (steamed rice cake), *appam*, *sambar*, *avial* (vegetable curry), fish curry | Coconut water, black coffee, tea |
| **Maharashtra** | Rice, wheat, jowar, bajra, pulses | *Bhakri*, *pav bhaji*, *vada pav*, *puran poli*, *misal pav* | *Solkadhi*, tea, buttermilk |
| **Manipur** | Rice, bamboo, soya bean | *Chamthong* (vegetable stew), *ngari* (fermented fish), *iromba* (mixture of mashed boiled vegetables, *ngari* and chilies), *singju* (mixed vegetable salad with perilla seeds), *hawaizar* (fermented soya bean) | Black tea |

# FOOD SECURITY

Food security is the assurance that every person has consistent access to sufficient, safe and nutritious food that meets their dietary needs for a healthy life. In many parts of the world, achieving food security is a significant challenge due to factors such as poverty, climate change and food wastage.

In India, diverse agricultural practices, influenced by varying soil types and climatic conditions, contribute to the richness of traditional foods across regions. However, ensuring that these foods reach everyone sustainably is essential for food security. Techniques such as freezing, drying, heating and canning (Fig. 5.12) help in preserving food and reducing wastage, thereby contributing to food security. Proper storage and management of food resources are vital to minimizing waste and ensuring that the population has access to nutritious food, thus strengthening the overall food security of the nation.

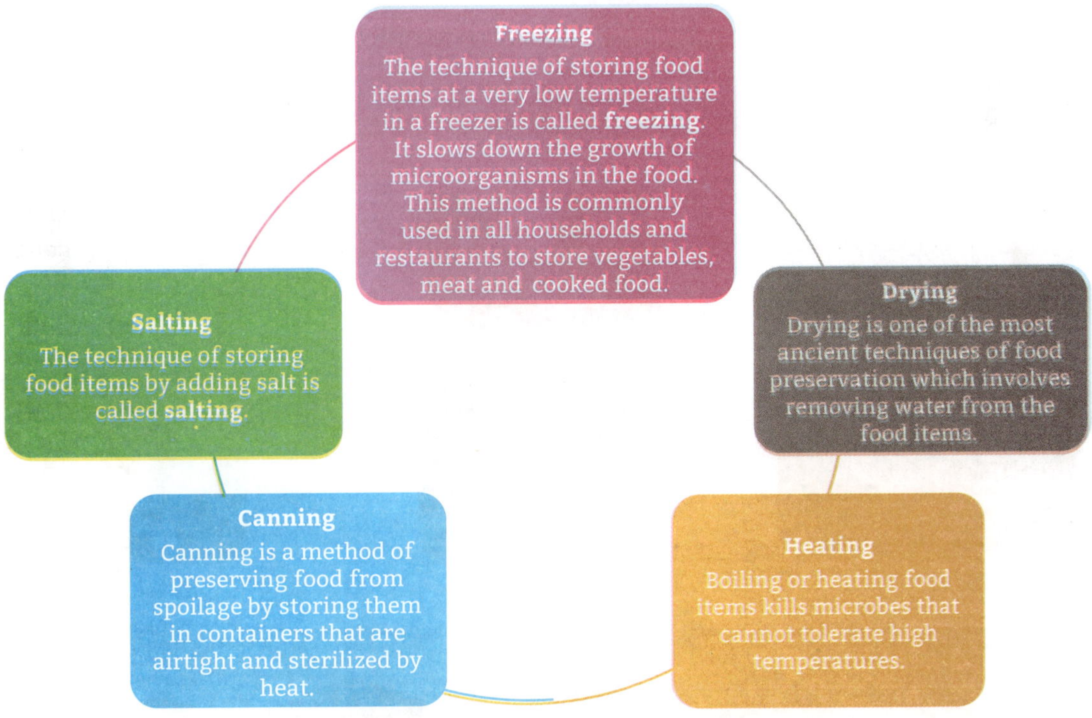


**Fig. 5.12:** Food preservation techniques

## Wonder!

**Fermentation** is a traditional food preservation technique that uses microorganisms to convert carbohydrates into acids or alcohols, extending shelf life and enhancing *umami* flavour. In Northeast India, fermentation is vital for food security, as it allows for the preservation of locally grown ingredients without refrigeration. Examples include fermented bamboo shoots, soya bean and fish, which offer extended storage and added nutritional benefits. This technique supports food availability and reduces waste, contributing significantly to the region's food security.

## Millets: Nutrient-Rich Cereals

Millets are small-seeded grasses that are highly nutritious and have been a staple food in many parts of India for centuries. They are:

- **Rich in nutrients:** Millets are packed with vitamins, minerals and fibre. They are also gluten-free and have a low glycemic index, making them suitable for people with certain dietary needs.
- **Climate-resilient:** Millets are hardy crops that can grow in arid and semi-arid regions with minimal water, making them an excellent choice for sustainable agriculture.

Common types of millets (Fig. 5.13) in India are given below:

- **Ragi (Finger Millet):** Rich in calcium, ragi is used to make porridge, bread and even *laddoos*.
- **Jowar (Sorghum):** Jowar is used to make rotis and is a good source of protein and fibre.
- **Bajra (Pearl Millet):** Bajra is used to make *bhakri*, a type of flatbread, and is rich in iron.

Finger millet

Sorghum

Pearl millet

**Fig. 5.13:** Types of millets

## Food Miles: From Farm to Our Plate

The concept of **food miles** refers to the distance food travels from the place where it is grown or produced to where it is consumed. The longer the food miles, the more energy is required for transportation, which can impact the environment. Thus, the significance of choosing local, sustainable food options to reduce our environmental impact and support regional farmers.

## Story of bread and chapati: from farm to plate

The concept of food miles helps us appreciate the journey our food takes before it reaches our plate. Let us see the journey of wheat to chapati (Fig. 5.14).

1. **Farming:** The journey of a bread or a *chapati* begins on a farm where wheat is grown.

2. **Storage:** The wheat grains are harvested, cleaned and stored.

3. **Milling and selling:** The wheat grains are sent to a mill, where they are ground into flour (*atta*). This flour is then packaged and sent to stores or directly to homes.

4. **Cooking**: The flour is kneaded into dough and baked into breads in bakeries. At home, the dough is rolled into flat discs and then cooked on a *tava* (griddle) to make chapati.

5. **Market**: In some cases, bread is produced in large scale and sold in supermarkets.

6. We consume this bread as breakfast at home or restaurants make sandwiches.

**Fig. 5.14:** Journey of wheat to chapati

## Revise and Recall

**Fill in the blanks.**

1. The variety of traditional food items in different states of India is closely related to the __________ grown in those regions.
2. Food security involves having __________, social and economic access to adequate, safe and nutritious food for a sustained healthy lifestyle.
3. In Northeast India, common techniques for preserving food include __________, drying and canning.
4. Examples of food preservation methods that help in extending the shelf life of foods are __________, boiling and freezing.
5. Food __________ occurs when food is lost or wasted, impacting global food security by increasing the number of hungry people.

## Keywords

**Carbohydrates:** The major part of the staple diet of people all over the world

**Fats:** Required for the proper development of the body, functioning of the brain and nervous system in children and for providing immunity

**Proteins:** The building blocks of a human body needed for growth and development of tissues and organs, immunity and body functions

**Vitamins:** Help us develop immunity against many disorders and assist in specific activities connected with growth and development of the body

**Minerals:** Required for making the bones strong, building muscles and proper functioning of the body

**Roughage:** Helps in the bowel movement (moves out the undigested food) and prevents constipation

**Balanced diet:** A diet that contains carbohydrates, proteins, fats, vitamins, mineral salts and fibre in proportions based on age and health

**Nutrient deficiency:** The condition resulting due to insufficient intake of specific nutrients in right amounts

**Symptoms:** The signs of a disorder or deficiency of nutrients in our body

**Toxins:** Substances that are harmful for our body

**Food diversity:** The variety of foods and food-related practices that exist within a given population, region or culture

# Summary

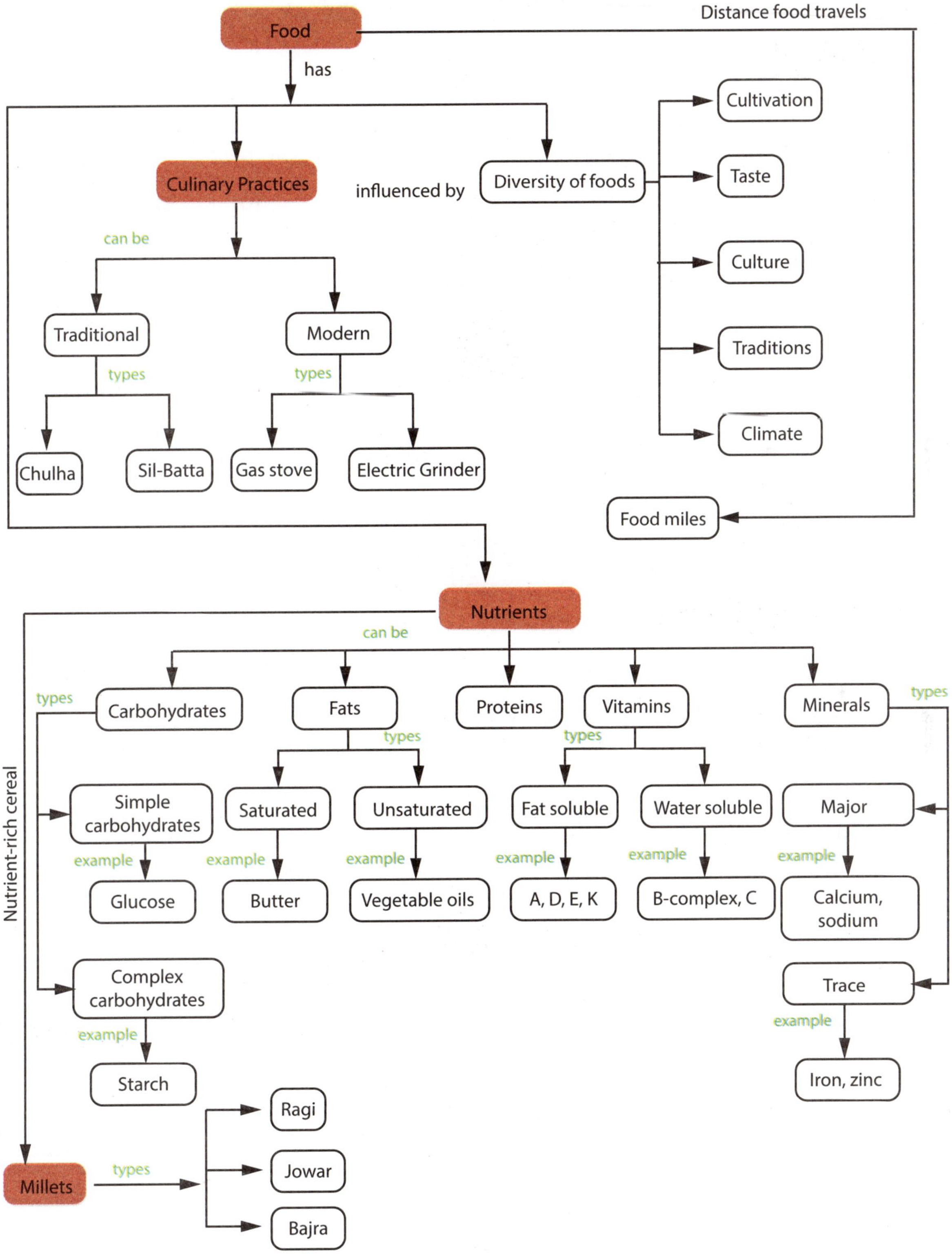

Food
Distance food travels
has
Culinary Practices
influenced by
Diversity of foods
Cultivation
Taste
Culture
Traditions
Climate
can be
Traditional
Modern
types
types
Chulha
Sil-Batta
Gas stove
Electric Grinder
Food miles
Nutrients
can be
Nutrient-rich cereal
types
Carbohydrates
Fats
Proteins
Vitamins
Minerals
types
types
types
Simple carbohydrates
Saturated
Unsaturated
Fat soluble
Water soluble
Major
example
example
example
example
example
example
Glucose
Butter
Vegetable oils
A, D, E, K
B-complex, C
Calcium, sodium
Complex carbohydrates
Trace
example
example
Starch
Iron, zinc
Millets
types
Ragi
Jowar
Bajra

# Exercise

W ia

**A. Choose the correct option.**

1. Which of the following food items is rich in carbohydrates?
   (a) Broccoli (b) Cakes (c) Carrots (d) Bell peppers
2. Which one of the following is a source of vitamins?
   (a) Rice (b) Potato chips (c) Oranges (d) Bread
3. Which of the following is a trace mineral?
   (a) Calcium (b) Chlorine (c) Iron (d) Phosphorus
4. Insufficient amount of vitamin A in the diet can cause __________.
   (a) beriberi (b) poor vision (c) scurvy (d) simple goitre
5. Deficiency of vitamin D causes __________.
   (a) rickets (b) scurvy (c) kwashiorkor (d) marasmus

**B. Fill in the blanks.** ia

1. Butter is rich in __________. (fat/carbohydrate)
2. The vitamin that is called the sunshine vitamin is __________. (vitamin A/vitamin D)
3. Cobalt belongs to the group of __________ mineral. (trace/major)
4. Anaemia is caused by lack of __________ in the body. (iron/copper)
5. A person suffering from swollen glands in the neck has __________. (rickets/goitre)

**C. State whether the following statements are true (T) or false (F).**

1. As fats have higher energy than carbohydrates, they can be consumed in place of carbohydrates in equal amounts.
2. Thirteen kinds of vitamins are found in the animal sources of food.
3. Eating only one type of food provides the body with all the required nutrients.
4. Calcium makes the bones strong.
5. Lack of a particular nutrient in the body can cause disorders.

**D. Name each of the following in one word.**

1. Lack of this vitamin leads to scurvy __________
2. The other name given to dietary fibre __________
3. Swollen glands in the neck is a symptom of this disorder __________
4. A source of fat __________
5. A way by which water removes toxins from the body __________

**E. Give reasons for the following.**

1. Consuming moderate quantity of butter is good for health.
2. Frozen yogurt must be chosen instead of an ice cream.
3. Too much oily and fatty food causes obesity.
4. Dietary fibres are essential part of our diet.
5. It is important to consume a balanced diet on a regular basis.

**F. Answer the following questions briefly.**

1. Discuss traditional versus modern culinary practices in India.
2. Give two examples of carbohydrate-rich food.
3. Name four protein-rich food.
4. Why are dietary fibres important?
5. What is a balanced diet?
6. What are deficiency disorders? Name the disorder caused by the deficiency of carbohydrates and proteins.

**G. Answer the following questions.**

1. Write a note on the main nutrients required by our body. Give one source of each.
2. Describe the cooking practices that help retain the nutrients in the food.
3. What do you understand by food diversity? Briefly explain the different dimensions of food diversity.
4. Why are millets considered a healthy food choice? Can eating only millets meet all the body's nutritional needs? Discuss.
5. What are food miles? Illustrate with the help of an example or a food item available in your region.

# Cognitive Corner

## Critical Thinking

1. If you consume only fried food and cold drinks, will you remain healthy?
2. Who will need more carbohydrates in the diet—an athlete or an office worker? Why?
3. Which is better—eating the fruit or having it as a fruit juice? Discuss the reasons for your answer.

## Picture Study

**Identify the deficiency disorders shown in the following pictures.**

1. ______________

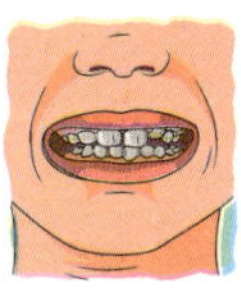

2. ______________

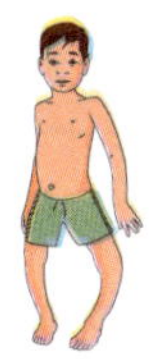

3. ______________

## Project

1. Form a Nutrition Club at your school. Then, work together to create a diverse and nutritious meal plan for a week that includes ingredients from different cultures and cuisines. Research the nutritional value of each ingredient and share your findings with the club. Then, organize a potluck where everyone brings a dish inspired by the meal plan, and discuss the cultural significance and health benefits of each dish. **(C-4.2)**
2. People often say that one should not take water while eating food—is this true? Find out about this and prepare a report based on your findings. **(C-7.1)**

## In the Library

Read about balanced diet and then prepare a chart on the balanced diet (breakfast, lunch, teatime and dinner) for MS Dhoni (the cricketer), your classmate and your grandfather. **(C-6.2)**

## Life Skills

Write the number of servings of nutrients you consume daily in the blank space provided next to the nutrient pyramid. Compare the proportions of nutrients consumed with the recommended servings given in the reference table. Based on your comparison, do you need to adjust your diet to better align with the recommended nutrient intake for a healthier lifestyle? If so, how would you make those adjustments? **(C-7.1)**

| | Cereals | Vegetables | Fruits | Dairy | Proteins |
|---|---|---|---|---|---|
| Children (4–7 years) | 3–4 | 4 | 2 | 3 | $\frac{1}{2}$–1 |
| Children (8–11 years) | 4–6 | 4–5 | 1–2 | 3 | 1–$1\frac{1}{2}$ |
| Adolescents (12–18 years) | 4–7 | 5–9 | 3–4 | 3–5 | 1–2 |

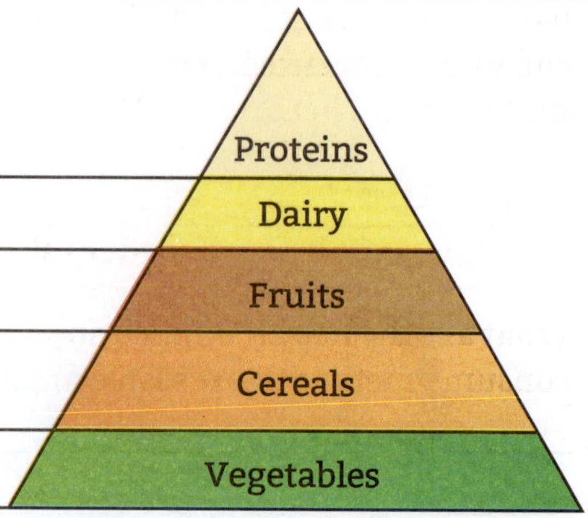

2 ZERO HUNGER

# Worksheet

In India, despite achieving self-sufficiency in crop production, malnutrition remains prevalent among a significant portion of the population, primarily affecting impoverished individuals with limited access to adequate food. Even those who have access to sufficient food suffer from malnutrition due to intake of imbalanced diets. Pregnant mothers, in particular, lack essential nutrients, leading to the birth of weak babies and an increased risk of diseases and mortality. In contrast, individuals in towns and cities experience overnutrition, consuming excessive carbohydrates, proteins and fats, resulting in obesity, heart diseases, diabetes and various other disorders.

33.4% of children in India are underweight.

Malnourished child

Obese child

A. Given below are pictures of food items. Identify and tick the ones you think everyone should eat to avoid malnutrition or obesity.

Paneer

Rice

Samosa

Fruit bowl

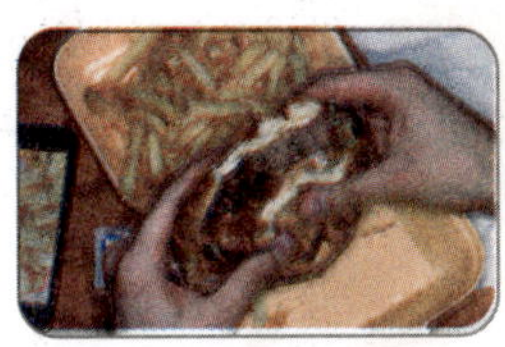
Burger and fries

B. In light of the contrasting health outcomes described for both undernourished babies and overnourished individuals, what are some potential strategies that can be implemented at the community and individual levels to promote balanced nutrition and healthy lifestyles for pregnant mothers and residents in towns and cities?

______________________________________________

______________________________________________

C. What are the health implications for individuals living in towns and cities who consume diets with excessive amounts of carbohydrates, proteins and fats?

______________________________________________

______________________________________________

# 6 Materials Around Us

## Curricular Goals

- Explore the world of matter and its constituents, properties and behaviour **(CG-1)**
- Understand the interface of science, technology and society **(CG-5)**

## Competencies

- Classify matter based on its observable physical properties (such as solid, liquid or gas; shape; volume; density; transparency—transparent, opaque or translucent; and magnetic properties—magnetic or non-magnetic) as well as its chemical characteristics (whether it is pure or impure) **(C-1.1)**
- Illustrate how science and technology can help to improve the quality of human life such as judicious consumption of resources **(C-5.1)**

## Let's Get Started

Look at the image given below and find the odd object. What is the basis for grouping things together? Write down in the space provided.

______________________________

______________________________

______________________________

______________________________

______________________________

______________________________

In our everyday life, we come across many instances where we need to arrange or sort materials into different groups or categories. For example, when you go to a library, you can see books organized in different sections such as fiction, encyclopaedia, magazines, maths, science and social science. At home, in the kitchen, you must have seen arrangement of groceries or utensils in different racks or cupboards. Sorting or arranging materials help us find things easily when we need them.

*The systematic arrangement of the objects into groups is called* ***classification***. In any classification, objects are grouped on the basis of the similarities or differences in their properties or characteristics.

## LUSTRE

Look at Figure 6.1. What is common between the objects shown in the figure? They all have a shine or lustre. **Lustre** is defined as the property of a material to shine.

*Materials that have a shiny surface are known as **lustrous materials***. Examples are metals such as gold, silver, bronze and iron. *Materials that lack shine are known as **non-lustrous materials***. Examples are paper, rubber, cardboard, wood and wool. Some lustrous materials can lose their shine and appear dull when they are exposed to air or moisture for a long duration.

Metal tap

Bronze

Gold

Pearl

**Fig. 6.1:** Materials that have lustre

### Activity 6.1

**Aim:** To classify the given materials as lustrous and non-lustrous

**Materials required:** Steel spoon, coins, a piece of pure cotton cloth, a piece of cotton cloth mixed with polyester, a piece of cinnamon, a few peppercorns, cardboard piece and aluminium foil

**Procedure:**

1. Observe the appearance of each material.
2. Record your observations in the following table.
3. Put a tick mark (✓) in the appropriate box.

**Observation Table:**

| Type of material | Lustrous | Non-lustrous | Type of material | Lustrous | Non-lustrous |
|---|---|---|---|---|---|
| Steel spoon | | | A piece of cinnamon | | |
| Coins | | | A few peppercorns | | |
| Pure cotton cloth | | | Cardboard piece | | |
| Cotton cloth mixed with polyester | | | Aluminium foil | | |

**Conclusion:** What do you conclude?

## TEXTURE

Texture of a material refers to how it feels when touched. Based on the texture, there are two categories of materials:

- **Rough materials** such as stones, wood, body scrubbers and sandpaper.
- **Smooth materials** such as marble, a piece of satin cloth, polished stainless steel spoon, soft toys and foam.

## HARDNESS

Materials can be hard or soft. Let us perform the following activity to understand this.

### Activity 6.2

**Aim:** To find the hardness of given materials

**Materials required:** Wax, pillow, stone, ceramic plate, chalk and ice cube

**Procedure:**

1. Try to compress each of the collected materials.
2. Record your observations in the following table.
3. Put a tick mark (✓) in the appropriate box.

**Observation:**

| Type of material | Easy to compress | Difficult to compress | Type of material | Easy to compress | Difficult to compress |
|---|---|---|---|---|---|
| Wax | | | Ceramic plate | | |
| Pillow | | | Chalk | | |
| Stone | | | Ice cube | | |

**Conclusion:** What do you conclude?

From Activity 6.2, you can see that some materials are very hard and difficult to compress, whereas others can be easily compressed.
*Materials that can be easily compressed are known as* ***soft materials****. Materials that are difficult to compress are known as* ***hard materials****.*

## STATE

Based on the state of existence, materials can be classified into three categories: **solids, liquids** and **gases**. The difference in the state of materials is due to the differences in the way the particles within them are arranged. The arrangement of particles in substances decides the way they change their volume and shape (Figs. 6.2 and 6.3).

a

Solids have a definite shape.

**Solids** have a definite shape and occupy a definite space and volume. A solid has no or least compressibility and maintains its shape even when subjected to an external force. For example, when we transfer a wooden block from one place to another, its volume and shape do not change.

**Liquids** do not have a definite shape but occupy a fixed volume. A liquid fills the container when at rest and flows freely when poured into another container. For example, when we transfer 100 mℓ of coffee from a kettle to a cup, it takes the shape of the coffee cup, but the volume of the coffee remains the same. Liquids can be compressed to a small extent as compared to solids.

Liquids flow easily.

**Gases** do not have a definite shape or volume. A gas can expand to fill any available space in a container. Gases are highly compressible as compared to solids and liquids. For example, when we pump air into a bicycle tyre, the air is compressed and pushed into the tyre. Then, the air expands to fill the tyre and takes its shape.

Gases expand to fill any available space.

**Fig. 6.2:** Properties of solids, liquids and gases

Table 6.1 summarizes the properties of the three states of matter.

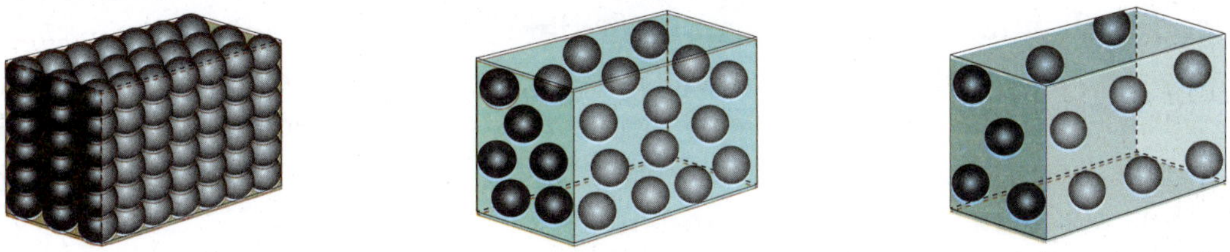

Solids—tightly packed particles | Liquids—not so tightly packed particles | Gases—loosely packed particles

**Fig. 6.3:** Arrangement of particles in solids, liquids and gases

**Table 6.1:** Properties of the three states of matter

| Properties | Solids | Liquids | Gases |
|---|---|---|---|
| Definite mass | Yes | Yes | Yes |
| Definite shape | Yes | No | No |
| Compressibility | Cannot be compressed | Can be compressed to a small extent | Highly compressible |
| Particle arrangement | Tightly packed | Less tightly packed | Loosely packed |

## Activity 6.3

Classify the following substances into solids, liquids and gases.

Oxygen, sugar crystals, paper, fruit juices, plastic box, nitrogen, water, pencil, wood, soup, tea, buttermilk, glass beaker, hydrogen, eraser, carbon dioxide, petrol, saliva, soda, smoke from camphor and sponge cake

## Revise and Recall

**Fill in the blanks.**

1. The systematic arrangement of the objects into groups is called ____________. (rearrangement/classification)
2. ____________ materials are shiny in appearance. (Lustrous/Non-lustrous)
3. ____________ of a material is how it feels when touched. (State/Texture)
4. Materials that are difficult to compress are known as ____________ materials. (hard/soft)
5. ____________ do not have a definite shape or volume. (Liquids/Gases)

# SOLUBILITY

*The property of a substance to dissolve in a given liquid is known as* ***solubility*** *of that substance.* Recall what you have learnt in earlier classes about solubility.

What happens to salt and sand when they are mixed with water? What about mixing sand in water? Salt dissolves completely in water as it is **soluble** in water. However, sand does not dissolve in water as it is **insoluble** in water. Are liquids also soluble in water? Let us perform an activity to find out.

## Activity 6.4

**Aim:** To check the solubility of some liquids in water

**Materials required:** Four beakers, four glass rods, lemon juice, coconut oil, milk and kerosene

**Procedure:**

1. Take 25 mℓ of water in four different beakers. Label them A, B, C and D.
2. Add one tablespoon of of lemon juice, coconut oil, milk and kerosene to the water in the beakers labelled A, B, C and D, respectively.
3. Stir the contents of the solution in each beaker with a glass rod.
4. Allow it to stand for five minutes.
5. Observe whether all the liquids mix with the water.
6. Record your observations in a tabular form as shown below.

**Observation Table:**

| Type of liquid | Mixes well | Does not mix |
|---|---|---|
| Lemon juice | | |

**Conclusion:** What do you conclude? Are there liquids that can dissolve in water?

From Activity 6.4, it is clear that some liquids dissolve in water completely. Such liquids are known as **miscible liquids**. For example, alcohol, lemon juice, honey and vinegar.

Some liquids do not dissolve in water (Fig. 6.4). Such liquids are known as **immiscible liquids**. For example, kerosene, coconut oil, diesel and petrol.

Some gases are also found dissolved in water. Gases such as oxygen and carbon dioxide dissolve in water.

**Fig. 6.4:** Oil does not dissolve in water.

**Science in Context**

Oxygen and carbon dioxide dissolved in the water are used by aquatic animals and plants, respectively.

**Go Green**

We know that oil is immiscible in water. Human activities that lead to oil spills in oceans should be prevented as they can result in the death of aquatic plants and animals and have long-term adverse effects on human life.

# FLOTATION

*The property of a material to float on water is called **flotation**. In your earlier classes, you have learned about mass and volume. The mass per unit volume of a substance is known as **density**.*

Look at Figure 6.5. When we place a paper boat on water, it floats. However, when we put an iron nail in a glass of water, it sinks to the bottom of the glass. Have you ever thought why this happens? Materials may float or sink depending on their density. Some materials such as paper are less dense than water and thus float. On the other hand, some materials such as iron are denser than water and thus sink.

(a) (b)

**Fig. 6.5:** A paper boat floats on water but an iron nail sinks in water

Hence, we can say that materials that are denser than water will sink in water. For example, stone. Materials that are less dense than water will float on water. Examples are empty plastic bottles, dried leaves and cotton. Some liquids such as kerosene oil, petrol, diesel and vegetable oils also float on water as these liquids are less dense than water.

## Activity 6.5

**Aim:** To identify whether the given materials can float or sink in water

**Materials required:** 1000 m$\ell$ Beaker, 500 m$\ell$ water, paper clip, marble, plastic bead, dried leaf, glycerine/oil and small rubber ball

**Procedure:**

Before you start the activity, predict and write down in the first column of the table given below whether the following materials—paper clip, marble, plastic bead, dried leaf, glycerine/oil, and small rubber ball—will float or sink in water. Then, begin your activity.

1. Take 500 m$\ell$ water in a beaker.
2. Put the given materials one by one in the beaker and observe whether they float or sink.
3. Record your observations as given in the table below.

**Observation Table:**

| S. No. | Material | Prediction Will it float/sink? | Whether it floated/sank | Was the prediction correct? (Yes/No) |
|---|---|---|---|---|
| 1 | Paper clip | | | |
| 2 | Marble | | | |
| 3 | Plastic bead | | | |

**Note:** Perform the above activity using other liquids such as glycerin or oil in a beaker instead of water. Find out whether your observation is the same as above or different.

**Conclusion:** In this activity, whether a material floats or sinks depends on its density compared to the liquid. What do you conclude?

# MAGNETIC PROPERTY

A magnet is a substance that can attract pieces of iron and materials made out of iron (Fig. 6.6).

**Fig. 6.6:** A magnet attracts iron

Based on the attraction of materials towards a magnet, they can be classified into two categories: magnetic and non-magnetic.

*Materials that get attracted towards a magnet are known as* ***magnetic materials****, for example, iron. Materials that do not get attracted towards a magnet are known as* ***non-magnetic materials****, for example, rubber.*

# CONDUCTIVITY

*The property of a material to allow heat or electricity to pass through it is known as* ***conductivity****.*

**Fig. 6.7:** Copper utensils used for cooking

## Conductivity of Heat

Copper utensils are used for cooking (Fig. 6.7) instead of wooden cookware. Do you know why? It is because copper utensils heat up very quickly.

Based on the property of materials to pass heat through them, they can be classified into two categories: conductors and insulators of heat.

*Materials that allow heat to pass through them are called* ***conductors*** *of heat. Examples are metals such as copper, aluminium and iron.*

> **Science in Context**
>
> Mercury is used in thermometers as it is a good conductor of heat.

*Materials that do not allow heat to pass through them easily are called* ***insulators*** *of heat*. Examples are wood and thick cotton cloth such as oven mittens.

## Conductivity of Electricity

Based on the property of materials to pass electricity through them, they can be classified into two categories: conductors of electricity and insulators of electricity.

*Materials that allow electricity to pass through them are called* ***conductors*** *of electricity*. Examples are metals such as copper and iron.

*Materials that do not allow electricity to pass through them are called* ***insulators*** *of electricity*. Examples are wood and plastic.

For instance, electrical appliances are connected by copper wires to electrical sources because copper is a good conductor of electricity. These wires have an outer covering of rubber (Fig. 6.8), which is an insulator, to prevent us from getting an electric shock.

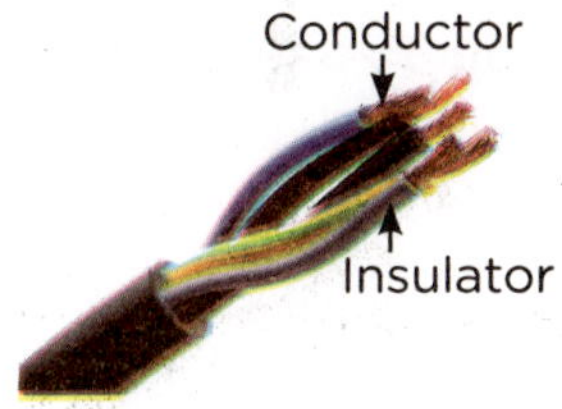


**Fig. 6.8:** Copper wires with plastic covering

> **Wonder!**
>
> Human body is a conductor of electricity. The condition that results when electricity passes through our body is called an electric shock. This may be a temporary condition but it can be life-threatening. Hence, one must be careful while dealing with electricity.

## TRANSPARENCY

Look at Figure 6.9. Three identical toys are placed in three different tumblers. Can you see the toys in all the three tumblers?

You can see that in the first tumbler, the toy is clearly visible. In the second one, the toy is partially visible. In the third tumbler, the toy is not visible at all.

**Fig. 6.9:** Transparent, translucent and opaque objects

Depending on the amount of light that can pass through materials, they can be classified into three categories: **transparent**, **translucent** and **opaque**. This property is known as **transparency**. *Materials that allow light to pass through them completely are called* ***transparent materials***. We can see clearly through transparent materials, for example, air, clear glass and water. *Materials that allow light to pass through them partially are called* ***translucent materials***. We can see through translucent materials but not clearly as compared to transparent materials. Coloured glass, butter paper and fog are examples of translucent materials. *Materials that do not allow light to pass through them at all are called* ***opaque materials***. We cannot see through opaque materials at all, for example, wood, stone and cardboard.

### Science in Context

Translucent objects are semi-transparent; some ultraviolet rays can pass through them. Thus, a person behind a translucent object can get sunburns.

## Activity 6.6

**Aim:** To classify the given objects as transparent, translucent and opaque

**Materials required:** Lamination sheet, waxed paper, plywood, cloth, clear glass, tissue paper, cardboard, aluminium foil, X-ray sheets and molten glass

**Procedure:**

1. Take the given materials one by one.
2. Keep a pencil or pen behind each material. Determine if the object is clearly visible (transparent), partially visible (translucent) or not visible at all (opaque).
3. Record your observations in your notebook by creating a similar table as shown below.
4. Tick the appropriate column based on your observation for each material. Then, identify the type of material based on your observation.

**Observation Table:**

| Material | Light passes completely | Some light passes | Blocks all light |
|---|---|---|---|
| Lamination sheet | ✓ | | |
| Cardboard | | ✓ | |
| Molten glass | | | ✓ |

**Conclusion:** Transparent materials allow light to pass through them completely, so objects behind them can be seen clearly. Whereas translucent materials allow some light to pass through but scatter it, making it difficult to see objects behind them clearly. Opaque materials block all light, preventing any view of objects behind them. This activity is useful in everyday life for selecting appropriate materials based on their light properties. For example, transparent materials are used in windows and lenses where clear visibility is needed, translucent materials for privacy screens and lampshades where you want to diffuse light and opaque materials such as cardboard are used in packaging.

## GROUPING MATERIALS BASED ON THEIR PROPERTIES

We use a large variety of materials in our daily lives. Different kinds of materials have different sets of properties. They may have different appearances and be transparent, opaque or translucent. They may float or sink in water.

So, for our convenience in everyday life, we often group materials based on similarities or dissimilarities in their properties. Grouping of materials has the following benefits.

- It makes the study of properties of materials convenient. Grouping fabrics as cotton, wool and polyester allows us to compare their durability, warmth and comfort, making it easier to choose the right material for clothing.
- It helps to find useful patterns in the properties. By grouping metals such as iron, copper and aluminum, we can observe that they conduct electricity well, which is why they are used in electrical wiring.
- It helps to understand materials better and use them more effectively. For example, understanding that glass is transparent and fragile helps us use it for windows but handle it carefully to avoid breakage.
- It promotes sustainable development by optimizing material usage and minimizing waste. Grouping recyclable materials such as paper, plastic and metal helps in recycling efforts, reducing waste and conserving resources.

### Activity 6.7

**Aim:** To identify suitable materials for making a tumbler

**Materials required:** Paper, plastic, metal, cloth and glass

**Procedure:**

1. List possible materials that could be used to make a tumbler (e.g., paper, plastic, metal, cloth, wood and glass).
2. Consider the properties of each material, such as whether it is waterproof, durable and safe for holding liquids.
3. Record your data and observation in the table.
4. Discuss why certain materials are more suitable than others for making a tumbler.

**Observation Table:**

| Material | Waterproof (Yes/No) | Durable (Yes/No) | Safe (Yes/No) | Suitable for Making a Tumbler (Yes/No) |
|---|---|---|---|---|
| Paper | No | No | No | No |
| Plastic | | | | |

Some materials, such as plastic, metal and glass, can hold water effectively without leaking. Materials such as cloth or paper allow water to pass through.

**Inference:** The choice of material for making a tumbler depends on its properties such as being waterproof, durable and safe.

**Conclusion:** Materials are chosen for making objects based on their properties and the purpose for which the object will be used. Grouping materials based on their properties helps in selecting the most suitable one for a specific use.

## Activity 6.8

**Aim:** To understand why different materials are used for making balls for various sports

**Materials required:** Tennis ball, cricket ball, hand exercise ball, a ruler or measuring tape and a flat surface

**Procedure:**

1. Gather balls of the same size but made of different materials (e.g., tennis ball, cricket ball, hand exercise ball).
2. Drop each ball from a fixed height onto a flat surface.
3. Measure the height to which each ball bounces using a ruler or measuring tape.
4. Record the bounce height (very high, slightly high/low but noticeable/barely bounces) for each ball in a table as shown below.
5. Discuss why different materials are used for making balls for different sports.

**Observation Table:**

| Ball | Material | Bounce Height | Suitable for Sport (Yes/No) |
|---|---|---|---|
| Tennis ball | Rubber/Felt | Very High | Yes |
| Cricket ball | | | |
| Hand exercise ball | | Low | No |

The balls made from different materials bounce to different heights.

**Inference:** The material of the ball influences its bounce. Balls used in different sports are made from materials that suit the specific requirements of that sport. For example, tennis balls are made of rubber with a fuzzy outer layer to provide the right amount of bounce and grip on the court.

**Conclusion:** Different materials have different properties, which make them suitable for specific uses. In sports, the choice of material for a ball is crucial for its performance, and grouping materials based on their properties helps in making the right choice.

## WHAT IS MATTER?

As you have seen in the previous sections, in our daily lives, we use different materials, each with unique properties. While different materials might have different uses, one thing they all have in common is that these are made of matter. What exactly is matter? ***Matter*** *is anything that occupies space and has mass.* This means that if something takes up space and can be weighed, it is considered matter. Matter includes everything you see, touch or even things you cannot see such as air.

Matter has the following properties:

- **Mass:** The mass of an object tells us how much matter is present in it. The more mass an object has, the heavier it feels. Mass is measured in grams (g) or kilograms (kg).
- **Volume:** Volume is the amount of space that matter occupies. Volume is measured in litres ($\ell$) or millilitres (m$\ell$).

## Space and Volume

Imagine you have two identical glass tumblers, meaning both have the same size and can hold the same amount of liquid. Now, let us see what happens when you pour water of different quantities (about 100 mℓ and 250 mℓ) into each glass tumbler.

**Tumbler 1:** In the first tumbler, pour about 100 mℓ water.

**Tumbler 2:** In the second tumbler, pour about 250 mℓ water.

Even though both tumblers are the same size and can hold the same amount of water, the amount of water in each tumbler is different. The first tumbler has less water (100 mℓ), so the water takes up less space. The second tumbler has more water (250 mℓ), so it takes up more space.

- **Volume of water:** The term *volume* refers to the amount of space that the water occupies inside the tumbler. In Tumbler 1, the water occupies less space, so its volume is smaller. In Tumbler 2, the water takes up more space, so its volume is greater.
- **Space in the tumbler:** The total *space* available inside the tumbler is the same for both, but how much of that space is filled with water depends on the volume of water you pour. If a tumbler is only half-filled, it means there is still empty space inside that has not been taken up by the water. If a tumbler is almost full, most of the space inside is occupied by the water.

The more water you pour into the tumbler, the more space it takes up, and the greater the volume of water. So, volume is simply the measure of how much space a substance (water) occupies within a container (a tumbler).

### Know the Scientist

**Acharya Kanada**

Acharya Kanada was an ancient Indian philosopher who introduced the concept of "paramanu," the smallest indivisible particle of matter. He proposed that these particles combine to form larger entities, which make up the physical world. His ideas laid the foundation for understanding matter and the creation of the universe, emphasizing that everything is made of eternal, indivisible particles that aggregate to form complex substances.

## Keywords

**Solubility:** The property of a substance to dissolve in a given liquid
**Magnetic materials:** Materials that get attracted towards a magnet
**Non-magnetic materials:** Materials that do not get attracted towards a magnet
**Conductors:** Materials that allow heat or electricity to pass through them
**Insulators:** Materials that do not allow heat or electricity to pass through them
**Transparent:** Materials that allow light to pass through them completely
**Opaque:** Materials that do not allow light to pass through them at all
**Translucent:** Materials that allow light to pass through them partially
**Matter:** Anything that occupies space and has mass.

## Summary

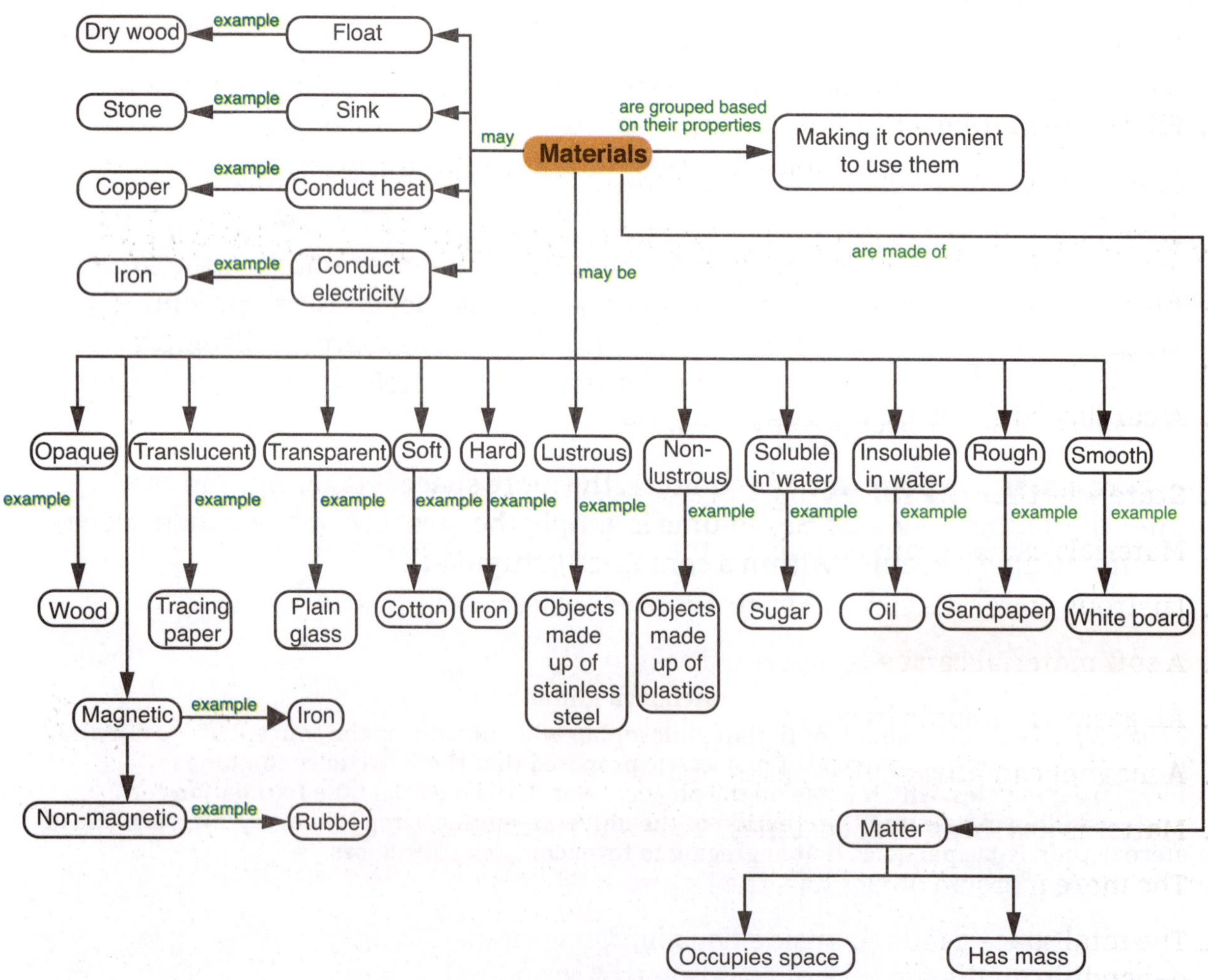

# Exercise

W

ia

**A. Choose the correct option.**

1. Which of the following is not a physical property to describe the appearance of materials?

   (a) Lustre (b) Hardness (c) Roughness (d) Reactivity

2. The property of a material to shine is called ____________.

   (a) texture (b) solubility (c) lustre (d) hardness

3. Which of the following is immiscible in water?

   (a) Alcohol (b) Oil (c) Lemon juice (d) Honey

4. Which of the following objects does not sink in water?

   (a) Stone (b) Plastic ball (c) Key (d) Coin

5. Metals are ____________.

   (a) lustrous (b) hard

   (c) conductors of heat (d) All of these

ia

**B. Fill in the blanks.**

1. Cotton is a ____________________ material. (lustrous/non-lustrous)
2. Rubber is ____________________. (magnetic/non-magnetic)
3. An empty plastic bottle ____________________ in water. (floats/sinks)
4. Plastic is ____________________ of electricity. (a conductor/an insulator)
5. A cardboard sheet is ____________________. (opaque/transparent)

**C. State whether the following statements are true (T) or false (F).**

1. Materials can be grouped only on the basis of their shapes and colours.
2. Lustrous materials can lose their shine when exposed to air or moisture.
3. A soft material can be compressed easily.
4. All gases are soluble in water.
5. A magnet can attract all types of materials.
6. Matter is anything that occupies space and has mass.
7. The more mass an object has, the lighter it feels.
8. The total space available inside two identical tumblers is different, depending on the amount of water poured into them.

**D. Give two examples for each of the following.**

1. Miscible liquids ______________ ______________
2. Translucent materials ______________ ______________
3. Smooth materials ______________ ______________
4. Non-lustrous materials ______________ ______________
5. Insulators of heat ______________ ______________

**E. Give reasons for the following.**

1. We cannot see through a wooden plank.
2. Stone settles down in water.
3. A cooking pan is made of metal but its handle is made of wood.
4. Ghee does not dissolve in water.
5. Grouping of materials is important.

**F. Answer the following questions briefly.**

1. What is classification?
2. Why should we sort or arrange materials?
3. Distinguish between lustrous and non-lustrous materials.
4. Define density and give an example to explain the same.
5. Distinguish between magnetic and non-magnetic materials.

**G. Answer the following questions.**

1. What are the properties of solids, liquids and gases? Explain with a diagram.
2. Distinguish between transparent, translucent and opaque materials. Give examples for each.
3. Define conductivity. How can materials be classified based on their conductivity?
4. Write and explain any four properties of materials.
5. What is matter? Why is it important to understand its properties of mass and volume in relation to the materials we use daily?

# Cognitive Corner

## Critical Thinking

1. What would happen if you rub lustrous materials with a sandpaper?
2. Imagine you have two mysterious materials, X and Y. When you expose material X to heat, it changes colour significantly. On the other hand, material Y does not change colour when exposed to heat.

Now, when you expose both materials to sunlight, only material Y maintains its original colour, while material X undergoes noticeable fading.

What could materials X and Y be? Can you identify whether material X is heat-sensitive or light-sensitive? What about material Y? Justify your answer.

3. We see our face when we look in a mirror. Is the mirror a transparent object?

## Picture Study

**Identify the property of materials shown in the following pictures.**

1. ______________________

2. ______________________

## Project

1. Collect information by conducting a research on how cooking utensils have evolved over time. Find out the reasons for the changes they have undergone. Present your findings in a creative way to share with the History and Innovation Club. **(C-5.1)**
2. Visit a nearby jewellery shop and collect information on how a goldsmith retains the natural colour of gold while making gold ornaments. Write a report based on your findings in a scrapbook for the Science Club. **(C-6.1)**

## In the Library

There is a story that Archimedes ran out of his bath and on to the street, shouting 'Eureka' when he discovered the principle behind flotation. Is this a true story? Find out more about the details of his discoveries on flotation. **(C-6.2)**

## Life Skills

When you are in a hurry and you need something, it feels so good if the things are organized and you find it quickly. What if the things are not organized?

Do you feel sorting and organizing things is important?
If yes, then suggest some places where you can implement them in your life. For example, helping your school librarian in organizing books. **(C-7.3)**

9 INDUSTRY, INNOVATION AND INFRASTRUCTURE

# Worksheet

Since the beginning of time, humans have looked at birds in the sky and longed to fly. On 17 December 1903, Wilbur and Orville Wright made their first flight. The structure of the aeroplane has changed a lot since then. Now, each part of the plane is designed using a specific material for a definite purpose. They can fly for long hours at great speeds high up in the sky.

First aeroplane

Modern aeroplane

**Look at the pictures of parts of a modern aeroplane. Explain why the mentioned materials were chosen to build these parts of an aeroplane.**

1.

Window of an aeroplane is made of plexiglass, a kind of plastic.

______________________________

______________________________

2.

Aeroplane tyres are made from rubber along with other materials.

______________________________

______________________________

3.

Tail fin of an aeroplane is made of aluminium.

______________________________

______________________________

# 7 Methods of Separation

**Curricular Goals**

- Explore the world of matter and its constituents, properties and behaviour **(CG-1)**
- Understand the interface of science, technology and society **(CG-5)**

**Competencies**

- Classify matter based on observable physical and chemical characteristics **(C-1.1)**
- Describe changes in matter (physical change) and use particulate nature to represent the properties of matter **(C-1.2)**
- Illustrate how science and technology can help to improve the quality of human life such as health care and judicious consumption of resources **(C-5.1)**

## Let's Get Started

Substances can exist in different forms and combinations, often found mixed together. Separation of these substances is necessary depending on our requirements. Different methods of separation are based on their distinct properties such as state, size and weight. Separation of substances allows us to isolate specific components as needed.

There is a bowl filled with cereals, pulses and seeds (see the picture below). Write down the method you would use to separate these three things in the space given below.

___________________________________________

___________________________________________

# PURE SUBSTANCE AND MIXTURE

A **pure substance** is a substance that is made up of only one kind of atoms or molecules, for example, copper and water.

A **mixture** is a substance that contains two or more different substances mixed together in no fixed proportions. The different types of substances present in a mixture are called its components or constituents.

## Types of Mixtures

Based on the physical state of components that are mixed together, mixtures can be classified into three types: (a) solid–solid mixture (for example: salt and pepper), (b) solid–liquid mixture (for example: sugar and water) and (c) liquid–liquid mixture (for example: water and milk).

Now, can you write one more example from your day-to-day life for each of the three mixtures mentioned above?

Based on the extent to which two or more components mingle with one another, mixtures can be classified as homogeneous and heterogeneous.

**Homogeneous mixtures:** *The mixtures in which the components that make up the mixture are distributed uniformly and cannot be seen clearly or separately are called **homogeneous mixtures**.*

Air is an example of a homogeneous mixture. We cannot see the different gases present in the air distinctly. Another example is ink.

**Heterogeneous mixtures:** *The mixtures in which the components that make up the mixture are not distributed uniformly and can be seen separately are called **heterogeneous mixtures**.*

A mixture of oil and water is an example of a heterogeneous mixture. We can see the oil and water distinctly in the mixture.

# NEED FOR SEPARATION

Separation of mixtures into their constituents or components is necessary for the following reasons:

- To separate different useful components from a mixture. For example, by churning milk, the cream is separated from milk so that both components can be used.
- To remove unwanted materials or impurities from a mixture. For example, the separation of husk from rice grains, unwanted stones from rice grains or pulses and separation of unwanted leaves from raw leafy vegetables before cooking.
- To get pure substances. For example, in the preparation of tea, tea leaves are separated from brewed tea.

# METHODS OF SEPARATION

Different components of a mixture have different chemical and physical properties. Hence, selecting the appropriate method of separation for a mixture depends on the characteristic properties of each component.

## Separating Solid—Solid Mixtures

- **Handpicking:** This method of separation is based on the difference in the sizes, shapes or colours of the components to be separated. In this method, the component that is lesser in number is picked out using hands (Fig. 7.1). Substances that can be separated by handpicking from all types of food grains and pulses are stones, dirt, husk, etc.

**Fig. 7.1:** Handpicking

- **Threshing:** *The process of separating grains from stalks of harvested crops either by beating the stalks against a hard surface or by using a threshing machine is called* ***threshing*** (Fig. 7.2).

  Substances that can be separated by threshing are all types of grains such as millets, wheat, oats, barley and rice.

**Fig. 7.2:** Threshing

- **Winnowing:** *The process of separating grains (heavier components) from chaff (lighter components) by the action of blowing wind is called* ***winnowing*** (Fig. 7.3).

  Substances that can be separated by winnowing are all types of grains that are covered by husk such as rice and wheat.

  This method of separation is based on the difference in the weights of the components to be separated.

**Fig. 7.3:** Winnowing

- **Sieving:** This method of separation is based on the difference in the sizes of the components to be separated (Fig. 7.4).

  The larger component is left behind in the sieve, while the smaller component passes through the pores of the sieve. The component to be separated should have particles having size smaller than the sieve pores.

**Fig. 7.4:** Sieving

Substances that can be separated by sieving are the ones that have **bran**[1] or impurities in them such as flour and semolina. Wheat flour is sieved before it is used for making dough. During construction of buildings, stones and pebbles are removed from sand by sieving.

- **Magnetic Separation:** This method (Fig. 7.5) is used to separate magnetic substances, such as iron, from non-magnetic substances. For example, if iron filings get mixed with sand, a magnet can be used to attract and separate the iron filings from the sand. The magnet pulls the iron filings because iron is a magnetic material, while the sand, being non-magnetic, remains behind. This method is commonly used in industries to separate scrap iron from waste materials, making it easier to recycle and reuse the iron.

### Word Web

[1]**Bran:** the outer skin of cereal grains that remains after the grains have been processed into flour

**Fig. 7.5** Magnetic separation

## Revise and Recall

**Fill in the blanks.**

1. Handpicking is a method to separate _________ mixtures. (solid–solid/ solid–liquid)
2. Stones can be separated from pulses by _________. (handpicking/sieving)
3. _________ is the method used by farmers to separate lighter husk particles from heavier seeds of grains. (Winnowing/Handpicking)
4. The mixture of rice flour and husk can be separated by _________. (threshing/sieving)
5. Iron filings can be separated from sand by _________. (sieving/magnets)

## Separating Solid—Liquid Mixtures

- **Sedimentation and decantation:** ***Sedimentation*** *is the process of separating insoluble solid components mixed in a liquid by allowing them to settle down at the bottom of the container before draining away the liquid.* This method of separation is based on the difference in the weights of the components of a solid–liquid mixture. In this method, the mixture is kept undisturbed for some time so that the heavier, insoluble solid components settle down at the bottom of the container containing the mixture. *The solid component that settles down during sedimentation is called the* ***sediment****.*

  Sedimentation is then followed by decantation in which the liquid is poured out carefully into another container without disturbing the sediment. Thus, the solid components are separated from the liquid.

  *The process of pouring out the layer of clear liquid without disturbing the sediment is called* ***decantation****.*

  Sedimentation and decantation methods are used at home while washing pulses in water. The upper layer of water that contains impurities is decanted and sediments (pulses) are retained for further use.

## Activity 7.1

**Aim:** To separate a mixture of sand and water using sedimentation and decantation methods

**Materials required:** Two beakers, sand, water and a glass rod

**Procedure:**

1. Take a beaker and fill half of it with water.
2. Add one tablespoon of sand to it. Mix the contents using a glass rod.
3. Keep the beaker undisturbed for some time.
4. You will notice that the sand particles settle down at the bottom of the beaker. This happens because the sand particles are heavier than water.
5. A clear layer of water will be seen above the settled sand.
6. Without disturbing the sediment of sand, gently pour out the top layer of water into another beaker.

**Observation:** Clear water gets collected in the second beaker while the sand is left behind in the first beaker.

**Conclusion:** Sedimentation and decantation methods can be used to separate heavier insoluble components from a solid–liquid mixture.

### Science in Context

In nature, solid substances such as sand, clay and gravel get transported along with the waves and water currents. These substances get deposited as sediments resulting in the coastline formation. This is the main cause for the formation of beaches.

- **Filtration:** *The process of separating fine, insoluble solid components suspended in a liquid by using a porous medium (filter) is known as* ***filtration*** (Fig. 7.6). The pores of the filter should be smaller than the size of the components that have to be separated. Substances that can be filtered are dust particles, sediments, insoluble particles, etc. We use this method at home to separate tea leaves from prepared tea, and seeds and pulp from lemon or orange juice.

**Fig. 7.6:** Filtration

## Activity 7.2

**Aim:** To separate a mixture of sand and water using filtration method

**Materials required:** Two beakers, sand, water, a glass rod, filter paper, a funnel and a stand with a ring clamp (for supporting the funnel)

**Procedure:**

1. Take a filter paper and make a cone as shown in the figures i to iv and keep it aside.
2. Take two tablespoons of sand in a beaker.
3. Add 100 mℓ water to it and mix the contents using a glass rod as shown in figures (a) and (b).
4. Place the stand with the ring clamp on a stable surface, adjust it to hold the funnel securely above the empty beaker, and ensure the funnel is stable as shown in figure (c).
5. Place the paper cone in the funnel.
6. Gently pour the mixture into the funnel as shown in figure (c).

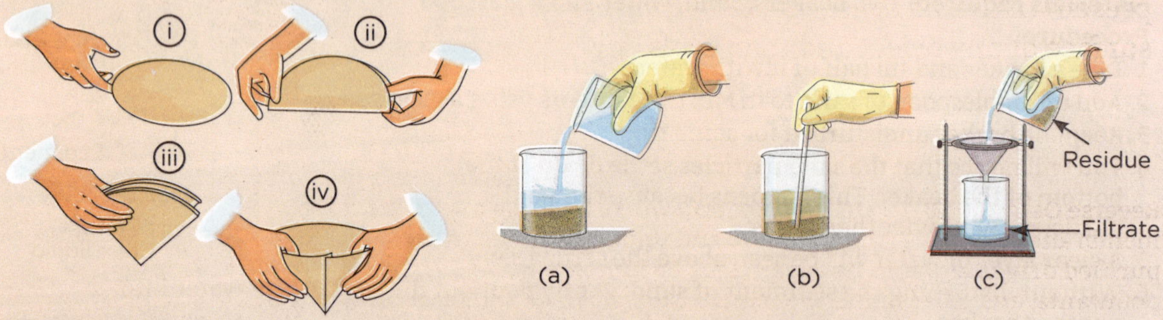


**Observation:** Clear water collects in the beaker after passing through the filter paper and sand particles are left behind in the filter paper.

**Conclusion:** Sand can be separated from water using filtration method.

- **Evaporation:** *The process in which a liquid changes into its gaseous state is called* ***evaporation***. This method is used to separate soluble solids from a solution of solid–liquid mixture. In this method, the liquid component is allowed to evaporate from the mixture, leaving behind only the solid component.

Evaporation is used to obtain common salt from seawater (Fig. 7.7). Seawater contains large amounts of salt dissolved in it. It is allowed to flow through narrow channels near coastal areas to be then collected in shallow ponds called salt pans. The water in these salt pans is allowed to dry in the sun. As the water evaporates, solid crystals of salt are left behind. The salt collected is further purified and is used for various purposes.

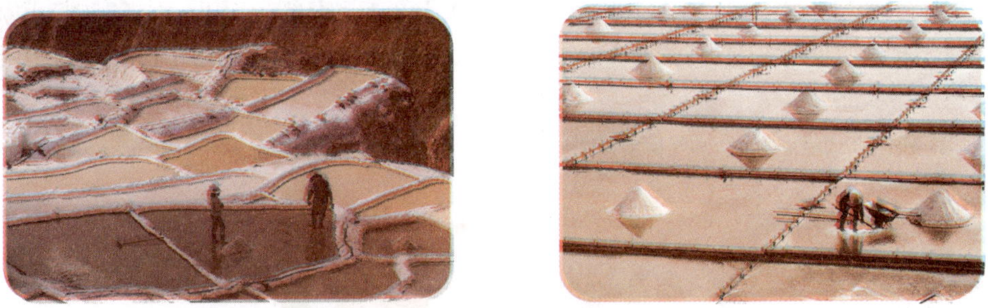

**Fig. 7.7:** Separation of salt from sea water by evaporation

- **Condensation:** *The process in which a gas changes to its liquid state is called **condensation**.*

The process of condensation is the opposite of evaporation. You might have seen tiny water droplets (dew) on the leaves of plants and on the mirrors of vehicles (Fig. 7.8) early in the morning. These water droplets are the results of the condensation process. This occurs when the water vapour present in the air comes in contact with a relatively cold surface of any object and then cools down to form dew.

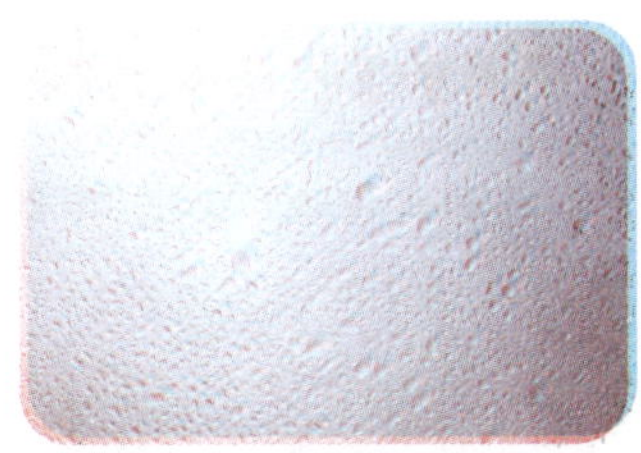

**Fig. 7.8:** Condensation

### Tech Update

Reverse Osmosis (RO) water purification works by using a semi-permeable membrane to remove contaminants and impurities from water, providing purified drinking water. Its advantages include effective removal of pollutants, and disadvantages include water wastage and the elimination of some essential minerals.

### Wonder!

To search for tiny particles of gold in rivers, a mixture of sand, mud and gravel is scooped up in a pan and swirled around. Gold particles are heavier than the other particles, so they settle down at the bottom of the pan. The lighter particles stay suspended in water, which are then decanted.

## Separating Liquid—Liquid Mixtures

- **Churning:** This method is used to separate butter from curd. In this process, curd is vigorously stirred or churned using a tool called a churner (Hindi: *mathni. What is a churner called in your mother tongue?*). As the curd is churned, the butter, which is lighter, starts to separate and float to the top. The remaining liquid, known as buttermilk, stays behind. Churning (Fig. 7.9) is a traditional and effective way to obtain butter, especially in rural areas where this method is still widely used.

**Fig. 7.9:** Churning

## Revise and Recall

**State whether the following statements are true (T) or false (F).**

1. Decantation is the best method for removing seeds from lemon juice.
2. A mixture of milk and water can be separated by sedimentation and decantation.
3. The preferred method to recover clear water from a bucket of muddy water is filtration.
4. Evaporation is used to obtain salt from seawater.
5. During the process of churning, butter separates from curd because butter is heavier than the buttermilk left behind.

### Know the Scientist

**Dr Thalappil Pradeep**
**(Born on 8 July, 1963)**

Dr Thalappil Pradeep, a professor at IIT Madras, is renowned for developing low-cost water purification technologies using nanomaterials to remove toxic elements such as arsenic and lead. His innovations, which have been commercialized and widely adopted in India, have significantly improved access to clean drinking water and public health. He has received several prestigious awards, including the Padma Shri, the Nikkei Asia Prize, the Shanti Swarup Bhatnagar Prize for Science and Technology and the VinFuture Prize.

## Keywords

**Mixture:** A substance that contains two or more different substances mixed together

**Homogeneous mixtures:** The mixtures in which the components are distributed uniformly and cannot be seen clearly

**Heterogeneous mixtures:** The mixtures in which the components are not distributed uniformly and can be seen clearly

**Threshing:** The process of separating grains from stalks of harvested crops either by beating the stalks against a hard surface or by using a threshing machine

**Winnowing:** The process of separating heavier components of a mixture from lighter components by the action of blowing wind

**Sieving:** The process of separating bigger particles from finer particles by passing them through a sieve

**Sedimentation:** The process of separating insoluble solid components mixed in a liquid by allowing them to settle down at the bottom of the container

**Decantation:** The process of pouring out the layer of clear liquid without disturbing the sediment

**Filtration:** The process of separating fine, insoluble solid components suspended in a liquid by using a porous medium

**Magnetic Separation:** A method used to separate magnetic materials, such as iron, from non-magnetic materials using a magnet

**Churning:** A process where curd is stirred to separate butter (solid) from butter-milk (liquid)

## Summary

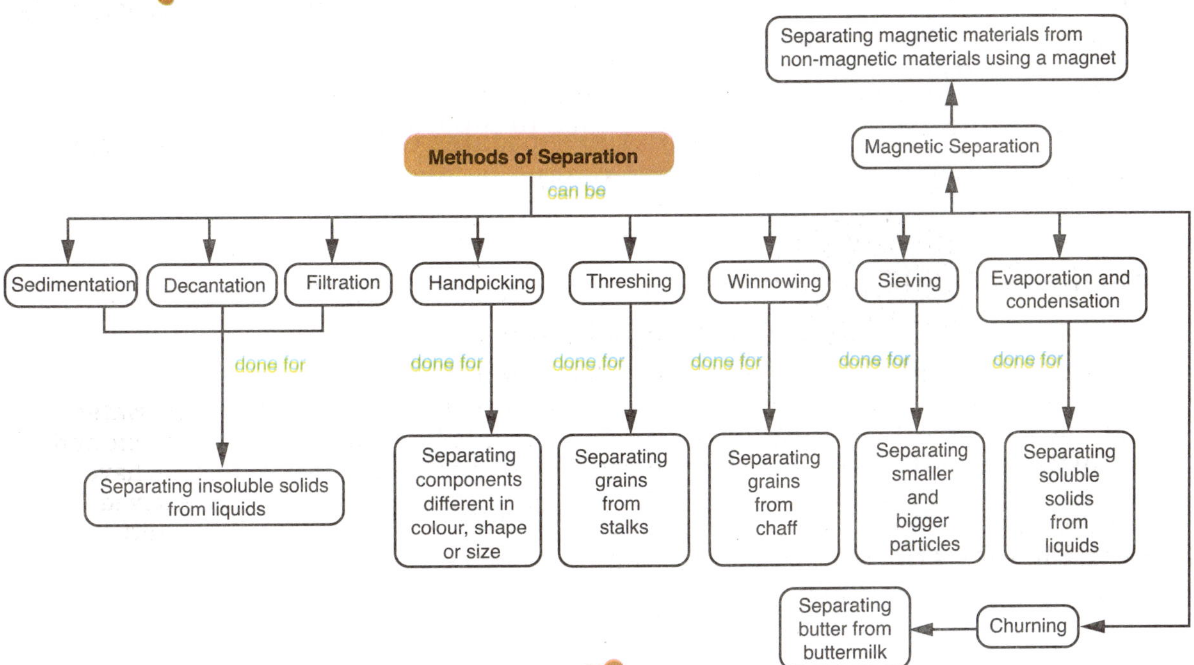

# Exercise

w

ia

**A. Choose the correct option.**

1. Substance that contains two or more components mixed together is a ________.
   (a) compound (b) mixture (c) element (d) molecule
2. Which of the following method will you use to clean flour before using it to make cookies?
   (a) Handpicking (b) Sieving (c) Winnowing (d) Filtration
3. Which of the following properties is used to separate a mixture of two solids by sieving?
   (a) Colour difference (b) Size difference (c) Weight difference (d) All of these
4. What type of separation is used to remove iron nails from sawdust?
   (a) Churning (b) Filtration
   (c) Magnetic Separation (d) Evaporation
5. Which of the following is a method used to separate butter from curd?
   (a) Filtration (b) Churning
   (c) Magnetic separation (d) Evaporation

**B. Fill in the blanks.**

ia

1. ________ is needed for the process of winnowing. (Wind/Water)
2. Impurities and bran can be removed from flour by using a ________. (filter/sieve)
3. Sieving is used when the components to be separated are different in ________. (size/weight)
4. Dissolved solid can be separated from its solution by ________ method. (evaporation/sedimentation)
5. In magnetic separation, a ________ is used to separate magnetic substances from non-magnetic ones. (magnet/iron)

**C. State whether the following statements are true (T) or false (F).**

1. Handpicking method is chosen when the quantity of impurities in the mixture is more than the required components.
2. Grains are separated from fresh stalks by using the threshing method.
3. Sieving allows the fine flour particles to remain on the sieve while the bigger impurities pass through the holes of the sieve.
4. The process of evaporation is used to obtain common salt from seawater.
5. Magnetic separation can be used to separate iron from a mixture of iron nails and sawdust.

**D. Match the following.**

| | |
|---|---|
| 1. Winnowing | (a) Separation of sand particles from sand and water solution |
| 2. Filtration | (b) Separation of salt from seawater |
| 3. Sedimentation | (c) Change of water vapour back into water |
| 4. Evaporation | (d) Separation of tea leaves from tea |
| 5. Condensation | (e) Separation of grains from husk |

**E. Give one word for each of the following.**

1. A substance that can be separated using threshing ____________
2. An example of solid–solid mixture ____________
3. An example of heterogeneous mixture ____________
4. The solid component that settles down during sedimentation ____________
5. Remaining liquid after churning curd ____________

**F. Give reasons for the following.**

1. A strainer is used to separate brewed tea from tea leaves.
2. Different sieves are used to separate different mixtures.
3. In a sand solution, particles settle down after sometime in the container.
4. Butter floats to the top during churning.
5. A magnet is useful in separating iron from other non-magnetic materials.

**G. Answer the following questions briefly.**

1. What is filtration?
2. Mary was asked to use sedimentation process to clean rice that her mother had brought from the mill before cooking. Why?
3. What is magnetic separation used for?
4. Describe the process of churning in simple terms.
5. Mention the appropriate methods for the separation of the following mixtures:
   (a) A mixture in which the components have different weights.
   (b) A mixture that has components of different sizes.
6. Rajesh is sweating because it is a hot sunny day. How does sweating help his body stay cool?

**H. Answer the following questions.**

1. What are the different methods used to separate a solid–solid mixture?
2. You are given a mixture of flour, bran and sand. How will you separate all the three components from this mixture? Name the method(s) that can be used to separate the components of the mixture.
3. Distinguish between homogeneous and heterogeneous mixtures.
4. Distinguish between evaporation and condensation.
5. Explain the processes of magnetic separation and churning. Describe the types of materials each method is used to separate. Give examples of where these methods might be applied in everyday life or industry.

# Cognitive Corner

## Critical Thinking

1. Masks are commonly made from various materials such as fabric, paper or plastic. Considering their design and material composition, what are the essential functions of masks in preventing the spread of airborne particles? How might different materials affect their effectiveness?
2. What will happen if evaporation did not take place at all?
3. What is the purpose of using air purifiers? How do air purifiers use filtration methods to improve air quality?

## Picture Study

**Name the methods you would use to separate the components from the following mixtures.**

1. Mixture: Pebbles, gravel, sawdust and sand

2. Mixture: Plastic beads, confetti balls and ball bearings

## Project

1. As a part of your Science Club activity, visit a water treatment plant and find out how many methods are used to treat the water before it is let into the taps for use at home. Write a report on the entire process involved in the purification of water. **(C-5.1)**
2. Conduct a research study to assess the awareness and knowledge of consumers regarding food adulteration. Based on the findings, propose educational campaigns and initiatives to empower consumers to identify and report adulterated food products. **(C-5.1)**
3. How can technology be used to enhance transparency and traceability of food adulteration? Develop a comprehensive strategy for a food manufacturing company to ensure the integrity of its supply chain and prevent food adulteration. **(C-5.1)**

## In the Laboratory

**Aim:** To separate a mixture of salt and water by evaporation and condensation methods **(C-7.2)**

**Materials required:** Two beakers, a Bunsen burner, salt, water, a teaspoon, tripod stands, wire gauze, a matchbox, ice cubes, a laboratory stand and a lid

**Procedure:**

1. Take a beaker containing the mixture of salt and water.
2. Use a teaspoon and mix the salt completely.
3. Place the beaker on the Bunsen burner and start heating the mixture.
4. Set up the apparatus as shown in the picture.

After some time, you will see the evaporation of water and formation of white residue.
The water vapours can be collected in a separate beaker by keeping a watch glass or a lid containing ice above the beaker. By using this method, the salt can be separated from the mixture of salt and water.

## Life Skills

Separation techniques have become a part of our daily activities. Some of these techniques are easily distinguishable while we use some separation techniques without realizing that we are using them. For instance, washing of hair. This is separation of dust and dirt from hair.

List some other separation techniques that we use in our daily life? **(C-7.3)**

______________________________

______________________________

______________________________

# Worksheet

Food adulteration is the method of adding harmful substances to food items to make more profit. Though such methods are punishable by law, many traders or manufacturers still practise this illegally.

Milk is often adulterated with water, detergent and fat.
Green vegetables are dyed with green colour to make them appear fresh.
Some pulses are coloured with very harmful yellow dyes.

A. Match the picture of food items on the left with what you think can be added as an adulterant on the right.

1. 

Rice grains

(a) 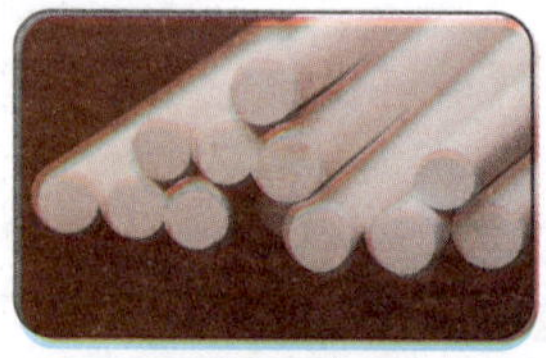

Chalk

2. 

Salt

(b) 

Papaya seeds

3. 

Pepper

(c) 

Small stones

B. Discuss the potential health risks associated with food adulteration and its impact on public health. What measures can governments take to strengthen food safety regulations and deter such practices?

C. Analyse the ethical implications of food adulteration for businesses and the broader society. How can consumers make informed choices to avoid purchasing adulterated food products?

D. Compare and contrast food adulteration regulations and enforcement mechanisms in different countries. What are some successful case studies of countries effectively combating food adulteration?

# 8 Measurement of Length and Motion

## Curricular Goals

- Explore the world of matter and its constituents, properties and behaviour **(CG-1)**
- Explore the physical world in scientific and mathematical terms **(CG-2)**

## Competencies

- Explain the importance of measurement and measure physical properties of matter in indigenous, non-standard and standard units using simple instruments **(C-1.3)**
- Describe one-dimensional motion (uniform, non-uniform, horizontal, vertical) using physical measurements (position, distance) through mathematical and diagrammatic representations **(C-2.1)**

## Let's Get Started

We use different devices to measure quantities such as distance, time, volume, mass and length. Given below are pictures of some devices used for measuring certain quantities. Name the quantities that can be measured using these devices. One has been done for you.

Mass ____________

____________

____________

____________

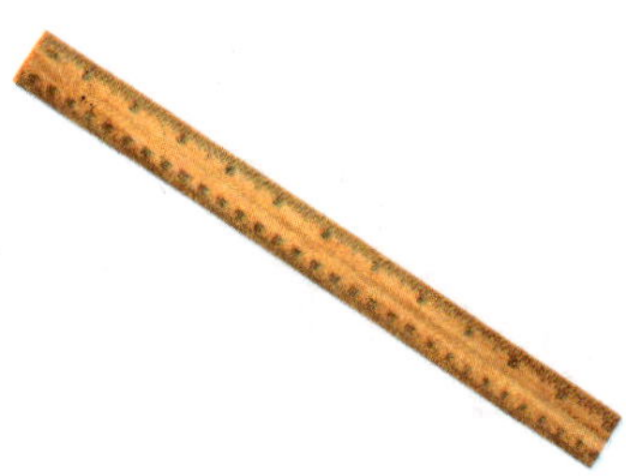

____________

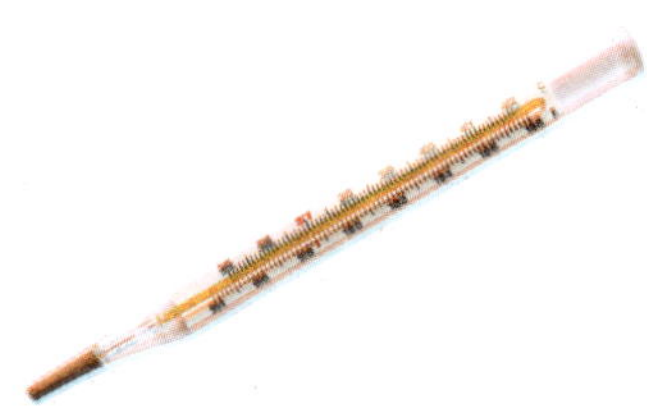

____________

# WHAT IS MEASUREMENT?

**Measurement** is the process of assigning (or giving) a numerical value to a **physical quantity** such as length, weight, volume and distance. The physical quantity measured is expressed in two parts—a numerical value and a unit. The numerical value is the magnitude of the measured quantity. A **unit** is a fixed quantity used as a standard of measurement. For example, metre is the standard unit of length, kilogram is the standard unit of mass and second is the standard unit of time.

## Need for Standard Units

In ancient times, people used their body parts for measurement (Fig. 8.1). For example, the length of one's foot and the width of a palm were accepted units of measurement.

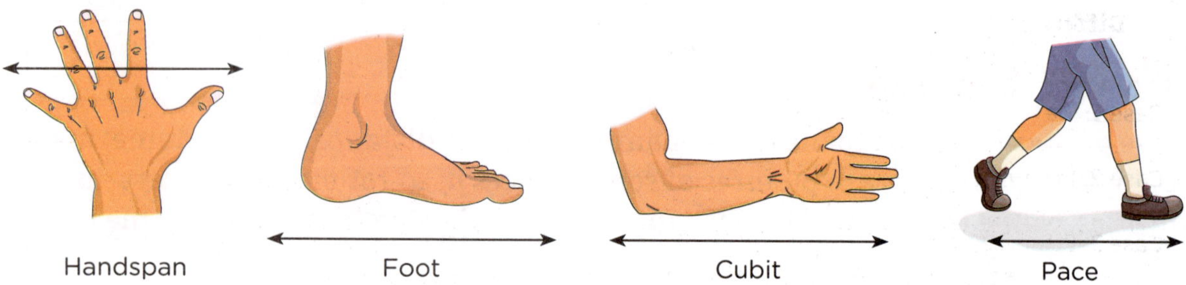


**Fig. 8.1:** Different units of measurements used in ancient times

Do you think the methods used in ancient times gave accurate measurements? If people used their handspans for measurement across the world, would it generate the same result? Let us look at an example.

Akhil needs a nylon string of length two handspans for his art project at the school. He asks his father to get it. Akhil's friend Abdul goes to a shop and buys a nylon string of length two handspans for himself. The next day, they compare the length of their strings. Do you think the length of their nylon strings are the same?

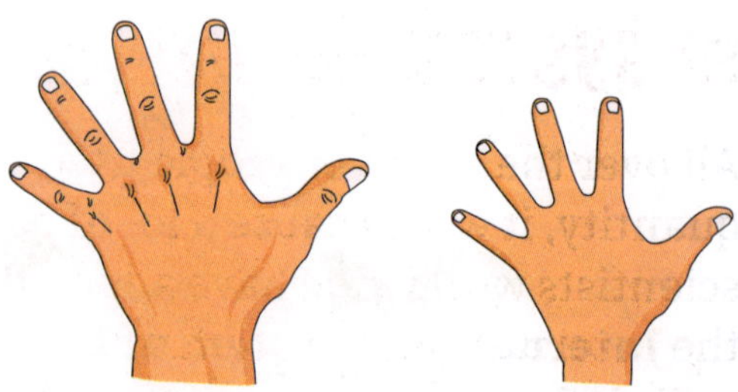

**Fig. 8.2:** Different handspan

The length of the two strings would probably differ as the handspan of Akhil's father is likely to be bigger than that of Abdul's (Fig. 8.2).

**Science in Context**

*Yojana* was the unit of length used in Vedic times in India.

## Activity 8.1

**Aim:** To prove the need for standard unit (centimetre for measuring the length)

**Materials required:** Table/desk, ruler and the help of two of your friends

**Procedure:**

1. Measure the length of a desk in your classroom with your handspan.
2. Ask two of your friends to measure the length of the same desk using their handspan.
3. Compare the results.
4. Now, measure the length of the same desk using a ruler.
5. Ask the same friends to measure the length using their rulers.
6. Enter the results in the table and compare them.

**Observation:**

Write your observations in the table given below. Are the values same in all the cases? Which method of measurement is the accurate one?

| Different Cases | Measured Value | |
|---|---|---|
| | Using Handspan | Using Ruler |
| Case 1: Me | | |
| Case 2: Friend 1 | | |
| Case 3: Friend 2 | | |

**Conclusion:** What do you conclude from this activity?

From the above activity, we can conclude that ancient methods of measurement were not always accurate. Therefore, standard units of measurement that do not vary from one person to another evolved.

## SI SYSTEM OF UNITS

All over the world, if people used diverse units to measure a specific physical quantity, it would cause a lot of confusion. Thus, to ensure uniformity and accuracy, scientists worldwide have adopted a standard set of units for measurement called the **International System of Units** or **SI units**. It consists of a set of standardized, well-defined units for measurement of physical quantities. For example, the unit of length in the SI system is metre, the unit of mass is kilogram and the unit of time is second.

There are also other systems of measuring units used by people in different parts of the world such as the FPS system, MKS system and CGS system.

Table 8.1 shows the units of length, mass and time in different systems of units.

**Table 8.1:** Different systems of units

| ↓ Quantity / System → | CGS | MKS | FPS | SI |
|---|---|---|---|---|
| Length | centimetre | metre | foot | metre |
| Mass | gram | kilogram | pound | kilogram |
| Time | second | second | second | second |
| Temperature | Kelvin | Kelvin | Fahrenheit | Kelvin |

## MEASUREMENT OF LENGTH

The SI unit of length is metre (m). One metre is divided into 10 decimetres, each decimetre is divided into 10 centimetres and each centimetre is divided into 10 millimetres. The unit of length is chosen based on how conveniently one can express the quantity being measured. For example, length of a book is measured in centimetres, dimensions of a room are measured in metres and the distance between two cities is measured in kilometres.

1 kilometre (km) = 1000 metres (m)

Now, let us express 3.5 km in other units of length.

3.5 km = 3.5 × 1000 m = **3500 m**

3.5 km = 3.5 × 1000 m = 3500 × 10 dm = **35,000 dm**

3.5 km = 3.5 × 1000 m = 3500 × 10 dm = 35,000 × 10 cm = **3,50,000 cm**

3.5 km = 3.5 × 1000 m = 3500 × 10 dm = 35,000 × 10 cm = 3,50,000 × 10 mm = **35,00,000 mm**

### Instruments Used to Measure Length

There are different types of instruments used to measure length. Length can be measured using a ruler (Fig. 8.3) or a measuring tape. Vernier calipers (Fig. 8.4) and screw gauge (Fig. 8.5) are used to make accurate measurements when the lengths are smaller than a millimetre. Laser rangefinder is a device used to measure long distances. Sound navigation and ranging (SONAR) is used to determine the depth of oceans.

**Fig. 8.3:** Ruler

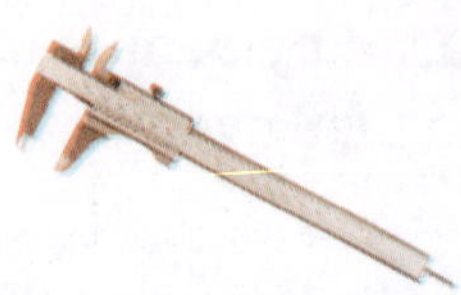

**Fig. 8.4:** Vernier calipers

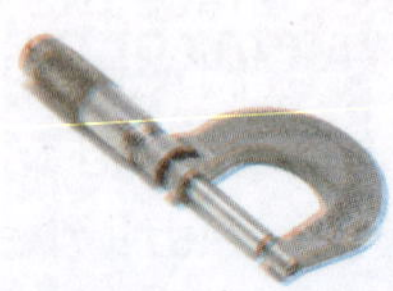

**Fig. 8.5:** Screw gauge

**Correct method of measurement using a ruler (Fig. 8.6):**

1. Keep the ruler on the object so that zero of the scale is at the starting point from where the length is to be measured.
2. Note the reading on the ruler on the other end, that is, the point till where the length is to be measured. Make sure your eyes are straight in line with the markings on the ruler.
3. If the zero marking on the ruler is not clear or the ruler is broken [Fig. 8.6 (b)], start the measurement from the next clear marking and find the difference between the two readings.

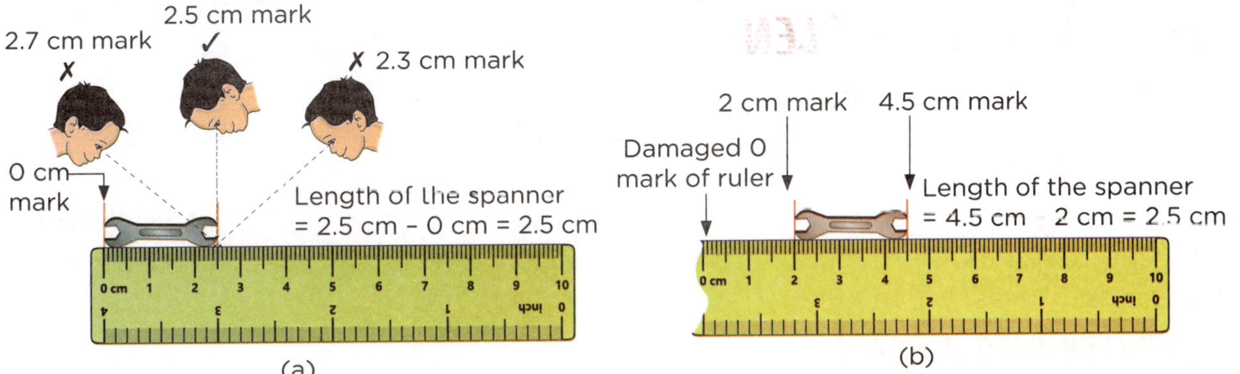


**Fig. 8.6:** Measurement using a ruler

Using a divider and a ruler, we can measure the length of a line segment easily. Keep the divider on the line so that its tips are at the two ends X and Y of the line segment [Fig. 8.7 (a)]. Then place the divider on a scale as shown in Figure 8.7 (b). Take the reading on the ruler, which is 4 cm. So, the length of the line segment XY is 4 cm.

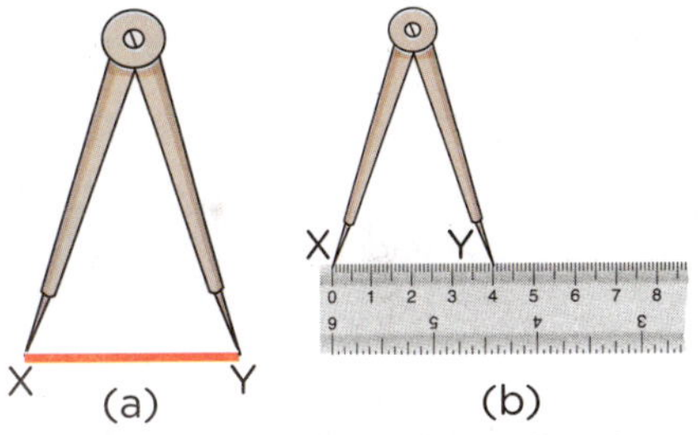


**Fig. 8.7:** Measuring length using a divider

## Measuring the Length of a Curved Line

The length of a straight line can be measured using a ruler, but how will you measure the length of a curved line? A flexible and non-stretchable string or thread can be used to measure the length of a curved line (Fig. 8.8). Place the thread along the curved line. Start from the beginning of the curved line and follow the entire length of the curve. Mark the starting point and ending point of the curve on the

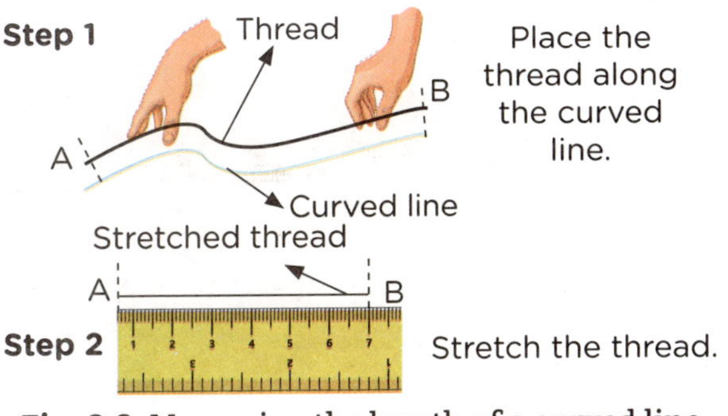


**Fig. 8.8:** Measuring the length of a curved line

thread. Put the thread straight on a flat surface and use a ruler to measure the length of the thread, where the starting point of the thread is kept at 0 unit and the marked end portion will give the measure of the length. The measured value gives the length of the curved line.

## Estimations

Estimation is the process of making a rough guess or calculation of a measurement, such as length, volume or mass. For example, if you are wondering how much a plant has grown, you might make a rough estimate by concluding it has grown a hand's length. Then to find out if you have estimated or guessed correctly, you can take a ruler to measure your hand's length and the plant's height to verify your calculation. If your teacher gives you a small packet of toffees and asks you to guess its weight, you pick it up and estimate its weight. To know how correct you were, you then weigh it using a balance. Estimation helps in making rough calculations when a measuring equipment is not available or a rough calculation is enough to meet your requirements.

### Revise and Recall

**Answer the following questions.**

1. What are the shortcomings of the units used in ancient times?
2. What are the advantages of having a standard set of units?
3. What is a fixed quantity used as a standard of measurement called?
4. What is the SI unit of length?

## MOTION AND REST

There is motion all around us. Every day, we come across motion of people and various objects such as vehicles, animals, birds, etc. When do we say that an object is in motion? Let us find out. Figures 8.9 (a) and (b) show the positions of a car in intervals of a few seconds.

(a) (b)

**Fig. 8.9** Positions of a moving car

Observe the positions of the car. The position of the car changes with time with respect to its surroundings. Therefore, the car is moving.

***Motion** is defined as a change in a person's or object's position with regard to time.* If the position of a body does not change with time with respect to its surroundings, then we say the body is at **rest**.

## Types of Motion

Motion of objects is classified based on the nature of the motion they undergo. For example, the nature of motion of a boy sitting in a moving car is different from the motion of a boy sitting in a roller coaster. Let us learn about the different types of motion.

## Translational Motion

Consider the motion of a car moving on a road. The position of the car changes continuously with time with respect to its surroundings. Moreover, during its journey all parts of the car move equal distances in equal intervals of time. Such motion is called *translational motion*. Translational motion can be of two types—rectilinear motion and curvilinear motion.

**Rectilinear motion:** If the motion of an object is along a straight line, it is called *rectilinear motion*. In rectilinear motion, the direction of the motion of the object remains the same as it is moving along a straight path (Fig. 8.10).

Examples are the motion of a car on a straight road, the motion of a stone falling down and an athlete running on a straight track.

**Curvilinear motion:** If an object moves along a curved path, it is called *curvilinear motion*. In curvilinear motion, the direction of the motion of the object changes with time, but the orientation of the object remains the same. A car moving on a curved road is an example of curvilinear motion (Fig. 8.11).

**Fig. 8.10:** Rectilinear motion

**Fig. 8.11:** Curvilinear motion

## Rotational Motion

Consider the motion of a fan. The fan rotates continuously about an axis. The distance moved by different points on the fan is not the same but all the points complete the rotation in the same time. Such motion is said to be *rotational motion*. Rotation of the Earth about its axis, motion of a spinning top and rotation of a flywheel are examples of rotational motion (Fig. 8.12).

**Fig. 8.12:** Rotational motion

> **Science in Context**
>
> The Earth rotates about its axis with certain speed. It also revolves around the sun with a certain speed called orbital speed. How wonderful it is to realize that we are moving at a great speed even while sitting still at a place.

## Periodic Motion

If the motion of an object is repeated along the same path at regular intervals of time, such motion is said to be *periodic motion*. Motion of the hands of a clock (Fig. 8.13), motion of a simple pendulum, motion of the moon around the Earth, rotation of the Earth about its own axis and revolution of the Earth around the sun are examples of periodic motion.

**Fig. 8.13:** Periodic motion

Now, consider the motion of a simple pendulum. After each regular interval of time, the metal bob of the pendulum repeats its motion by retracing its path, that is, the pendulum moves in a to-and-fro manner in regular intervals of time. Such motion is called **oscillatory motion** (Fig. 8.14). Moving pendulum of a clock and motion of a swing are examples of oscillatory motion.

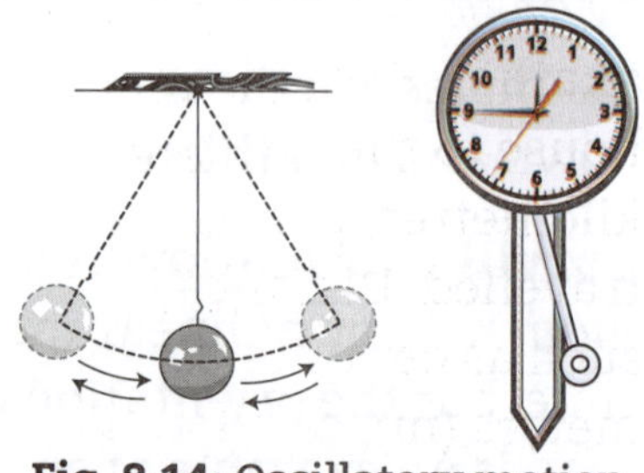

**Fig. 8.14:** Oscillatory motion

In some situations, we can observe a combination of different types of motion. For example, in the case of a moving car (Fig. 8.15), the wheels of the car undergo rotational motion while the car itself is in translational motion at the same time. As the Earth rotates about its own axis, it also moves around the sun. Therefore, it undergoes rotational as well as periodic motion. When a batsman hits a cricket ball, it undergoes both translational motion and rotational motion at the same time as it spins and goes high.

**Fig. 8.15:** A car in motion

## Activity 8.2

Make small groups of 4–5 students. Plan a visit to a nearby park or playground. (*If a visit is not possible, use images or videos of a children's park.*) Then, for each of your group, choose a minimum of two activities of an object or person(s) in motion (e.g., swings, merry-go-rounds, kids running) and note down your observations in a table as shown below. Classify each observed motion into linear, circular or oscillatory motion.

Discuss the reasoning behind each classification.

| Object/Person in Motion | Type of Motion |
|---|---|
| Swing | |
| Seesaw | |
| Merry-go-round | |
| Child sliding | |
| Child running | |

# DISTANCE AND POSITION

In our daily lives, we move from one place to another, whether it is going to school, visiting a friend or travelling to a different city. Understanding the concepts of distance, position, reference point and milestones can help us better understand how we measure and describe these movements.

## Distance

**Distance** *is the total length of the path travelled by an object*. It tells us how far one place is from another. For example, if you walk from your house to the school and cover a distance of 2 kilometres, that is the total distance you have travelled. Distance is usually measured in units such as centimetres (cm), decimetres (dm), metres (m), or kilometres (km), depending on how long the path is.

**Fig. 8.16:** Distance between three cities

Imagine you are travelling by "Chennai Express" train from Bengaluru to Chennai *via* Katpadi Junction. The train covers 230 km from Bengaluru to Katpadi Junction and 130 km from Katpadi Junction to Chennai. The total distance you travelled is 230 km + 130 km = 360 km.

## Position

**Position** *is the location of an object at a particular point in time*. It tells us where something is present at a given moment. For example, if you are standing at your school's entrance, your position is at the school entrance.

When position is described relative to something else, then another important concept to learn is about the reference point.

## Reference Point

*A **reference point** is a fixed place or object used to determine the position of an object.* It acts as a "starting point" from which we measure distance or describe the location of something.

Let us say you are at home and want to go to the park. If you say, "The park is 500 metres from my house," your house is the reference point (Fig. 8.17). If all your friends use their homes as reference points, each might describe the distance to the park differently, depending on how close or far their homes are from the park.

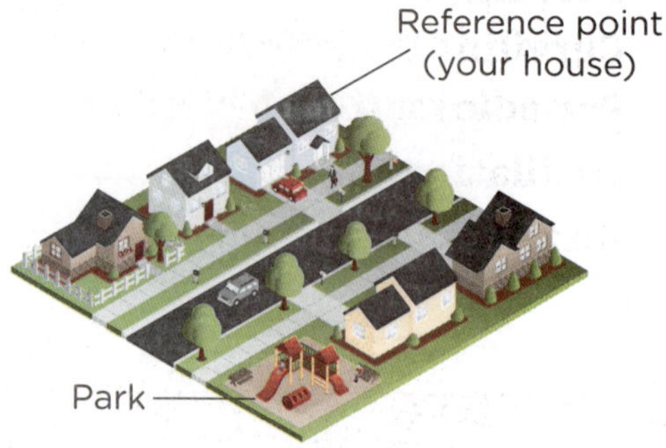


**Fig. 8.17:** A neighbourhood

## Milestone

*A **milestone** is a type of reference point.* It is a numbered marker placed on a road, canal, along railway lines or property boundaries. It indicates the distances to places and/or gives their positions on a route relative to a place.

For instance, if you are travelling by bus and you see a milestone (Fig. 8.18) that reads "Leh 107," it means you are 107 kilometers away from Leh. As you travel, the distance decreases, indicating you are getting closer to your destination.

**Fig. 8.18:** Milestone

Milestones act as reference points along a journey, helping travellers or navigators determine their current location relative to their destination. They allow travellers to find how much distance has been covered and how much remains. What we see on the milestones are the distances between the Head Post Offices of the two places.

### Know the Scientist

**Aryabhata**
**(476–550 CE)**

Aryabhata, a renowned ancient Indian mathematician and astronomer, made significant contributions to the understanding of motion, time, and celestial mechanics. He introduced precise time calculations, developed methods to predict the positions of planets and stars, and provided insights into the relativity of motion. His work laid the foundation for advancements in ancient Indian astronomy.

## Keywords

**Physical Quantity:** A quantity that can be measured
**Unit:** A fixed quantity used as a standard for measurement
**Rectilinear motion:** Motion of an object along a straight line
**Curvilinear motion:** Motion of an object along a curved path
**Periodic motion:** Motion of an object repeated at regular intervals of time
**Oscillation:** To-and-fro motion along the same path
**Distance:** The total length of the path covered by an object

## Summary

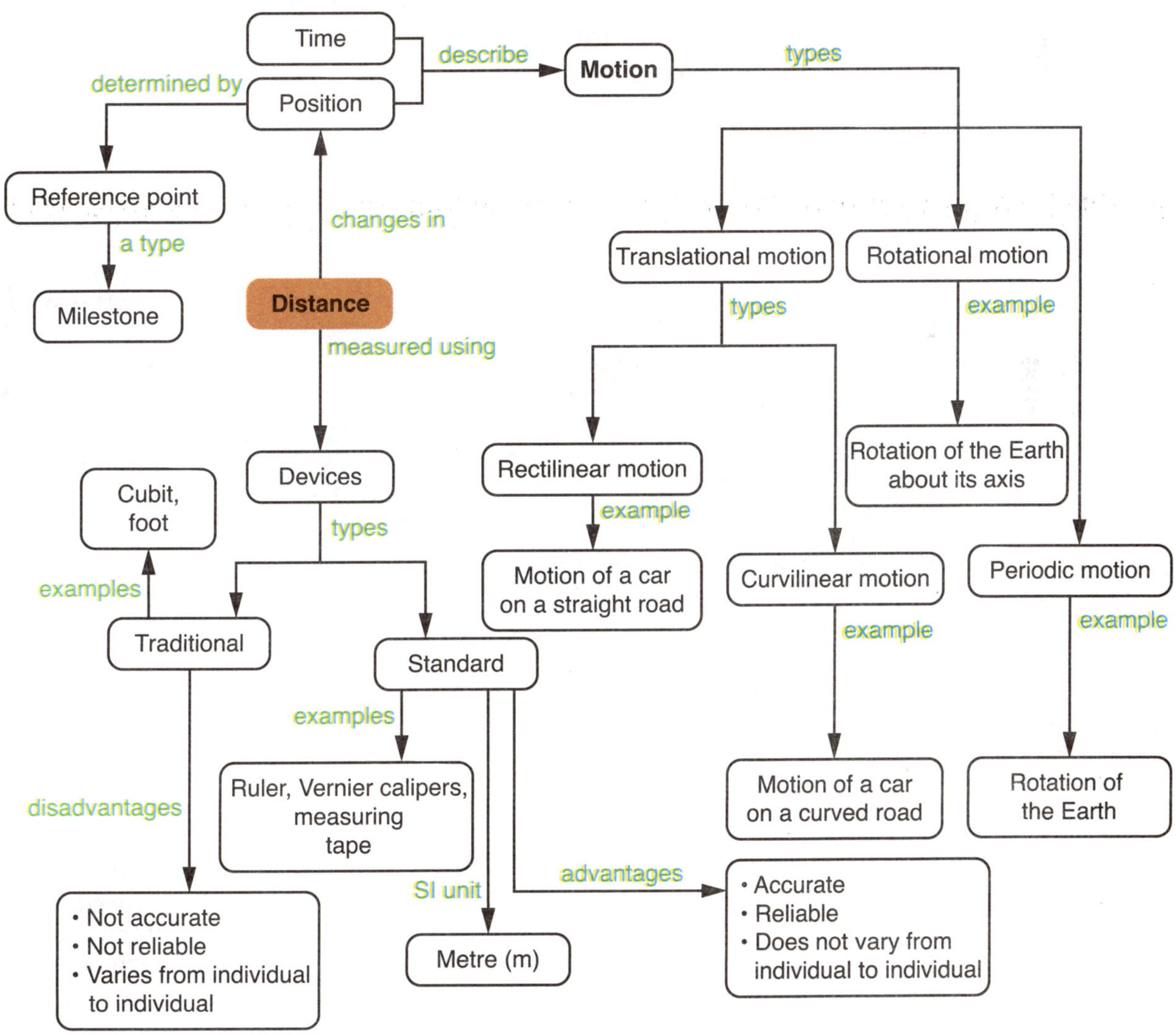

# Exercise

**A. Choose the correct option.**

1. Which of the following would be appropriate to measure the length of a football field?
   (a) Cubit (b) Handspan (c) Pace (d) Footstep
2. Which of the following would be appropriate to measure the length of a curved line?
   (a) Wooden scale (b) Measuring tape
   (c) Vernier calipers (d) Non-elastic thread and a ruler
3. In how many equal parts should one metre be divided to get a centimetre?
   (a) 100 (b) 1000 (c) 10 (d) 10,000
4. Which of the following is true with respect to the motion of the legs of a person walking on a straight footpath?
   (a) Only rectilinear (b) Rectilinear and rotational
   (c) Only rotational (d) Oscillatory and rectilinear
5. Which of the following is true with respect to the motion of the tyres of a bicycle on a straight road and a ceiling fan?
   (a) Both undergo rotational motion
   (b) Both undergo rectilinear motion
   (c) Both undergo rotational and rectilinear motion
   (d) None of these

**B. Fill in the blanks.**

1. One kilometre is equal to ________________ metres. (1000/10,000)
2. The SI unit of length is ________________. (kilometre/metre)
3. Five metres are equal to ________________ mm. (500/5000)
4. Motion of a child on a swing is ________________. (periodic and rectilinear/ periodic and oscillatory)
5. The total length of the path covered by an object is called ____________. (motion/distance)

**C. State whether the following statements are true (T) or false (F).**

1. The SI unit of length is kilometre.
2. Pace or a footstep can be used as a standard unit of length.
3. Motion is the change in position of an object with respect to time.
4. The motion of the minute hand of a clock is oscillatory.
5. A group of soldiers marching during guard of honour depicts periodic motion.

**D. Give reasons for the following.**

1. A cubit cannot be used as a standard unit for the measurement of length
2. Diameter of a ball cannot be measured using a ruler.
3. When sitting inside a moving bus, we are at rest as well as in motion.
4. Motion of the Earth around the sun is a periodic motion.
5. It is not recommended to use an elastic tape to measure distance.

**E. Answer the following questions briefly.**

1. Why do we need standard units for measurement?
2. What is periodic motion? Give one example seen in nature.
3. What is rotational motion? Give an example from your daily life.
4. The measurements given below are incomplete. Complete them.
   (a) The length of Ryan's hair is 10.
   (b) The bus took approximately 30 to reach school.
5. What is the role of a reference point in determining the position of an object?
6. How does a milestone help travellers on a highway?

**F. Answer the following questions.**

1. Traditional methods of measurement are not reliable compared to standard methods of measurement. Explain.
2. Give five examples of different types of measurements we need in our day-to-day life.
3. What are the different types of motion? Give two examples of each.
4. Can a body have rotational motion and rectilinear motion at the same time? Justify.
5. Explain the types of translatory motion with one example for each.
6. Explain the relationship between distance, position, reference point and milestones with examples.

# Cognitive Corner

## Critical Thinking

1. "All oscillatory motions are periodic while all periodic motions are not oscillatory." Is this statement correct? Justify your answer.
2. We know that the Earth moves around the sun. However, when we look at the sky we see that the sun rises in the east, slowly moves towards the west and sets there. Why?

## Picture Study

**Look at the pictures given below and identify the type of motion.**

1. ____________

2. ____________

## Project

1. Estimate the lengths of any five objects in your surroundings. Measure them and find out their actual lengths. List your findings in a table and compare your list with the lists of your classmates. **(C-1.3)**
2. Have you ever seen or heard about the Jantar Mantar in New Delhi? As a part of the Science Club activity, collect information and images of instruments used at Jantar Mantar and their functions. Make a PowerPoint presentation in a group and present it in your class. **(C-1.3)**

## In the Library

Although millimetre is a small unit of length, it is not convenient for expressing very small lengths such as the size of microbes, the wavelength of light and intermolecular distances in solid substances. Collect information about smaller units of length that are used to express length at the molecular and atomic levels. **(C-7.1)**

## Life Skills

1. We have learned about different types of motion. Observe a tailor stitching clothes using a sewing machine. Out of the different types of motion, what are the types we can see in stitching using a sewing machine? **(C-6.2)**
2. With your friends, dismantle a damaged clock or toys. Examine the arrangements in them for producing different types of motion. **(C-6.2)**
3. Milestones on Indian highways have different colours. Conduct a research to find out the significance of these colours and how they help travellers. What do these different coloured milestones indicate? Why is it important for drivers and travellers to be aware of these distinctions?

   After completing your research, create a road trip chart map that includes the meaning of these milestones, highlighting how they can guide you on your journey. How would this information be useful on a real road trip? **(C-5.1)**

9 INDUSTRY, INNOVATION AND INFRASTRUCTURE

# Worksheet

The main source of light on Earth is the sun. Sunlight travels through space and lights up all the members of the solar system. In space, the speed of light is 3,00,000 kilometres per second. This means that light takes only one second to cover 3,00,000 km.

Yet, it takes light about 8 and a half minutes to reach the Earth. This illustrates just how far the sun is from the Earth!

Let us calculate the distance between the sun and the Earth.

There are 60 seconds in a minute.

First, find out the number of seconds in eight and a half minutes.

______________________________________________

______________________________________________

You know that the sunlight travels 3,00,000 km in one second.

Now, multiply the number of seconds you found in 8 and a half minutes by 3,00,000 to find the distance light travels.

______________________________________________

______________________________________________

This gives the approximate distance of the sun from Earth.

However, in summer, it is difficult to stand in the sunlight, especially during the afternoon. Now imagine how hot the sun really is!

# 9 Temperature and Its Measurement

## Curricular Goals

- Explore the world of matter and its constituents, properties and behaviour **(CG-1)**
- Explore the nature and processes of science through engaging with the evolution of scientific knowledge and conducting scientific inquiry **(CG-6)**

## Competencies

- Describe changes in matter and use particulate nature to represent the properties of matter **(C-1.2)**
- Observe and explain the phenomena caused due to difference in temperature and density **(C-1.4)**
- Formulate questions using scientific terminology and collect data as evidence **(C-6.2)**

## Let's Get Started

Look at the pictures given below and write "SUMMER" against the clothing that you prefer to wear during summer and "WINTER" against the clothing that you prefer to wear during winter.

______________________

______________________

______________________

______________________

Temperature changes with the seasons. So, our preferences like the types of clothes we wear and the foods we eat also changes. The degree of hotness or coldness of any object is called its temperature. Let us learn more about temperature and its measurement in this chapter.

## HEAT

When you hold a glass of hot milk, the warmth you feel is because heat is moving from the hot milk to your cooler hand. **Heat** is a type of energy that always moves from something warmer to something cooler. The amount of heat is measured in joules (J), which is the SI unit for heat.

We get heat energy from the sun and by burning fuels such as coal, petrol and kerosene. We use heat energy in many ways, such as cooking food and keeping ourselves warm.

## TEMPERATURE

Temperature is a way to measure how hot or cold something is. It tells us how much heat energy is in an object or the air around us.

*The degree of hotness or coldness of an object is called its* ***temperature***. The SI unit of temperature is kelvin (K). A hot object has more heat energy than a cold object of same mass.

We often touch objects to decide how hot or cold they are. But is our sense of touch reliable? Let us perform a simple activity to understand this.

### Activity 9.1

**Aim**: To understand whether our sense of touch is reliable to determine how hot or cold objects are (*Note*: This activity needs to be performed only in the presence of teacher/instructor.)

**Materials required**: Three glass beakers labelled as A, B and C, warm water, cold water and normal water

**Procedure**:

1. Take three glass beakers (A, B and C). Pour warm water at 40 °C in beaker A and cold water at 10 °C in beaker C. In beaker B, pour water at room temperature.
2. Dip the index fingers of your left and right hands in beakers A and C, respectively, for about a minute. Then dip both the fingers in beaker B.

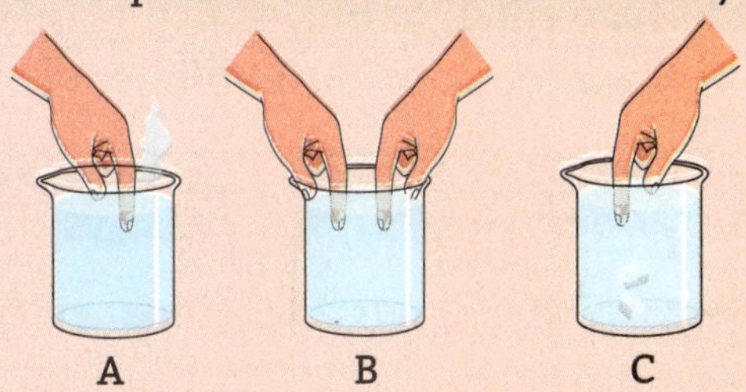


**Observation**: You will notice that the water in beaker B feels cold to the left index finger and warm to the right index finger.

**Conclusion**: This shows that the terms 'hot' and 'cold' are relative. There should be a reference temperature with respect to which we can say whether a given object is hot or cold. Our sense of touch is therefore not reliable in determining how hot or cold objects are.

As shown in Activity 9.1, our sense of touch is not very reliable in deciding how hot or cold objects are. There are more reliable ways to measure the temperature of an object. Let us learn more about them.

## Measurement of Temperature

A **thermometer** is a device used to measure temperature. It works by using substances that expand or contract with temperature changes.

> **Science in Context**
>
> In 1593, Galileo Galilei invented a water thermoscope, which, for the first time, measured the variations in temperature.

A thermometer consists of the following parts (Fig. 9.1).

**Bulb**: The bulb made of glass contains mercury or alcohol. It is the part of the thermometer that comes into contact with the object or body whose temperature is being measured.

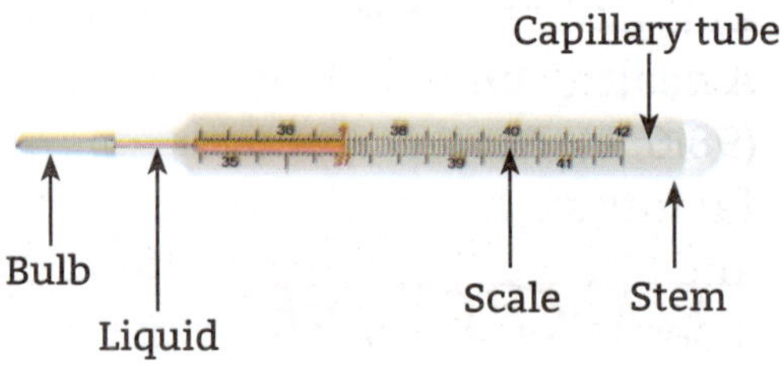


**Fig. 9.1**: Parts of a thermometer

Mercury is commonly used in thermometers because it remains in liquid state across a wide range of temperatures, from about –39 °C to 357 °C. Its silvery grey in colour makes it easy to read against the graduated scale and it does not stick to the glass of the thermometer. However, the disadvantage of using mercury is its toxicity. Even small amounts of mercury can be very harmful to health, so it is important to handle it with care and avoid exposure.

On the other hand, alcohol is used in thermometers because it is not toxic. It remains in a liquid state at temperatures ranging from approximately –100 °C to 78 °C allowing it to accurately measure very low temperatures. Alcohol is dyed with bright colours (e.g., red or blue), making it easy to see and read against the graduated scale. Additionally, it is less expensive than mercury. However, the disadvantage of using alcohol is that it cannot measure temperatures above 78 °C.

**Capillary tube:** A thin, sealed glass tube connected to the bulb. It allows the expansion and contraction of the liquid inside the bulb to be visibly displayed as a change in height.

**Scale:** A series of markings on the capillary tube, usually in degrees Celsius (°C) or Fahrenheit (°F). The scale allows the user to read the temperature.

**Steps to be followed to measure temperature using thermometer:**

1. Make sure the thermometer is clean and, if needed, shake it down to reset the mercury or alcohol to the lowest point.
2. Place the thermometer in the area where you want to measure temperature. This could be under your tongue tongue, or in the armpit, or rectally.
3. Leave the thermometer in place for a few minutes to allow mercury or alcohol to adjust to the temperature.
4. Remove the thermometer and look at the level of mercury or alcohol in the glass tube. The level will indicate the temperature.

# Types of Thermometers

Some commonly used thermometers are discussed below.

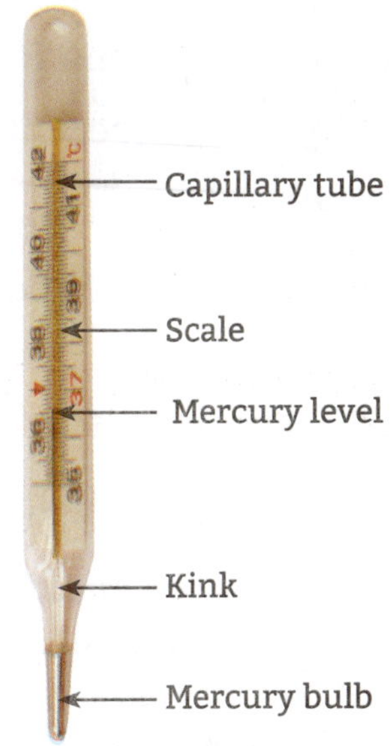


**Fig. 9.2**: Clinical thermometer

**Clinical thermometer**: A clinical thermometer (Fig. 9.2) is used to measure a human body temperature. Mercury is used in clinical thermometers. The temperature range of a clinical thermometer is 35 °C to 42 °C or 94 °F to 108 °F. A healthy human body has a temperature of about 37 °C (98.6 °F). However, body temperature can vary based on factors such as age, physical activity, the time of day and environmental conditions. It can also change when a person is ill. A body temperature that exceeds 40 °C (104 °F) is considered as a medical emergency and needs immediate medical attention.

The capillary tube of a clinical thermometer has a kink or bend, which acts as a barrier to stop the liquid from moving back down the tube once the temperature has been measured.

While using a clinical thermometer, the following precautions should be taken:

- The thermometer should be washed before and after use, preferably with an antiseptic solution.
- It should be ensured that before use, the mercury level is below 35 °C or 95 °F.
- The thermometer should be read keeping the level of mercury along the line of sight.
- The thermometer should be handled with care. If it hits against some hard object, it can break.
- The bulb of a thermometer should not be touched while taking a reading. Hold the thermometer by its glass body.

**Digital thermometer**: Electronic thermometers called digital thermometers (Fig. 9.3) are widely used for measuring temperature. Probe is the part of the thermometer that comes into contact with the body or the substance being measured. Shows the temperature reading on a display screen. Small batteries are used to enable them to function. Does not contain toxic materials like mercury.

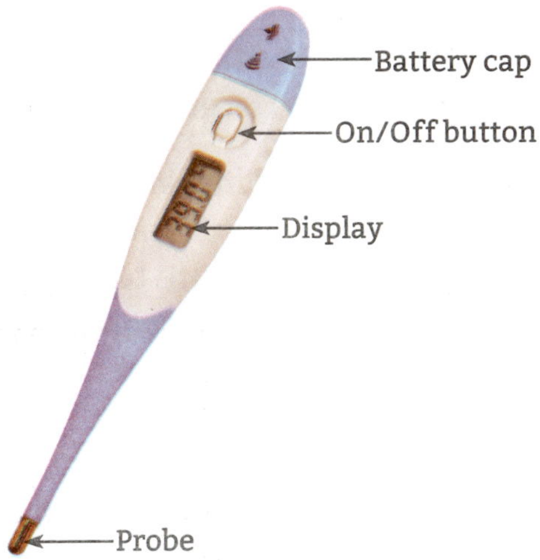


**Fig. 9.3**: Digital thermometer

The following steps are to be followed while using a digital thermometer:

- Wipe the probe with alcohol-based wipes and dry it using a soft cloth.
- Turn it on by pressing the power button.
- Place the probe under the tongue, or in the armpit, or rectally. For other purposes, place it in a liquid or environment.
- Wait until the thermometer beeps or the display shows a stable reading.
- Look at the digital display to read the temperature.

**Laboratory thermometer**: Laboratory thermometers (Fig. 9.4) are designed for use in laboratories during experiments. They are capable of measuring temperatures within a range of –10°C to 110°C. Alcohol is used in laboratory thermometers.

The following are some precautions to be taken while using a laboratory thermometer:

- Handle the thermometer with care. If it hits against some hard object, it can break.
- Do not hold the thermometer by the bulb while taking a reading.
- The thermometer should be kept upright, not tilted.
- The bulb should be surrounded on all sides by the substance whose temperature is to be measured.
- The bulb should not touch the surface of the container.
- Removing the thermometer from a boiling water bath and immediately immersing it in an ice bath may cause the thermometer to break.

**Fig. 9.4**: Laboratory thermometer

**Infrared thermometer:** Non-contact thermometers, also known as infrared thermometers (Fig. 9.5), are special tools that can measure temperature without needing to touch the person or object. This type of thermometer allows for safe and efficient temperature measurement, especially in places such as hospitals, airports or schools. It helps to check temperatures quickly and safely, reducing the chance of spreading germs or infections.

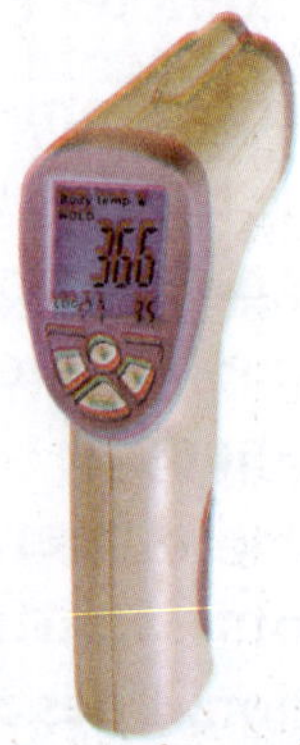

**Fig. 9.5**: Infrared thermometer

An infrared thermometer works by detecting the heat emitted from an object or person's surface. Here's how it works:

- Detection: The thermometer has a lens that collects infrared radiation (heat) emitted by the object or person's body.
- Conversion: This infrared radiation is then converted into an electrical signal.
- Measurement: The signal is processed by the thermometer's electronics to calculate the temperature.
- Display: The result is shown on the thermometer's screen, providing a quick and accurate temperature reading without any contact.

**Science in Context**

Nowadays, a digital thermometer is recommended for routine use over the traditional glass mercury thermometer. This is because mercury is a toxic substance and is very difficult to dispose off, if a thermometer breaks.

## Temperature Scales

Temperature is measured using different temperature scales. Each scale is based on two reference temperatures, usually the freezing and boiling points of water. The temperature range between these two points is divided into a specific number of divisions. Each division is taken as one unit of the scale.

The commonly used scales are the Celsius scale, the Fahrenheit scale and the Kelvin scale.

**Celsius scale**: This scale was developed by Anders Celsius. The unit of this scale is °C (read as degree Celsius). On this scale, the divisions fall between the freezing point of water taken as 0 °C and the boiling point of water taken as 100 °C.
0 °C is also called the lower fixed point, whereas 100 °C is called the upper fixed point. There are 100 divisions between these two points (Fig. 9.6).

**Fahrenheit scale**: This scale was developed by Daniel Gabriel Fahrenheit. The unit of this scale is °F (read as degree Fahrenheit). The Fahrenheit scale sets the freezing point and boiling point of water at 32 °F and 212 °F, respectively. The lower fixed point is 32 °F and the upper fixed point is 212 °F. There are 180 divisions between these two points (Fig. 9.6).

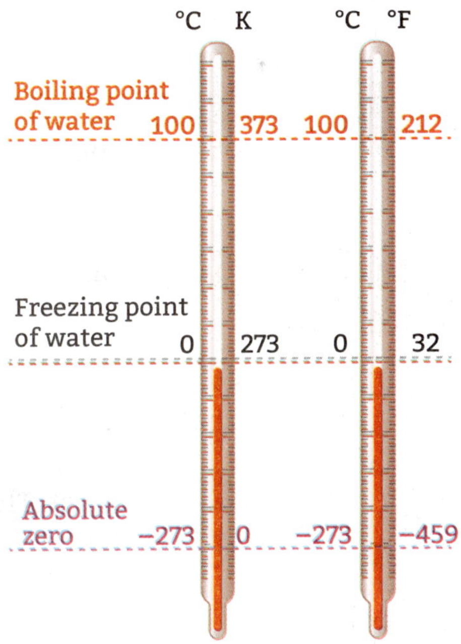


**Fig. 9.6**: Kelvin, Celsius and Fahrenheit scales

**Kelvin scale**: This scale was invented by Lord Kelvin. The unit of this scale is K and is the SI unit for measuring temperature. On this scale, the freezing point of water is 273.16 K (approx.) and the boiling point of water is 373.16 K. For convenience it is approximated and written as 273 K and 373 K. It is called the absolute scale of temperature since its 0 K is the absolute zero, that is, the lowest attainable temperature in the universe.

**Conversion of scales**

The three temperature scales (Celsius, Fahrenheit and Kelvin) can be converted from one to the other, using the following formulae:

$°F = [°C \times \frac{9}{5}] + 32$ is used to convert Celsius to Fahrenheit scale

$°C = [°F - 32] \times \frac{5}{9}$ is used to convert Fahrenheit to Celsius scale

$K = °C + 273$ is used to convert Celsius to Kelvin scale

## Revise and Recall

**Fill in the blanks.**

1. The degree of hotness or coldness of objects is called __________. (heat/temperature)
2. The SI unit of heat is __________. (kelvin/joule)
3. A __________ thermometer uses mercury to measure temperature. (laboratory/clinical)
4. The unit of the Celsius scale is __________. (°C/K)
5. The freezing point of water on the Fahrenheit scale is __________. (32°F/45°F)

## Activity 9.2

**Aim:** To measure and record the body temperature using a digital thermometer

**Materials required:** Digital thermometer, notebook and pen for recording temperatures and sanitizing wipes (to clean the thermometer after each use)

**Procedure:**

1. Ensure the digital thermometer is clean and functioning correctly. Turn it on by pressing the power button. Place the probe under the tongue, or in the armpit, or rectally. Wait until the thermometer beeps or the display shows a stable reading. Look at the digital display to read the temperature.
2. Find at least 10 participants and take the temperature of each participant by placing the probe of thermometer under their tongue (or follow the specific instructions for the thermometer being used).
3. Wait for the thermometer to beep or the display shows a stable reading.

4. Look at the digital display and write down the temperature readings for each person in the notebook.
5. Wipe the thermometer with a sanitizing wipe after each use.

**Observation:** Record the temperature readings of each participant in a table.

**Table: Body Temperature Measurements**

| Participant | Temperature (°C) | Observations |
|---|---|---|
| 1. | | |
| 2. | | |
| 3. | | |
| 4. | | |

Summarize the range of body temperatures observed. Discuss any factors that might affect body temperature and the importance of using a digital thermometer for accurate readings.

## Activity 9.3

**Aim**: To understand the markings on a laboratory thermometer by measuring the temperature of different substances

**Materials required:** Laboratory thermometer, Beaker, Warm water, Ice, burner (under teacher supervision), stopwatch or timer

**Procedure:**

**Part 1: Observing the Range of a Laboratory Thermometer (To be demonstrated by teacher)**

1. Show the laboratory thermometer to the students.
2. Show the lowest temperature reading and highest temperature reading.
3. Subtract the highest temperature reading by lowest temperature reading and explain that the subtracted value is the range of the thermometer.

**Part 2: Finding the Smallest Division of a Laboratory Thermometer (To be demonstrated by teacher)**

1. Choose any two consecutive temperature readings on the laboratory thermometer (e.g., 30 °C and 40 °C) and show it to the students.
2. Find the temperature difference between them by subtracting the highest temperature by the lowest lowest temperature.
3. Show that there are 10 smaller divisions between 30 °C and 40 °C.
4. Explain that by dividing the temperature difference value by number of smaller divisions, we can find the smallest temperature value that one small division represents.

**Part 3: Measuring Temperature Using a Laboratory Thermometer**

1. Take a stand and fix the thermometer to its clamp. Place a beaker filled with some warm water on the base of the stand.
2. Immerse the thermometer in the water by positioning the clamp on the stand, ensuring that the bulb is fully submerged but not touching the sides or bottom of the beaker.
3. Observe the rise of the liquid column in the thermometer.
4. Wait until the column stops rising and then note the temperature reading. Ensure you read the temperature while the thermometer is still immersed in the water, keeping your eyes in line with the liquid column.

**Part 4: Measuring Temperature of Boiling Water (To be demonstrated by teacher)**

1. Take a stand with the thermometer and a beaker fixed to its clamps.
2. Pour some water to the beaker and use a burner to heat water until it boils.
3. Observe the temperature reading on the thermometer and record the temperature.
4. Explain that the temperature remains constant during phase changes.

**Part 5: Measuring Temperature of Ice**

1. Fill a beaker with crushed ice and immerse the thermometer in it.
2. Record the temperature and observe how the temperature remains constant as the ice melts.

**Observation:**

**Table 1: Range and Smallest Division of a Laboratory Thermometer**

| Range of Thermometer | Smallest Division (°C) |
|---|---|
| | |
| | |

**Table 2: Temperature Measurements**

| Substance | Temperature (°C) | Observations |
|---|---|---|
| Warm Water | | |
| Boiling Water | | |
| Crushed Ice | | |

**Conclusion:**

- **Part 1:** The range of the thermometer determines the span of temperatures it can measure.
- **Part 2:** The smallest division helps in understanding the precision of the thermometer.
- **Part 3:** Correct technique is crucial for accurate temperature measurement.
- **Parts 4 and 5:** Temperature remains constant during phase changes (e.g., boiling water or melting ice).

Understanding the range and smallest division of a thermometer is essential for precise measurements. This activity demonstrates the importance of technique in scientific measurements.

## Activity 9.4

**Aim:** To measure and record the air temperature at different times of the day

**Materials required:** Laboratory thermometer, notebook and pen, clock or watch

**Procedure:**

1. Ensure the thermometer is cleaned and working properly.
2. Place the thermometer in the air where you want to measure the temperature. Ensure that thermometer is away from direct sources of heat or cold, such as heaters, air conditioners or sunlight.
3. Allow the thermometer to stabilize in the air. Once the thermometer has stabilized, read the temperature from the scale on the thermometer and record it.
4. At three different times of the day (morning, afternoon, and evening), measure the air temperature in the same location. Record the temperature at each time.

**Observation:** Write down the temperatures recorded at different times.

**Table: Air Temperature Measurements**

| Time of Day | Temperature (°C) | Observations |
|---|---|---|
| Morning | | |
| Afternoon | | |
| Evening | | |

**Inference:** The air temperature is cooler in the morning, warmer in the afternoon, and cooler again in the evening.

**Conclusion:** Air temperatures fluctuate throughout the day.

## Activity 9.5

**Aim:** To measure and record the maximum and minimum air temperatures over a specified period

**Materials required:** Maximum-minimum thermometer, notebook and pen, clock or watch

**Procedure:**

1. A maximum-minimum thermometer typically consists of two separate thermometers in one unit: one for measuring the maximum temperature and one for the minimum temperature.
2. Place the thermometer in a suitable location where it can accurately measure the air temperature. Ensure that it is located in a shaded area away from direct sunlight, heat sources and sources of cold.
3. Leave the thermometer in place for the desired period (usually 24 hours) to allow it to accurately record the maximum and minimum temperatures. The thermometer needs time to adjust to the ambient air conditions.
4. Identify which part of the thermometer is used to measure the maximum temperature. Observe and record the reading on the maximum thermometer.
5. Identify which part of the thermometer is used to measure the minimum temperature. Observe and record the reading on the minimum thermometer.
6. Repeat this for 5 days.

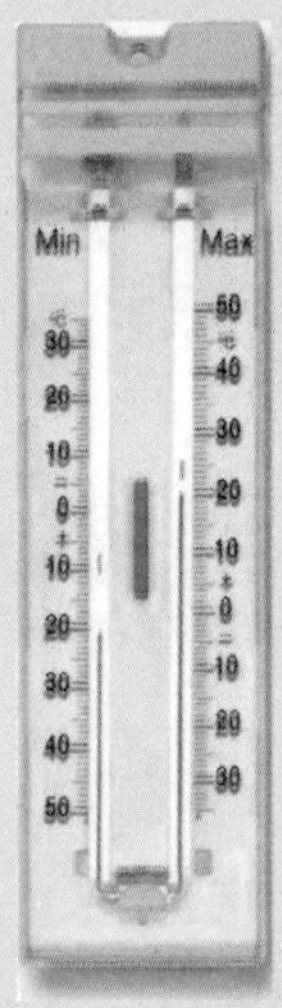


**Observation:** Record the maximum and minimum temperatures daily.

**Table: Maximum and Minimum Air Temperature**

| Date | Maximum Temperature (°C) | Minimum Temperature (°C) | Observations |
|---|---|---|---|
| Day 1 | | | |
| Day 2 | | | |

**Conclusion:** Air temperatures fluctuate daily and monitoring these changes helps in understanding about weather.

## Know the Scientist

**C. N. R. Rao**

**(Born on 30 June 1934)**

Chintamani Nagesa Ramachandra Rao is a renowned Indian chemist known for his research on materials, particularly their behaviour at different temperatures. His work on thermoelectric materials, which convert heat into electricity, has contributed to advancements in energy-efficient technologies. He also served as the chairperson of the Scientific Advisory Council to the Prime Minister of India and worked at prestigious institutions such as the Jawaharlal Nehru Centre for Advanced Scientific Research.

## Keywords

**Heat:** A form of energy that flows from a hot object to cold object

**Temperature:** The degree of hotness or coldness of an object

**Thermometer:** The instrument used to measure temperature

## Summary

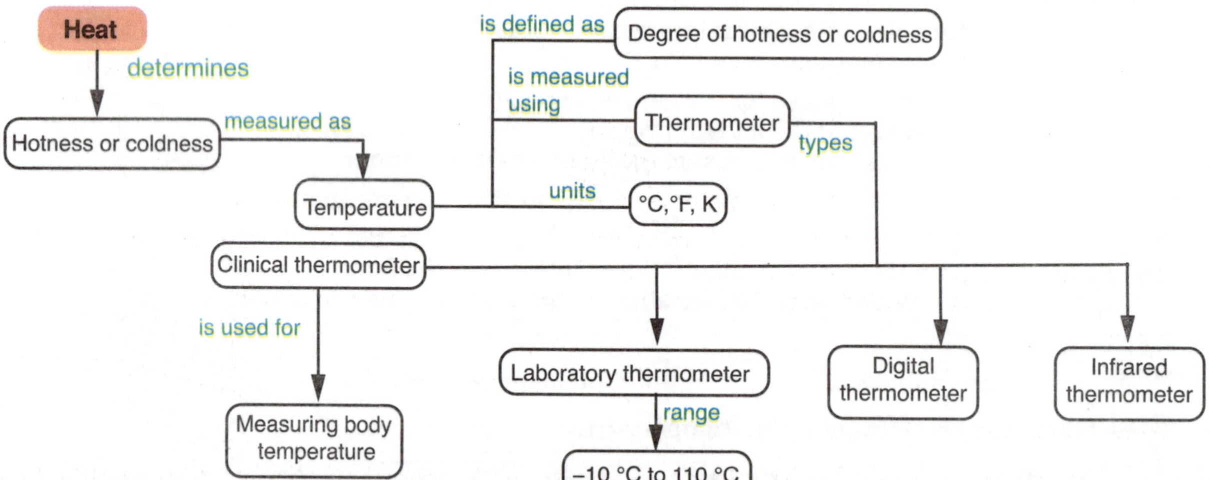

# EXERCISE

W

ia

**A. Choose the correct option.**

1. Which type of thermometer can measure temperature without direct contact?
   (a) Clinical thermometer
   (b) Digital thermometer
   (c) Infrared thermometer
   (d) Laboratory thermometer
2. Which of the following is not a common type of thermometer?
   (a) Clinical thermometer (b) Laboratory thermometer
   (c) Digital thermometer (d) Barometer
3. What is the SI unit of temperature?
   (a) Celsius (°C) (b) Fahrenheit (°F) (c) Kelvin (K) (d) Joule (J)
4. Which scale is used to measure absolute temperature?
   (a) Celsius (b) Fahrenheit (c) Kelvin (d) Rankine
5. What is the temperature at which alcohol can no longer be used in thermometers?
   (a) 0 °C (b) 100 °C (c) 78 °C (d) 110 °C

**B. Fill in the blanks.**

ia

1. The form of energy that flows from a hot object to a cold object is called ____________. (heat/temperature)
2. The ____________ point of water is 100 °C on the Celsius scale. (freezing/boiling)
3. The liquid used in most thermometers due to its wide temperature range is ____________. (mercury/alcohol)
4. The normal approximate temperature of a human body is ____________. (98.7°C or 37 °F/37 °C or 98.7 °F)
5. ____________ thermometers are used to measure temperature without contact. (Digital/Infrared)

**C. State whether the following statements are true (T) or false (F).**

1. The absolute zero is the lowest attainable temperature.
2. Digital thermometers do not contain mercury, making them safer to use than traditional thermometers.
3. The smallest division on a laboratory thermometer is always 1 °C.
4. The boiling point of water is 373.16 K on the Kelvin scale.
5. Mercury thermometers can be used to measure temperatures below –70 °C.

**D. Name each of the following in one word.**

1. Instrument used to measure temperature
2. SI unit of heat
3. SI unit of temperature
4. The primary liquid used in thermometers for measuring low temperatures
5. The minimum temperature that alcohol thermometers can measure

**E. Give reasons for the following.**

1. In a mercury thermometer, the level of mercury rises when its bulb comes in contact with a hot object.
2. We have to shake a clinical thermometer before taking a new reading.
3. Mercury is commonly used in thermometers despite its toxicity.
4. A thermometer is held vertically while measuring the temperature of a liquid.
5. The thermometer bulb should not touch the sides or bottom of the container when measuring temperature.

**F. Answer the following questions briefly.**

1. Write briefly about all the three temperature scales.
2. What is the relation between the Celsius scale and the Kelvin scale?
3. Explain why it is necessary to shake a clinical thermometer before use.
4. Describe how an infrared thermometer works.
5. List two precautions to take when using a laboratory thermometer.
6. What are the advantages of using a digital thermometer over a mercury thermometer?

**G. Answer the following questions in detail.**

1. Explain the parts of a thermometer with the help of a labelled diagram.
2. Compare and contrast the Celsius, Fahrenheit, and Kelvin scales of temperature.
3. Discuss the working of a clinical thermometer and how it differs from a laboratory thermometer.
4. Explain the process of measuring temperature using a laboratory thermometer with warm water.
5. How does the temperature of a substance change during phase transitions, such as boiling or melting, and why?
6. (a) Convert the given temperatures to °C. (i) 150 °F (ii) 48 °F
   (b) Convert the given temperatures to °F. (i) 150 °C (ii) 32 °C
7. Convert 25 °C to Fahrenheit.
8. If the temperature is 212 °F, what is the equivalent temperature in Celsius?
9. A thermometer shows a temperature of 300 K. What is this temperature in Celsius?
10. Convert 300 K to degrees Celsius and Fahrenheit.

# COGNITIVE CORNER

## Critical Thinking

1. Why do you think it is important to use different types of thermometers for different purposes? What could happen if the wrong type of thermometer is used?
2. Imagine you are conducting an experiment where you need to measure the temperature of a substance that changes rapidly. How would you ensure that your thermometer gives you the most accurate reading? What steps would you take to avoid errors in measurement?
3. If you had to design a new type of thermometer that could measure temperature in extreme conditions, such as on another planet or underwater, what features would you include? How would you ensure that it is both accurate and durable?
4. Why should we not use clinical thermometer for measuring the temperature of hot milk?
5. Why do we need three different scales of measurement for the temperature and not just one?

## Picture Study

**Observe the following image carefully.**

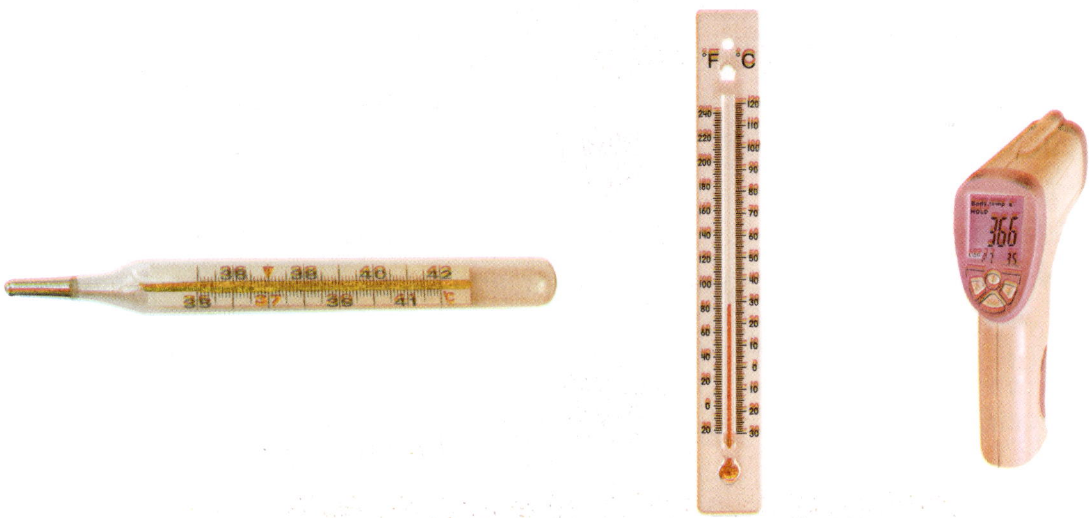

1. Identify each type of thermometer and where it is used.
2. Which thermometer is most suitable for measuring the temperature of a sick person? Explain why.
3. In which situation would you use an infrared thermometer instead of a laboratory thermometer, and why?
4. Describe the importance of handling thermometers correctly based on what you see in the image.

## Project

1. Understand how veterinarians measure the body temperature of different animals. Visit a veterinary hospital or clinic, if possible, to observe how the body temperature of animals such as cats, dogs, horses, camels, cows and buffaloes is measured.
   Interview a veterinarian or research online to learn about the different methods and tools used for measuring animal temperatures. Create a detailed report or a presentation describing the methods used for different animals, comparing them with how human temperatures are measured. Include diagrams or illustrations of the tools and techniques used, and explain why certain methods are preferred for specific animals. **(C-7.1)**
2. Investigate how temperature influences weather forecasts by collecting daily high and low temperatures from a local weather source over one week. Analyze the data for patterns and discuss how temperature changes affect weather conditions and energy use at home. Create a poster or an infographic illustrating how temperature measurement supports weather predictions and energy planning. Finally, share your research with your classmates, emphasizing the significance of accurate temperature measurement. **(C-6.2)**
3. Research key Indian institutions and scientists involved in meteorology and temperature measurement, focusing on inventions such as thermometers and weather stations. Discuss how these advancements have enhanced weather forecasting, climate studies and energy management, especially in agriculture and disaster management. Create a visual presentation, such as a poster or a presentation, to highlight these contributions. Finally, share your findings with your classmates, emphasizing India's significant role in advancing temperature measurement. **(C-8.1)**

## In the Library

Visit the library and use books, encyclopedias or online databases to find information about the coldest and hottest places on Earth. Record the minimum and maximum temperatures of these places and compare them with the extremes recorded in India. Present your findings in a report or as a poster, including maps and graphs to illustrate the temperature extremes. **(C-7.3)**

## Life Skills

1. Imagine you are going to visit one of the hottest or coldest places in India. What precautions would you take to ensure your safety in extreme temperatures? List the clothing, food and other items you would need to stay comfortable and safe. **(C-9.1)**
2. If you had a pet dog or cat, how would you take care of it during very hot or very cold weather? Describe the steps you would take to keep your pet healthy and comfortable, considering factors such as shelter, hydration and exercise. **(C-7.2)**

# Worksheet

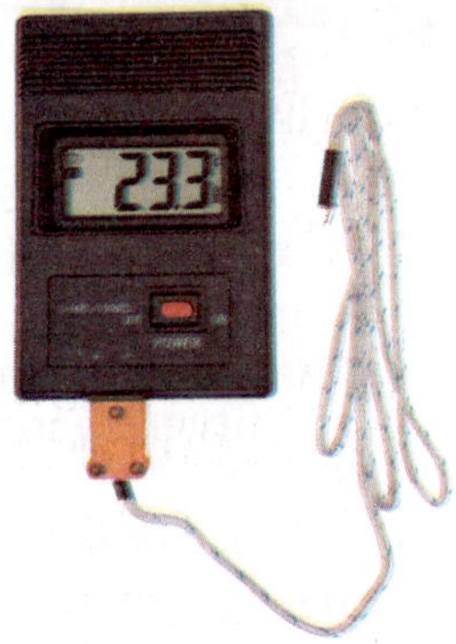

A thermocouple is a temperature-measuring device used in various industrial, scientific and engineering applications. It consists of two different metals joined together at one end to form a junction. When this junction is heated or cooled, it produces a voltage that can be measured and converted into a temperature reading.

A. How does the thermocouple work, and why is it important to use it carefully in different environments?

______________________________

______________________________

______________________________

B. What are its advantages and disadvantages compared with digital and laboratory thermometers?

______________________________

______________________________

______________________________

C. How does measuring temperature help us understand energy use in our homes? Can you think of ways we can save energy by keeping track of the temperature in different rooms?

______________________________

______________________________

______________________________

D. Some renewable energy sources, such as solar panels, work better at certain temperatures. How does temperature affect the efficiency of solar panels? What can we do to make sure we use them effectively?

______________________________

______________________________

______________________________

# 10 Magnets

### Curricular Goals

- Explore the world of matter and its constituents, properties and behaviour **(CG-1)**
- Explore the physical world in scientific and mathematical terms **(CG-2)**
- Explore the nature and processes of science through engaging with the evolution of scientific knowledge and conducting scientific inquiry **(CG-6)**

### Competencies

- Classify matter based on observable physical characteristics (magnetic and non-magnetic) **(C-1.1)**
- Describe the properties of a magnet (natural and artificial, earth as a magnet) **(C-2.3)**
- Formulate questions using scientific terminology (to identify behaviour of objects), and collect data that is usable as evidence (designing simple experiments) **(C-6.2)**

## Let's Get Started

Magnets have been used by humans for a very long time. They are commonly used in household things such as in toys, door bells, TVs, radios, refrigerators, fans, mixers, grinders, etc. Magnets are the objects that have the property of attracting materials that are generally metals such as iron and nickel.

Look at the pictures given below. Put a tick mark (✓) against each object you think will get attracted to a magnet and a cross (✗) against the ones that will not.

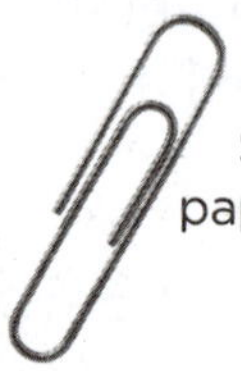

Steel paper clip ☐

Plastic bowl ☐

Iron lock ☐

Rubber tyre ☐

Log of wood ☐

Iron ring ☐

Rupee coin ☐

## DISCOVERY OF MAGNETS

Greeks discovered magnets before 500 BC. A shepherd named Magnes found that his stick with a small iron piece attached to the bottom end got stuck to a black stone (Fig. 10.1). This stone had the property of attracting small pieces of iron. Since the stone was first found in a place called Magnesia, it was named **magnetite**.

Magnetite is a naturally occurring substance mainly made up of **oxides**[1] of iron. It was also observed that when suspended freely, this stone always came to rest in the North–South direction. So, this stone was used to find directions while travelling and was named as **lodestone**, meaning leading stone.

**Fig. 10.1:** Discovery of lodestone

**Science in Context**

Magnets are made using a group of metals such as nickel, cobalt and iron. Substances such as neodymium and samarium are also used for making magnets.

**Word Web**

[1]**Oxides**: Substances formed when a material combines with oxygen

## NATURAL AND ARTIFICIAL MAGNETS

*A magnet obtained naturally from the Earth is called a* ***natural magnet***. For example, magnetite or lodestone.

***Artificial magnets*** *are human-made objects designed to exhibit magnetic properties.* Bar magnet, horseshoe magnet, spherical magnet, cylindrical magnet, ring magnet, disc magnet and magnetic needles are some examples of artificial magnets (Fig. 10.2).

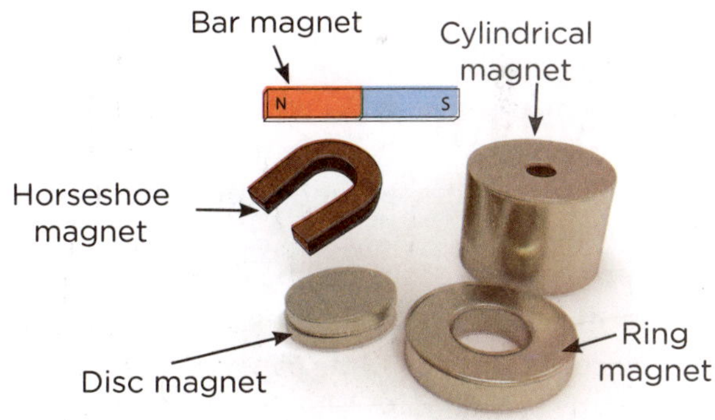


**Fig. 10.2:** Types of artificial magnets

## MAGNETIC AND NON-MAGNETIC MATERIALS

*Materials that are attracted towards a magnet are called* ***magnetic materials***. Materials made up of metals such as iron, cobalt and nickel are examples of magnetic materials. *Materials that are not attracted towards a magnet are called* ***non-magnetic materials***. Wood, plastic and rubber are examples of non-magnetic materials.

## Activity 10.1

**Aim:** To classify materials as magnetic and non-magnetic

**Materials required:** Bar magnet, iron nail, chalk, comb, paper clips, safety pin, eraser, iron key, wooden block, copper wire and aluminium vessel

**Procedure:**

1. Arrange all the items on a table one after the other.
2. Bring a bar magnet near each of these.
3. Observe what happens.
4. Record your observations in the table given below.

**Observation:**

| Materials | Attraction Towards Bar Magnet (Yes/No) | Materials | Attraction Towards Bar Magnet (Yes/No) |
|---|---|---|---|
| Chalk | | Paper clips | |
| Iron nail | | Comb | |
| Safety pin | | Aluminium vessel | |
| Wooden block | | Iron key | |
| Eraser | | Copper wire | |

**Conclusion:** The objects that got attracted towards the bar magnet are magnetic materials, those that did not are non-magnetic materials.

# POLES OF A MAGNET

a

Is the property of attraction in a magnet uniform throughout the magnet? Let us find out.

## Activity 10.2

**Aim:** To demonstrate that the property of attraction is more at the two ends of a magnet

**Materials required:** Iron filings, bar magnet and a sheet of white paper

**Procedure:**

1. Place the sheet of white paper on a flat surface to serve as a base.
2. Gently sprinkle a small amount of iron filings evenly over the paper.
3. Position the bar magnet horizontally on top of the paper. Make sure it is centered so that you can clearly observe the distribution of the filings.
4. Carefully lift the magnet from the paper. Notice the pattern formed by the iron filings.

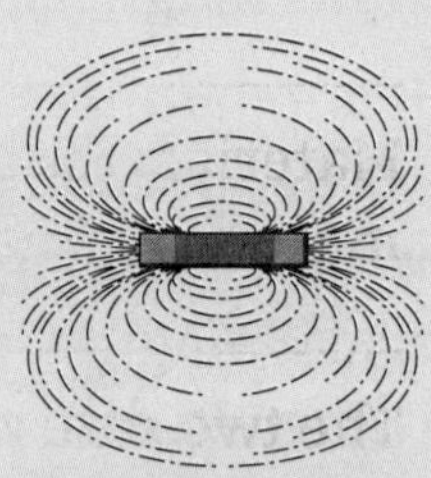

Iron filings aligned around the bar magnet

**Observation:** The iron filings get attracted to the magnet; they are concentrated at the ends.

**Conclusion:** The property of attraction in a magnet is concentrated at the two ends of the magnet.

From Activity 10.2, we see that the magnetic forces are stronger at the two ends of a magnet. The ends of a magnet where the magnetic forces are stronger are called the **poles of the magnet** or **magnetic poles**. Now, let us learn how the poles of a magnet are named.

## Activity 10.3

**Aim:** To demonstrate that a freely suspended magnet comes to rest in a North–South direction

**Materials required:** A bar magnet, a magnetic compass, thread and a stand

**Procedure:**

1. Tie a thread at the centre of a bar magnet.
2. Suspend the magnet from a stand by means of the thread.
3. Observe the direction of the alignment of the magnet. Now place a magnetic compass near that magnet to know which pole is directing towards which direction.
4. Disturb the alignment of the magnet and allow it to rest again.
5. Now, observe the alignment of the magnet.

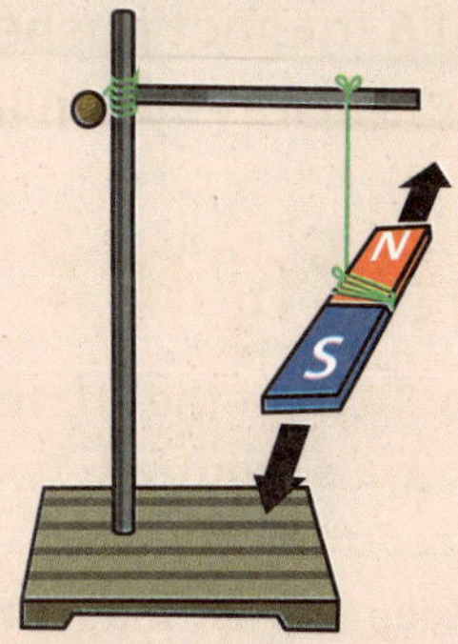

Freely suspended magnet aligned in the North-South direction

**Observation:** The bar magnet always aligns itself in the North–South direction.

**Conclusion:** Magnets possess directional property.

From the above activity, we saw that a freely suspended magnet always aligns in the North– South direction. This property of a magnet is called its *directional property*. The end of the magnet pointing towards North is called the **north pole** of the magnet. The end of the magnet pointing towards South is called the **south pole** of the magnet. All magnets have two poles irrespective of their shape. Usually these are marked as N (for North) and S (for South).

## Revise and Recall

**Fill in the blanks.**

1. ____________________ is a natural magnet. (Lodestone/Iron)
2. Materials that are attracted by a magnet are called ____________________ materials. (magnetic/non-magnetic)
3. ____________________ is an example of magnetic material. (Iron/Plastic)
4. The two ends of a magnet where the magnetic property is more are called ____________________. (points/poles)
5. A freely suspended magnet aligns itself in the ____________________ direction. (North–South/East–West)

# ATTRACTION AND REPULSION BETWEEN MAGNETS

Magnets show attracting or repulsing property among them. The north pole of a magnet and the south pole of another magnet always pull each other when brought close to one another. Unlike poles of magnets always attract each other. This is called the *attracting property* of magnets.

North pole of a magnet pushes away the north pole of another magnet. Similarly, south pole of a magnet pushes away the south pole of another magnet. That is, like poles of magnets always push away each other. This is called the *repulsing property* of magnets.

## Activity 10.4

**Aim:** To show the attracting and repulsing property of magnets

**Materials required:** Two bar magnets

**Procedure:**

1. Keep two bar magnets on a table in a line as shown in (a).
2. Move one magnet close to the other. What do you observe?
3. Now keep the magnets as shown in (b) and (c) and repeat the same. What do you observe in each case?

(a) (b) (c)

**Observation:** When the south pole of a magnet is brought close to the north pole of another magnet, a pull can be experienced as they attract each other. When the south pole of a magnet is brought close to the south pole of another magnet or the north pole of a magnet is brought close to the north pole of another magnet, no pull is experienced as they are not attracted to one another. They repel each other.

**Conclusion:**

1. Like poles of magnets repel each other.
2. Unlike poles of magnets attract each other.

These two statements form the fundamental laws of magnetism, namely: like poles of a magnet repel one another whereas unlike poles of magnets attract each another.

# Magnetic Poles Always Exist in Pairs

We cannot separate one magnetic pole from another pole. They always exist in pairs (Fig. 10.3). If you break a magnet into two pieces, you will get two magnets, each with a north pole and a south pole. That is, magnetic poles can never be isolated.

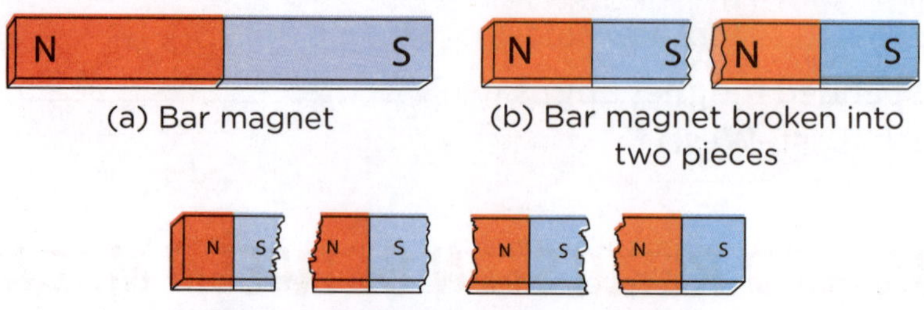


(a) Bar magnet

(b) Bar magnet broken into two pieces

(c) Bar magnet broken into four pieces

**Fig. 10.3:** Magnetic poles exist in pairs

# EARTH AS A MAGNET

We have seen that a freely suspended magnet aligns itself in the North–South direction. What may be the reason for this? This is because the Earth has magnetic properties and, therefore, acts like a huge bar magnet (Fig. 10.4).

The Earth's magnetic north pole is near the geographic South Pole of the Earth and the Earth's magnetic south pole is near the geographic North Pole of the Earth. When a magnet is suspended freely, its north pole is attracted by the magnetic south pole of the Earth and its south pole is attracted by the magnetic north pole of the Earth. Hence, it aligns itself in the geographic North–South direction.

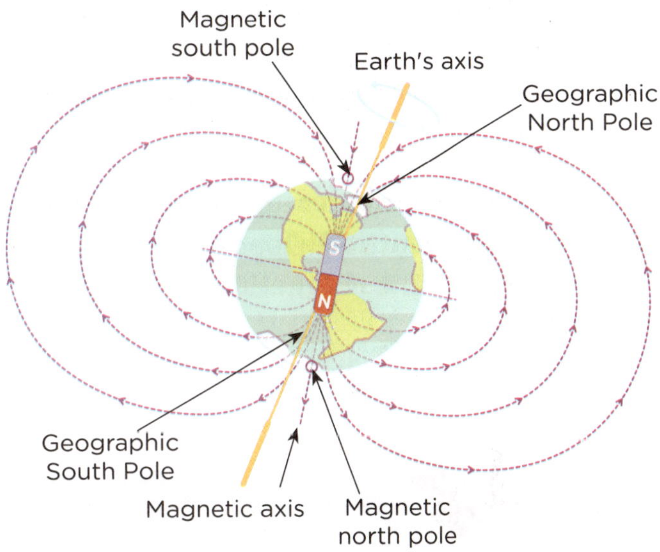


**Fig. 10.4:** Earth as a magnet

# MAGNETIC COMPASS

A compass is a device used to find directions (Fig. 10.5). It consists of a magnetic needle pivoted centrally on a sharp pointed support and free to rotate horizontally. The magnetic needle always points towards the North–South direction. Magnetic compass is mainly used by sailors, sea voyagers and explorers.

**Fig. 10.5:** Magnetic compass

The outer case of a compass is always made up of a non-magnetic material such as aluminium, brass or plastic. If this were to be made up of magnetic material such as iron, the magnetic needle would be attracted by the case and it would not point towards the North–South direction.

## Know the Scientist

**C. V. Raman**
**(1888–1970)**

Sir Chandrasekhara Venkata Raman, an Indian physicist, made significant contributions to the understanding of magnetic properties and the interaction of light with materials. He was awarded the 1930 Nobel Prize in Physics for discovering the "Raman Effect," which led to February 28 being celebrated as National Science Day in India. Raman also founded the Indian Academy of Sciences and the Raman Research Institute, cementing his legacy as one of the 20th century's most important scientists.

## MAKING MAGNETS

We can convert a small piece of iron into a simple magnet using a permanent bar magnet. *The process of making a substance magnetic (temporarily or permanently) is called* ***magnetisation***. There are many methods available for magnetisation. One such method is the touch method or stroke method. There are two different types of touch methods: single-touch method and double-touch method.

**Single-touch method:** A magnet is rubbed along the magnetic substance (iron bar) from one end to another and lifted vertically upwards [Fig. 10.6 (a)].

**Double-touch method:** Opposite poles of two magnets are placed next to each other at the centre of the magnetic substance (iron bar) and rubbed in opposite direction [Fig. 10.6 (b)].

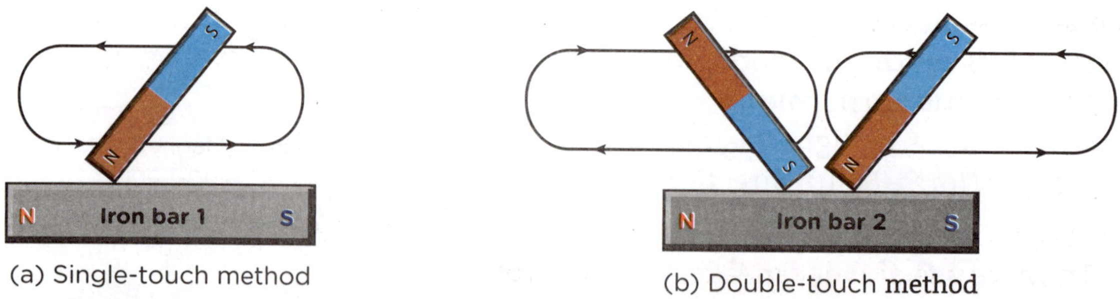


**Fig. 10.6:** Methods to magnetise the iron bar

### Activity 10.5

**Aim:** To magnetize an iron bar using the single-touch method

**Materials required:** A bar magnet and a piece of iron bar

**Procedure:**

1. Place the iron bar on a table.
2. Hold a bar magnet in your hand and put one end of a bar magnet on one end of the iron bar.
3. Rub the magnet along the iron bar from end to end.
4. Lift the magnet and put it back at the beginning.
5. Repeat the process 20–30 times.
6. Now, bring a paper clip close to the iron bar. What do you observe?

**Observation:** The iron bar behaves as a weak magnet after being stroked with the bar magnet.

**Conclusion:** A magnetic material can be magnetised by using a permanent magnet.

### Science in Context

Magnets made by stroke methods are weak in nature. Electrical methods are used to make strong magnets. The material that is to be made a magnet is kept inside a copper coil and electric current is passed through it for a specified amount of time. Then, the material becomes a strong magnet.

## Preserving Magnets

When magnets are kept for a long time leaving the magnetic poles free or exposed, they slowly lose their magnetic properties. Therefore, magnets have to be preserved to prevent the loss of magnetic properties.

Usually, bar magnets are stored as pairs with unlike poles close to each other. Two pieces of iron called keepers are kept at the two ends [Fig. 10.7 (a)]. A horseshoe magnet is preserved by keeping a single keeper on its two poles [Fig. 10.7 (b)].

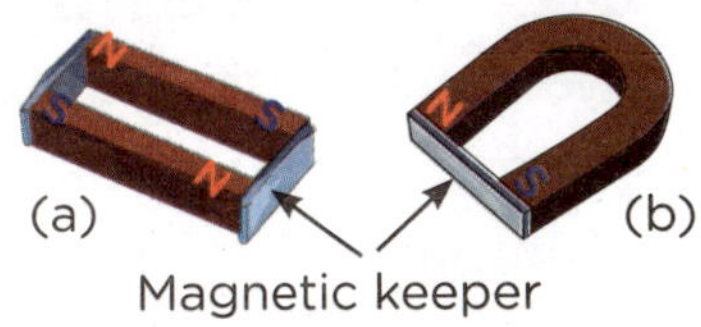


**Fig. 10.7:** Preserving magnets with magnetic keepers

## DEMAGNETISATION

*The process by which magnets lose their magnetic properties is called* ***demagnetisation***. A magnet slowly loses its magnetic properties if subjected to heat or any mechanical shocks such as dropping and hammering. While handling magnets we should not heat or drop them down.

## USES OF MAGNETS

- Magnets are used in electronic devices such as television and radio.
- They are used in loudspeakers and microphones.
- Electric motors and power generators have strong magnets inside them.
- They are used in magnetic storage devices such as hard disk of a computer, tape recorder, etc.
- Magnetic strips are used to store information on credit cards, ATM cards, etc.
- Magnets are used in many medical devices such as MRI scanning machines and CT scanning machines.

### Revise and Recall

**Fill in the blanks.**

1. Like poles of two magnets ________________ each other. (attract/repel)
2. ________________ is a device used to find the direction. (Compass/ATM)
3. The process of making a magnet from a magnetic material is called ________________. (magnetisation/demagnetisation)
4. The process by which a magnet loses its magnetic properties is called ________________. (magnetisation/demagnetisation)
5. Small iron pieces kept at the poles of magnets to preserve them are called ________________. (keepers/takers)

## Keywords

**Lodestone:** A naturally found stone that shows the properties of a magnet
**Magnetic materials:** Materials that are attracted by a magnet
**Non-magnetic materials:** Materials that are not attracted by a magnet
**Magnetic poles:** The two ends of a magnet where magnetic properties are stronger
**Compass:** A device used to find direction
**Magnetisation:** The process of acquiring magnetic properties
**Demagnetisation:** The process by which a magnet loses its magnetic properties

## Summary

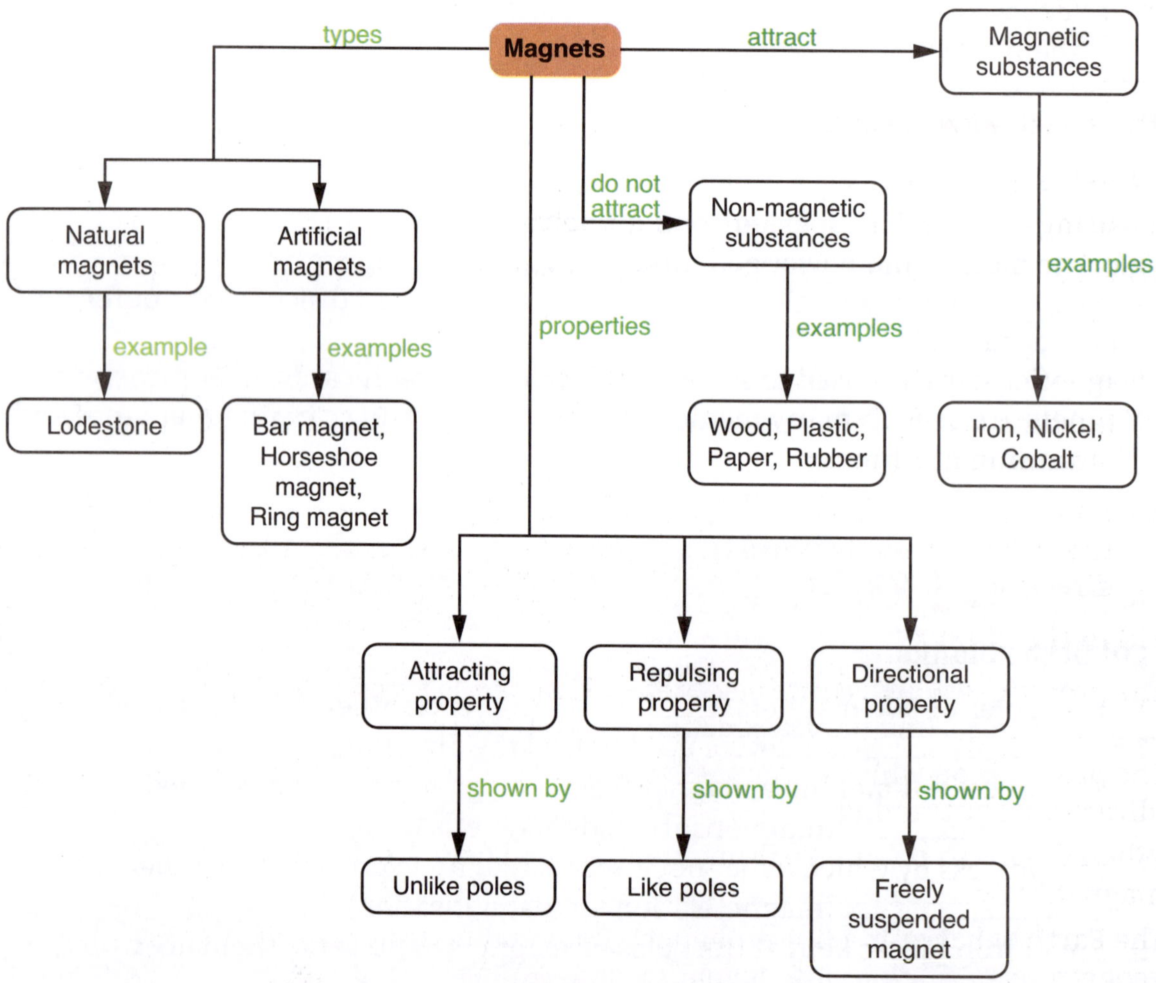

# Exercise

w

ia

**A. Choose the correct option.**

1. Which one of these is a magnetic material?
   (a) Iron (b) Carbon (c) Aluminium (d) Zinc
2. Which one of these is not a magnetic material?
   (a) Iron (b) Nickel (c) Cobalt (d) Zinc
3. What will happen if a bar magnet is broken into two pieces?
   (a) Both pieces will act as two separate magnets.
   (b) Only one piece will act as a magnet.
   (c) Both pieces will not act as magnets.
   (d) One piece will have both ends as North Poles and the other piece will have both ends as South Poles.
4. Copper has to be separated from a mixture of copper turnings and iron filings. An easy method to separate them is by ______________________.
   (a) using a magnet (b) using a solvent that dissolves only iron
   (c) using a filter (d) using a solvent that dissolves only copper
5. Which of the following is the best suitable method to make an iron strip into a magnet?
   (a) Placing the iron strip near a bar magnet for some time
   (b) Keeping the iron strip in contact with a bar magnet for some time
   (c) Rubbing the iron strip using any one pole of a magnet from one end to the other end many times
   (d) Rubbing the iron strip using one of the poles of the magnet from one end to the other end many times and then rubbing it using the other pole in the same direction

**B. Fill in the blanks.**

ia

1. The process by which a magnet loses its magnetic properties is called ______________. (magnetisation/demagnetisation)
2. The principle on which a compass works is ______________ property of magnets. (directional/attracting)
3. When the north pole of a bar magnet is placed near the north pole of another magnet, they ______________ each other. (attract/repel)
4. The Earth behaves as a huge magnet whose magnetic north pole is at the geographic ______________ Pole. (North/South)
5. Magnetite is ______________ magnet. (a natural/an artificial)

**C. State whether the following statements are true (T) or false (F).**

1. Mercury is not a magnetic material.
2. A compass can be used to find East–West direction.
3. The magnetic south pole of Earth is located at the geographic North Pole.
4. An iron bar can be magnetised by rubbing with a horseshoe magnet.
5. Electrical conductors can exhibit magnetic properties.

**D. Give reasons for the following.**

1. A freely suspended bar magnet always aligns itself in the North–South direction.
2. We cannot isolate north pole of a magnet from its south pole or vice versa.
3. When we keep a bar magnet in a heap of iron filings, more iron filings get attracted at the ends of the magnet.
4. In a magnetic compass box, the compass needle is kept in a closed non-magnetic container.
5. After using two bar magnets, these should be kept with keepers at the ends with a wooden piece between them.

**E. Answer the following questions briefly.**

1. What is the directional property of magnets?
2. Where are the poles of the Earth's magnet located?
3. What will happen if you break a bar magnet into two pieces?
4. The outer frame of a magnetic compass is made up of a non-magnetic material. Why?
5. What are the precautions to be taken while handling magnets?

**F. Answer the following questions.**

1. Explain why a freely suspended magnet aligns itself in the North–South direction. Use diagrams to support your answer.
2. Magnets should be preserved with magnetic keepers. Why?
3. Describe one activity to show that magnetic property of a magnet is more at its poles.
4. Explain how you can magnetise an iron needle using the single-touch method.
5. What is demagnetisation? List the methods of demagnetising a magnet.

# Cognitive Corner

## Critical Thinking

1. You are breaking a magnet AB, whose north pole is at A and south pole is at B, into two pieces $A_1B_1$ and $A_2B_2$ along its length. Where will be poles of the two newly formed pieces? Why?
2. You are given two identical metal rods out of which one is a magnet and the other is an iron rod. How will you identify which one is the magnet and which is the iron rod?

## Picture Study

**Identify the polarities of the magnetised iron bars given below.**

1. 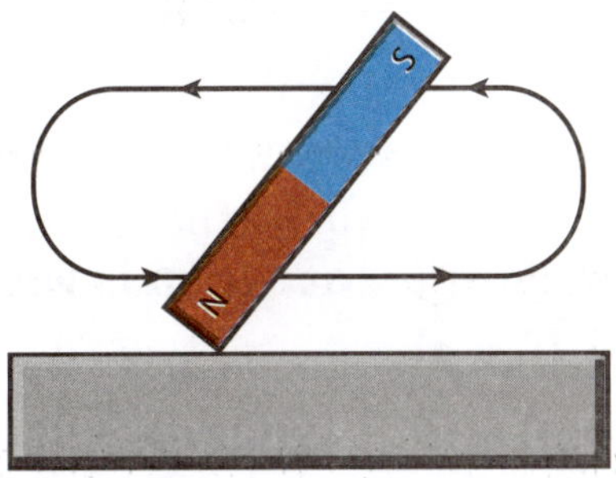


2. 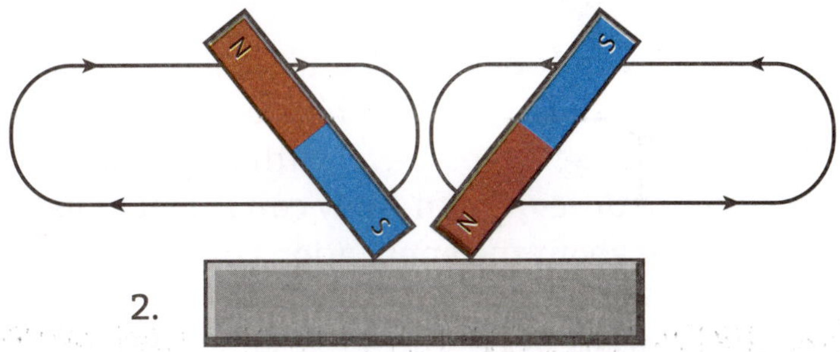


## Project

1. Create a magnetic fishing game where you can use magnets to "fish" for steel objects. You will need small steel objects (e.g., paper clips, small nuts and bolts), a large shallow container filled with water, a strong magnet, a fishing rod made from a stick or pencil with a string attached, a small magnet tied to the end of the string, coloured markers or paint, construction paper, scissors and glue.

   Steps:

   a. Prepare the Fishing Area: Fill the shallow container with water. Place small steel objects (such as paper clips or nuts) in the water, representing "fish."

   b. Create the Fishing Rod: Attach a string to the end of the stick or pencil to create a fishing rod. Tie a small magnet to the other end of the string.

   c. Decorate the Fish: Cut out fish shapes from construction paper. Use coloured markers or paint to decorate the fish shapes. Glue the decorated fish onto the steel objects.

   d. Play the Fishing Game: Takes turn using the fishing rod to catch the "fish" in the container.

The magnet on the rod will attract the steel objects, allowing you to "fish" them out of the water.

Challenge:

Time yourselves to see who can catch the most fish in a set amount of time.

Add obstacles or create a maze in the water using non-magnetic materials, making the fishing more challenging. **(C-7.2)**

2. Magnets are used in magnetic data storage devices. As a part of Science Club activity, form groups and collect information about magnetic storage devices and their applications. Find different magnetic storage devices we use in our day-to-day lives. **(C-5.1)**

## In the Library

Magnetic levitation or magnetic suspension is the method by which an object is lifted or suspended with the help of magnetic fields. Maglev trains work on magnetic levitation. These trains travel without touching the track. It floats above the track with magnetic levitation. They can travel at very high speeds of more than 500 km/h. Learn more about the applications of magnetic levitation. **(C-5.1)**

## In the Laboratory

1. Using a small bar magnet, a bowl of water and a piece of cork or styrofoam, create your own magnetic compass. How does the magnet behave when placed in water? Describe how this experiment shows the alignment of the magnet with the Earth's magnetic field. **(C-7.2)**
2. Take different sized magnets and try to pick up paper clips or small metal objects. Observe how many objects each magnet can lift. Based on your observations, explain how the size of a magnet relates to its magnetic strength. What does this tell you about how magnets work in real-world applications? **(C-9.1)**

## Life Skills

1. Dismantle any discarded electronic toys and speakers. In the dismantled objects, you may find magnets of different shapes and pieces of iron. How will you distinguish between the two? **(C-7.2)**
2. Some people believe that magnets can have an effect on the human body, such as improving health or healing. However, there is still no strong scientific evidence to support these claims. Research what scientists currently know about how magnets interact with the human body. Why is this an area where our scientific understanding is still limited? Can you propose any experiments to explore this further? **(C-9.2)**

9 INDUSTRY, INNOVATION AND INFRASTRUCTURE

# Worksheet

In ancient times, Indians were familiar with magnets and their properties, referring to them by different names such as *chumbakah, lohakantah* and *ayomanih*. They recognized that magnets not only attracted iron but also had other practical applications. Megasthenes, a Greek historian who visited India during the 4th century BCE, documented the use of magnets in Indian society. Moreover, the ancient Ayurvedic text, *Charaka Samhita*, referenced the use of magnets for healing purposes and promoting overall well-being.

A. Learn more about ancient Indian knowledge on the properties of magnets and their use in the treatment of some diseases. Write down your findings in the space below.

________________________________________________

________________________________________________

________________________________________________

B. How did the ancient Indians demonstrate an advanced understanding of magnets and their versatile applications?

________________________________________________

________________________________________________

________________________________________________

C. In what ways does the knowledge of ancient Indian civilizations, as exemplified by their understanding of magnets and their uses, challenge our perceptions about the advancements and capabilities of ancient societies compared to the present?

________________________________________________

________________________________________________

________________________________________________

D. How can we integrate and learn from the ancient Indian knowledge system to inform modern scientific research and innovations, recognizing the potential contributions of traditional practices in contemporary society?

________________________________________________

________________________________________________

________________________________________________

# 11 Water and Its States

## Curricular Goals

- Explore the world of matter, and its constituents, properties and behaviour **[CG-1]**
- Understand the interface of science, technology and society **[CG-5]**
- Communicate own questions, observations and conclusions related to science **[CG-7]**

## Competencies

- Describe changes in matter and use particulate nature to represent the properties of matter and the changes **(C-1.2)**
- Illustrate how science and technology can help to improve the quality of human life such as judicious consumption of resources **(C-5.1)**
- Design and build simple models to demonstrate scientific concepts **(C-7.2)**
- Represent real world events and relationships through diagrams **(C-7.3)**

## Let's Get Started

Water is one of the basic requirements for all living beings. Look at the pictures for clues and fill in the blanks.

①

②

③

④

1. A boat needs water to ________________________________.
2. A fire engine needs water to ________________________________.
3. A fish needs water to ________________________________.
4. Human beings need water to ________________________________.

The majority of Earth's water (97%) is found in seas and oceans, but it is unsuitable for drinking due to its high salt content. Only about 0.01% of total freshwater is available for consumption, making water a precious resource.

The freshwater we obtain from sources such as streams, lakes, rivers and groundwater is essential for various daily activities, including cooking, drinking and washing.

## USES OF WATER

We have been reading from the primary classes that water is essential for life. Given below are some uses of water.

**Bodily Functions:** Plants, animals and human beings need water for their survival. Plants need water to prepare food and for germination of seeds. Animals and humans need water for all their bodily functions (digestion, respiration, circulation, etc.)

**Agricultural Purposes:** Water is used for agriculture (growing crops such as rice, wheat, sugarcane and vegetables on a large scale). Rainwater alone is not sufficient for this purpose; thus, water from rivers, borewells and streams is also used for agricultural purposes. This practice is called **irrigation** (Fig. 11.1).

**Fig. 11.1:** Water for irrigation

**Domestic Purposes:** We use water for drinking, cooking, washing utensils, clothes, vehicles, watering plants, etc.

**Industrial Use:** Water serves as a raw material, ingredient and solvent in preparing various products in several industries. Cooling, heating, steaming and cleaning are other industrial activities for which water is extensively used.

**Generating Electricity:** In many parts of the world, water from rivers is used to produce electricity, which is known as **hydroelectric power**. The water from rivers is stored by constructing dams and reservoirs. This stored water is then used to generate electricity.

**Transportation:** Huge cargo ships (Fig. 11.2) transport goods such as oil, petroleum products and other essential supplies. Ocean liners and cruise liners are the ships that carry people on vacation all around the world through rivers, seas and oceans.

**Fig. 11.2:** Cargo ship in the sea

**Recreation:** Water is used in swimming pools, water parks and water games for recreation. Boating is a leisure activity that is done for relaxation. Yachting or fishing is a hobby for many people.

**As a Habitat:** You learned about the aquatic habitats in Chapter 3. Rivers, lakes and ponds are freshwater habitats for many kinds of fish, crocodiles, ducks, pelicans, lotus, etc. The huge and deep oceans are the marine habitats. They are home to fish, seagulls, turtles, crabs, seaweeds, etc.

## Activity 11.1

**Aim:** To observe how excess, deficient and sufficient water affects plant growth

**Materials required:** Three identical pots with drainage holes, potting soil, three identical young bean plants of same height and age, watering can and measuring cups

**Procedure:** Set up the experiment with the following conditions.

1. Fill each pot with an equal amount of the potting soil. (*Use the same soil type to fill all the three pots.*)
2. Plant one bean plant in each pot, ensuring they are at the same depth.
3. Label the pots as "Excess Water", "Deficient Water" and "Sufficient Water".
4. For the pot labelled "Excess Water", water the plant generously each day until the soil becomes waterlogged.
5. For the pot labelled "Deficient Water", water the plant very sparingly, just enough to slightly moisten the soil. Use about half a mug of water on alternate days.
6. For the pot labelled "Sufficient Water", water the plant with a consistent amount, using approximately one mug of water daily to keep the soil evenly moist.

**Observation:**

**Daily:** Check and note changes in the appearance of each plant, such as leaf colour and wilting.

**Weekly:** Measure and record the height of each plant using a ruler.

| Day | Condition | | | Appearance | Growth (Height in cm) |
|---|---|---|---|---|---|
| | Excess Water | Deficient Water | Sufficient Water | | |
| 1 | | | | | |
| 7 | | | | | |
| 14 | | | | | |

**Inference:**

**Excess Water:** Leaves turned yellow and the plant exhibited stunted growth.

**Deficient Water:** Plants appeared wilted and had dry leaves.

**Sufficient Water:** Plants were healthy with vibrant leaves and steady growth.

**Conclusion:**

Both excessive and insufficient watering negatively impact plant health. Adequate watering supports optimal growth and vitality.

**Discussion:**

1. What differences did you observe in the plants receiving excess water compared to the other two plants?
2. How did the appearance of the excessively-watered plant differ in terms of leaf colour and overall health?
3. What impact did deficient watering have on the plant's growth and leaf texture?
4. How did the plant with sufficient water differ in terms of height and leaf colour compared to the other two plants?

## WATER FROM SOURCE TO HOME

The water in our homes comes from a variety of sources depending on where we live. The water found below the ground is called **groundwater**.

The water found on the surface of the Earth is called **surface water**.

Some of us get water from deep in the earth in the form of groundwater, while others get water that originates as surface water in the form of streams and rivers.

The surface water is not fit for drinking, so it is first purified. Water treatment involves chemical and physical processes that filter out impurities and disinfect harmful microorganisms, thereby making the water suitable for drinking.

Once the water is treated, it is delivered to our homes from the public municipal water treatment system or a private well through a network of pipes.

## STATES OF WATER

a

The three states (or forms) of matter are solid, liquid and gas. In nature, water exists in all the three states (Fig. 11.3). The state of water depends on the temperature of the environment. If the water is kept in very cold conditions such as in a refrigerator, it turns into ice, which is its solid state. If water is heated in a vessel, it boils and becomes steam, which is the gaseous state of water.

**Fig. 11.3:** Forms of water

Liquid state of water, seen in rivers, lakes, seas and oceans, is the most prominent form of water on Earth. The ice in the polar regions, glaciers, hail, frost, etc., are the solid states of water in nature. Water vapour, steam and fog are the gaseous states of water in nature.

### Activity 11.2

**Aim:** To observe and compare the three states of water

**Materials required:** Three transparent containers, ice cubes of the same size (enough to fill one container), tap water (to fill another container), electric kettle, stove, spoon or stirrer and towels or paper towels (for cleanup)

**Procedure:**

1. Label the three beakers: one for ice, one for water and one for steam.
2. Place ice cubes into the first container.
   - What shape are the ice cubes? How does the ice feel when you touch it? (Touch carefully.)
   - What word would you use to describe the state (form) of ice?
3. Fill the second container with tap water.
   - How does it behave when you move the container? (Gently swirl or tilt the container.)
   - What word would you use to describe the state of water in the second container?

4. Observe your teacher heat water in an electric kettle or on a stove until it begins to produce steam.
    - What happens when steam enters the container? Can you see the steam? What do you notice on the container's surface?
5. Use the table given below to record your observations for each state of water.

| State of Water | Appearance | Shape | Ability to Spread |
|---|---|---|---|
| Ice | | | |
| Water | | | |
| Gas | | | |

**Conclusion:**

This activity effectively demonstrated and compared the three states of water: solid (ice), liquid (water) and gas (steam). Ice was observed to be rigid and maintained a fixed shape, while water flowed freely and adapted to the shape of its container. In contrast, steam expanded to fill its surroundings without a defined shape. These observations highlight the unique properties of each state and illustrate how temperature influences the behavior and transitions of water in its various forms.

## Changes in the Forms of Water

When you pour water in an ice tray and keep it inside a fridge, the water turns into ice cubes. The conversion of a liquid into solid is called **freezing**.

Take some ice cubes and put them in a steel container. You will see that the ice cubes begin to melt after some time. This happens because the steel container is warmer than the fridge. If you heat the ice cubes, they will melt faster into water. The conversion of a solid into liquid is called **melting**.

If you continue to heat the water formed out of the ice cubes for a longer duration, the water will start to become water vapour, which is the gaseous form of water. The conversion of a liquid into gas is called **evaporation**. When wet clothes are spread out on a clothesline, the water gets evaporated, leaving the clothes dry (Fig. 11.4).

**Fig. 11.4:** Clothes drying due to evaporation

When you put ice cubes in a glass of fruit juice or cola drink and leave it in the glass, you will notice drops of water forming on the outer surface of the glass (Fig. 11.5). These tiny drops of water are known as water droplets. Water droplets are formed when the vapour present in the air around comes in contact with the cool surface of the tumbler. The conversion of a gas into liquid is called **condensation**.

**Fig. 11.5:** Condensation of water vapour on the surface of the glass

## Activity 11.3

**Aim:** To investigate how different conditions affect the rate at which water evaporates

**Material required:** Three identical bowls, a 5 mℓ dropper or a teaspoon, water, a fan, a stopwatch or timer, a sunny spot, a shady spot and an indoor area with no direct sunlight

**Procedure:**

**1. Setting Up the Experiment:**
- Pour 5 mℓ (or one teaspoon) water into the three bowls.
- Place one bowl in direct sunlight (outdoor sunny spot).
- Place the second bowl in the shade (outdoor shaded spot).
- Place the third bowl indoors, with a fan blowing air directly over it.

**2. Recording Observations:**
- Start the timer as soon as the bowls are placed in their respective locations.
- Observe the bowls every 15 minutes and note the time taken for the water to completely evaporate in each case.
- Record your observations in the table given below.

| Condition | Time | | | Observation |
|---|---|---|---|---|
| | 15 minutes | 30 minutes | 45 minutes | |
| Bowl in sunny spot | | | | |
| Bowl in shaded spot | | | | |
| Bowl with blowing air | | | | |

**What conditions should be kept the same?**
- Type and size of the bowls used
- Amount of water taken in each bowl
- Start time for the experiment

**3. Inference:**

a. Based on your observations, which location caused the water to evaporate the fastest? Why do you think that is?

b. How did the airflow from the fan affect the rate of evaporation compared to the water in the shaded area?

**Inference:**

**Sunny Spot:** The bowl in the sunny spot exhibited the shortest time for complete evaporation.

**Shaded Spot:** The bowl in the shaded spot had the longest evaporation time.

**Blowing Air:** The bowl with the fan blowing air evaporated faster than the shaded bowl, though the rate may vary based on the speed of the airflow.

**Conclusion:**

The experiment shows that water evaporates fastest in direct sunlight, followed by airflow from a fan. Evaporation is the slowest in shaded areas. Heat and airflow speed up evaporation, while reduced heat and light slow it down.

**Discussion**

a. What might happen if you increased the amount of water in each bowl? How do you think this would affect the evaporation times?

b. How would you expect the results to differ if you used larger bowls? Why?

## Humidity and Cooling Effect

Evaporation plays a significant role in our daily lives, influencing how quickly things dry and how temperatures feel around us. One critical factor that affects evaporation is humidity. It refers to the amount of water vapour present in the air. On a rainy day, when the air is already saturated with moisture (high humidity), evaporation slows down, causing clothes to dry more slowly. To speed up drying in such conditions, you can increase air movement by using a fan or place the clothes in a well-ventilated area.

The cooling effect is another fascinating consequence of evaporation. For example, water stored in an earthen pot stays cooler than in a stainless steel pot. This happens because water seeps through the porous surface of the earthen pot and evaporates. As the water evaporates, it absorbs heat from the surroundings, cooling the water inside the pot. This principle is also at play when you rub sanitizer on your hands—it feels cool because the alcohol evaporates quickly, drawing heat from your skin.

### Revise and Recall

**Fill in the blanks.**

1. The water in the sea has a high content of ________________. (salt/sugar)
2. ________________ is a freshwater source. (Ocean/River)
3. Water turns into ice on ________________. (heating/cooling)
4. When water is ________________ it changes into water vapour. (heated/cooled)
5. Washed clothes dry in the sun due to ________________. (evaporation/condensation)

## WATER CYCLE

a

The continuous circulation of water from the Earth's surface to the atmosphere and back to the Earth is known as the **water cycle** (Fig. 11.6). This happens repeatedly and in a particular order to form a cycle. In this process, water turns into all the three states of matter in different steps.

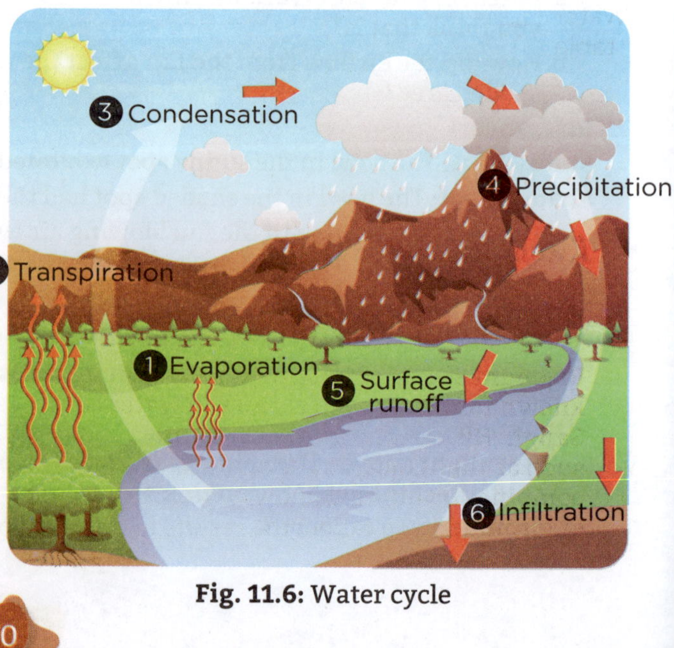


**Fig. 11.6:** Water cycle

1. Water from oceans, lakes, rivers, etc., **evaporates** to form water vapour.

2. Plants give out water vapour through their leaves by the process called **transpiration**.
3. Water vapour rises up in the atmosphere and **condenses** to form clouds.
4. Water in the clouds fall back on the Earth as rain, snow, hail or sleet. This is called **precipitation**.
5. **Surface runoff** refers to the flow of water, often from precipitation or melting snow, that travels over the ground and eventually returns to rivers, lakes or oceans. It occurs when the ground cannot absorb all the water, leading it to flow across the surface.

Some rainwater is absorbed by the soil and moves deeper into the soil to form **groundwater** (Fig. 11.7). The absorption or movement of water through the space between soil particles is known as **infiltration**. The level under the ground where all the spaces between soil particles are saturated with water is called the **water table**.

The groundwater may come out through natural openings or **crevices**[1] of the rocks to form natural springs. Natural springs are the sources of water found in many lakes.

**Word Web**

[1]**Crevices:** cracks in rocks

**Fig. 11.7:** Groundwater

**Science in Context**

During precipitation, water droplets can carry dust and harmful gases from polluted air, such as oxides of sulphur and nitrogen. These gases combine with raindrops to form acids, resulting in acid rain. Acid rain negatively impacts soil, plants and damages old monuments.

**Know the Scientist**

**Rajendra Singh**
**(Born on 6 August 1959)**

Rajendra Singh, a prominent river rejuvenator and environmentalist from Rajasthan, is known for his impactful work in water conservation through his organization, Tarun Bharat Sangh. His efforts have successfully revived five rivers in Rajasthan and earned him accolades such as the Magsaysay Award and the Stockholm Water Prize. Singh's innovative approach combines traditional knowledge with modern techniques to address water scarcity and environmental challenges.

## Revise and Recall

**Fill in the blanks.**

1. Water from the water bodies enters the atmosphere by the process of ___________. (condensation/evaporation)
2. Condensation of rising water vapour in the sky forms ___________. (clouds/snow)
3. The continuous circulation of water from water bodies to the atmosphere and back is called ___________. (water cycle/precipitation)
4. Some rainwater is absorbed by the soil and moves deeper into the soil to form ___________. (groundwater/precipitation)
5. The absorption or movement of water through the space between soil particles is known as ___________. (infiltration/condensation)

## Keywords

**Water cycle:** The continuous circulation of water between the Earth's surface and the atmosphere

**Surface water:** The amount of water found on the Earth's surface

**Transpiration:** The loss of water in the form of water vapour from plant leaves

**Groundwater:** Water that is found below the ground

**Humidity:** The amount of water vapour present in the air

**Water table:** The level under the ground where all the spaces between soil particles are saturated with water

## Summary

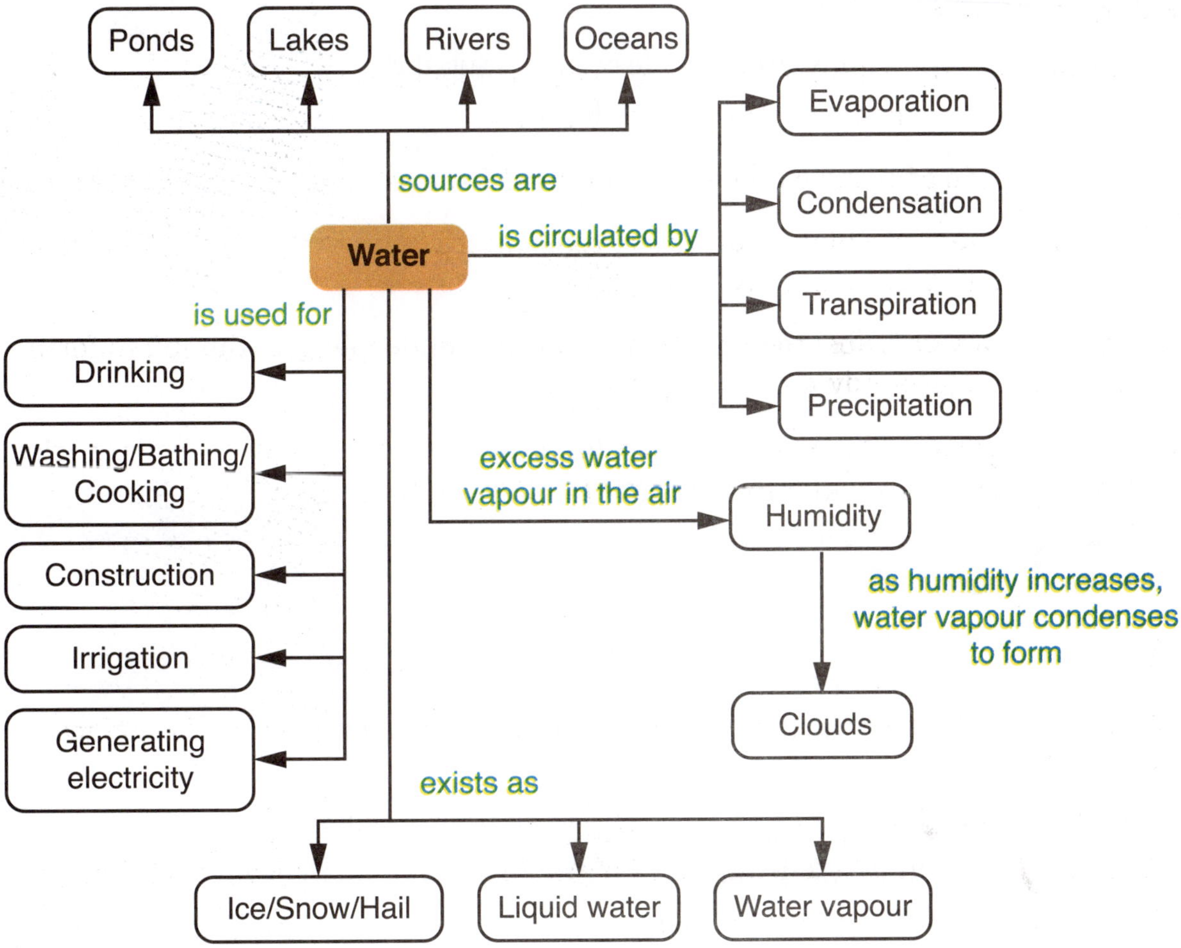
Ponds
Lakes
Rivers
Oceans
sources are
Water
is circulated by
Evaporation
Condensation
Transpiration
Precipitation
is used for
Drinking
Washing/Bathing/Cooking
Construction
Irrigation
Generating electricity
excess water vapour in the air
Humidity
as humidity increases, water vapour condenses to form
Clouds
exists as
Ice/Snow/Hail
Liquid water
Water vapour

# Exercise

w

ia

**A. Choose the correct option.**

1. Which of the following is an example of groundwater?
   (a) Pond (b) Lake
   (c) Natural springs (d) Ocean
2. Which of the following is not a freshwater source?
   (a) River (b) Rainwater
   (c) Ocean (d) Pond
3. Which of the following water sources does not support transportation?
   (a) River (b) Spring
   (c) Ocean (d) Sea
4. During evaporation, water changes its state from ____________.
   (a) solid to liquid
   (b) liquid to solid
   (c) gas to liquid
   (d) liquid to gas
5. Why does water in an earthen pot feel cooler than in a steel pot?
   (a) The pot cools the water.
   (b) Heat is absorbed by the pot.
   (c) Evaporation cools the water.
   (d) The pot blocks sunlight.
6. Which of the following depends on evaporation to write on paper?
   (a) Pencil (b) Ink pen
   (c) Ballpoint pen (d) Crayons

**B. Fill in the blanks.**

ia

1. The water present on the surface of the Earth is called ____________ water. (surface/ground)
2. Loss of water from the plants as vapour is called ____________. (transpiration/precipitation)
3. The content of water in the air is called ____________. (natural spring/water vapour)
4. Snowing is a form of ____________. (precipitation/condensation)
5. Water evaporates more slowly on a rainy day because the air is already high in ____________. (humidity/temperature)

**C. State whether the following statements are true (T) or false (F).**

1. Pond is a groundwater source.
2. Humidity refers to the amount of water vapour present in the air.
3. Surface runoff only occurs in dry regions where there is no rainfall.
4. The conversion of a liquid into gas is called evaporation.
5. Water evaporates faster in a humid environment compared to a dry environment.

**D. Define each of the following.**

1. Groundwater
2. Precipitation
3. Infiltration
4. Water cycle
5. Water table

**E. Give reasons for the following.**

1. Washed clothes are usually hung under sunlight.
2. A puddle of water is formed under a cold soda can kept on a table.
3. Steam cannot be seen during the process of evaporation from the lakes and ponds.
4. Clothes dry slower on a rainy day.
5. Metal playground equipment is is common in parks. Why does the area around metal equipment feel hotter than the area around wooden playground equipment on a sunny day?

**F. Answer the following questions briefly.**

1. How are clouds formed?
2. How does the exposure area of water affect its evaporation rate?
3. What happens to water when it undergoes condensation?
4. How does humidity affect the rate of evaporation?
5. What role does water play in hydroelectric power generation?
6. Air conditioners cool the air by removing heat from a room, which seems to contradict their use in drying clothes. How does using an air conditioner help in drying wet clothes if it typically makes the environment cooler, and evaporation requires heat?

**G. Answer the following questions.**

1. Write any five uses of water.
2. Explain the water cycle, describing each stage of the process.
3. Discuss how water is used for agricultural purposes and explain why rainwater alone is not always sufficient.
4. Describe the cooling effect of water and give examples where this principle is applied.
5. Discuss the properties exhibited by water in its three states with appropriate examples.
6. Describe the process of water treatment and why it is necessary before water reaches homes.

# Cognitive Corner

## Critical Thinking

1. How might the different states of water (solid, liquid, gas) affect the design and efficiency of a cooling system for a large building?
2. The sea gets water from the rain and rivers. Although rain and river water are the sources of freshwater, seawater is salty. Why?
3. A metal chair left outside in the sun feels very hot to sit on. What can you do to make it cooler before sitting?

## Picture Study

Look at the picture of a river flowing into a reservoir and a water treatment plant in operation.

Based on the picture, answer the following questions.

1. Identify and label the sources of water shown in the picture.
2. Explain why the water from the river needs to be treated before it reaches our homes. Use observations from the picture to support your answer.

## Project

1. As a part of Science Club activity, make models of the water cycle and groundwater (showing water table). Draw these on a chart or use cardboard and thermocol to design the model. **(C-7.2)**
2. Explore how different states of water (solid, liquid and gas) influence various life forms and environments. Investigate and analyse the effects of these states on polar regions, plant and animal life and weather patterns. Design experiments or research studies to observe how ice impacts environments, the role of liquid water in sustaining life and how water vapour affects climate and humidity. Summarize your findings and discuss the implications for health, agriculture and ecosystems. This project will help you understand the vital role of water in sustaining life and the importance of its management. **(C-6.2)**

## In the Library

Plants need soil, water and sunlight for their germination and growth. There is a new technique that does not require soil for growth of plants; it is called hydroponics. Read more about hydroponics and how it provides nutrition to plants. Share this knowledge with your family and neighbourhood. **(C-5.1)**

## Life Skills

1. Imagine you have a small load of clothes to wash, and you are considering using the washing machine. What steps can you take to make a responsible and ecofriendly decision, considering judicious use of water and electricity? How can you incorporate the habit of waiting for a full load before using the washing machine into your daily life to promote sustainability? **(C-5.1)**
2. How can you ensure your safety while visiting water spots such as rivers and lakes, especially when the rocks may be slippery due to slush, mud and lichens? Describe the responsible actions you should take to protect yourself and avoid potential hazards in such situations. How can you effectively communicate with your parents or elders to inform them about your plans and ensure your safety during the visit? **(C-1.4)**

# Worksheet

India relies heavily on its rivers as a source of drinking water, but pollution has become a major concern. This pollution not only affects human health but also poses a significant threat to aquatic life. The contamination often results from toxic discharges from factories and untreated sewage, emphasizing the relevance of SDG 6 (Clean Water and Sanitation) in addressing water pollution. Traditional Indian knowledge systems, such as rainwater harvesting, can play a role in promoting sustainable practices and raising awareness about water conservation and pollution prevention.

A. How can you implement practical water conservation strategies at home?

____________________________________________________________

____________________________________________________________

B. Reflect on the impact of your daily choices on the environment and aquatic life. List any three mindful habits to reduce plastic waste and use ecofriendly products.

____________________________________________________________

____________________________________________________________

C. Analyse the causes of water pollution in your local community and brainstorm innovative solutions to raise awareness and prevent further contamination. List any two solutions.

____________________________________________________________

____________________________________________________________

D. How can you develop empathy for the well-being of aquatic life and become an advocate for cleaning rivers? Mention any two ways.

____________________________________________________________

____________________________________________________________

# 12 Natural Resources

## Curricular Goals

- Explore the living world in scientific terms **(CG-3)**
- Understand the interface of science, technology and society **(CG-5)**

## Competencies

- Explain the conditions suitable for sustaining life on earth **(C-3.4)**
- Illustrate how science and technology can help to improve the quality of human life such as judicious consumption of resources **(C-5.1)**

## Let's Get Started

Identify any three natural resources shown in the picture.

1. ______________________________

2. ______________________________

3. ______________________________

## NATURAL RESOURCES

**Natural resources** are materials and substances that occur naturally within the environment and are essential for life on Earth. These include renewable resources and non-renewable resources.

Resources, such as air, water and forests, which can be replenished naturally over time are called ***renewable resources***. Resources, such as fossil fuels, which are finite and take millions of years to form, are called ***non-renewable*** resources.

In our daily lives, we rely on these natural resources. For example, we need air to breathe, use water to wash clothes, soil to grow plants and wood to make furniture. These resources are vital for our everyday activities. It is important to use them wisely to avoid wastage and preserve them for the future.

## AIR IS EVERYWHERE AROUND US

Air is present all around us. We cannot see it but we can feel its presence. For example, we feel the presence of air in the form of leaves of trees rustling, or the clothes hanging on a clothes-line swaying. The moving air is called **wind**.

The Earth is surrounded by a blanket or layer of air called the **atmosphere**. The atmosphere extends up to many kilometres above the surface of the Earth.

### Activity 12.1

**Aim:** To prove that air is present all around us

**Materials required:** A polythene bag, one small pin and a string

**Procedure:**

1. Open the polythene bag and move it around quickly from side to side. This action allows air to fill the bag.
2. Once the bag is filled with air, close the top and tightly tie it with a string.
3. Examine the bag. Note how its size has increased due to the air inside.
4. Carefully use the pin to make a small hole in the bag.
5. Watch how the bag's size changes as the air escapes through the pinhole.

**Observation:** The size of the bag initially increases as it fills with air and decreases after the pinhole is made, showing air escaping.

**Conclusion:** The experiment demonstrates that air is present around us. The bag expands when filled with air and shrinks when air is released, proving that air occupies space and is all around us.

## Activity 12.2

**Aim:** To prove that water contains air

**Materials required:** A clean sponge, a clear glass or beaker and water

**Procedure:**

1. Submerge the sponge in the water until it is fully soaked. Allow it to sit for a minute to ensure it absorbs as much water as possible.
2. Take the sponge out of the water and gently squeeze it over the glass or beaker.
3. As you squeeze the sponge, watch for small bubbles forming and rising in the water.

**Observation:** Small air bubbles will be released from the sponge into the water as you squeeze it.

**Conclusion:** The presence of bubbles indicates that air was trapped in the sponge along with the water. This demonstrates that air is present in water and can be released from objects that have absorbed it.

## Composition of Air

a

Air is a mixture of gases consisting of 78% nitrogen, 21% oxygen and the remaining 1% consists of carbon dioxide, dust, smoke and other gases (Fig. 12.1). The amount mentioned here is with regard to the volume of the particular gas in the total amount of air in the atmosphere. The pie chart given alongside shows the composition of air.

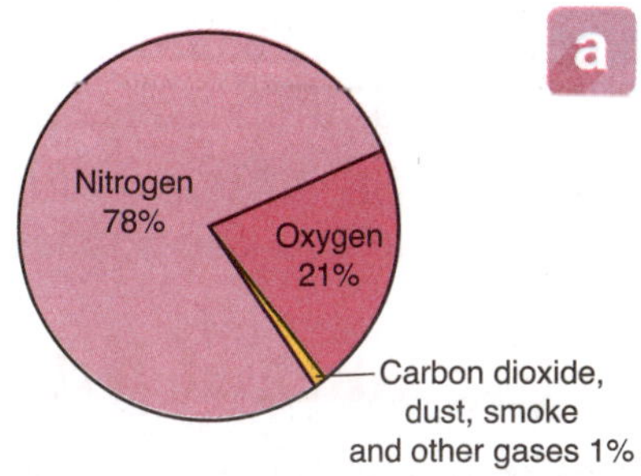


**Fig. 12.1:** Composition of air

Along with the constituents mentioned, small quantities of water vapour, dust and smoke are also present in the air. The amount of these constituents varies in different regions from time to time. The cities have a high amount of pollutants due to the increased smoke and dust from vehicles, factories, etc.

| Gas | Composition by Volume |
|---|---|
| Nitrogen | 78% |
| Oxygen | 21% |
| Carbon dioxide | 0.03% |
| Other gases | 0.97% |

## Importance of Oxygen

All living beings breathe in oxygen and breathe out carbon dioxide. The oxygen that living beings inhale is used to obtain energy from the food they eat.

**Animals:** Different animals use different organs and mechanisms for breathing (Fig. 12.2).

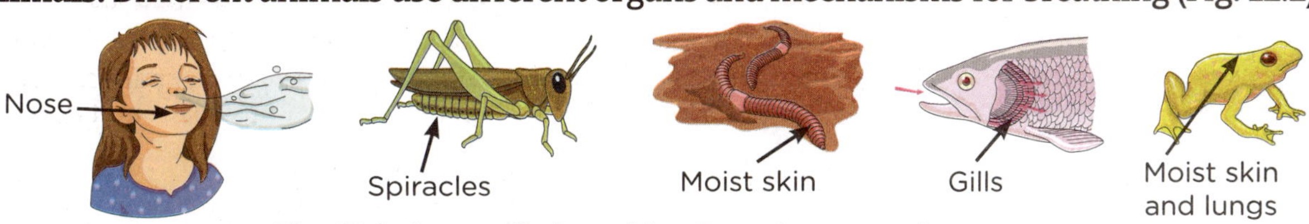


**Fig. 12.2:** Organs for breathing in various organisms

***Mammals*** such as human beings, elephants and lions breathe through their nose. The air taken in goes to the lungs.

**Insects** such as grasshoppers and cockroaches breathe through tiny openings called spiracles, which lead to a network of tubes known as the trachea, where air is distributed directly to their tissues.

**Earthworms** breathe through their moist skin.

***Aquatic animals*** such as fish and crab breathe through gills. Aquatic mammals such as whales and dolphins have air holes for breathing.

***Amphibians*** such as frog and salamander have separate mechanisms for breathing underwater and outside water. On land, frogs use their lungs to breathe in air. In water, they breathe with the help of their moist skin.

**Plants:** Plants take in carbon dioxide for photosynthesis. The oxygen released during photosynthesis is utilized for breathing. They have tiny holes called **stomata** on the underside of their leaves through which exchange of gases takes place (Fig. 12.3). Water plants such as lotus have stomata on the upper side of their leaves.

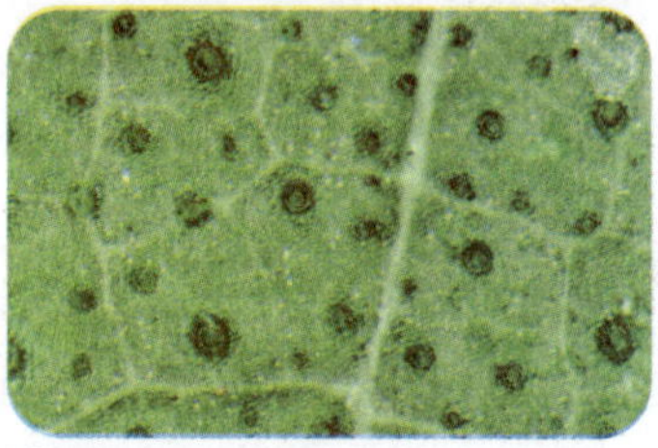

**Fig. 12.3:** Stomata present on the underside of a leaf

## Importance of Nitrogen

Nitrogen is essential for the growth of plants but plants cannot obtain nitrogen directly from the air. Nitrogen in the air is converted into nitric acid through a series of chemical reactions caused by both lightning and rain. Some bacteria present in the soil convert the nitric acid into usable forms such as nitrates that are absorbed by the roots of plants.

## Importance of Carbon dioxide

Carbon dioxide is a very important gas for plants and also for animals. Plants use carbon dioxide for preparation of food, through photosynthesis. This food is then consumed by all animals.

## Balance of Carbon dioxide and Oxygen in Nature

Carbon dioxide is released by all living organisms that breathe in oxygen. If all the oxygen is used up, then there will be a shortage of oxygen. However, this does not happen because of plants and trees present in nature.

Photosynthesis is the process in which plants take in carbon dioxide from the air to prepare their food in the presence of sunlight. In this process, oxygen is produced and released into the atmosphere.

Figure 12.4 shows the balance between carbon dioxide and oxygen in the atmosphere.

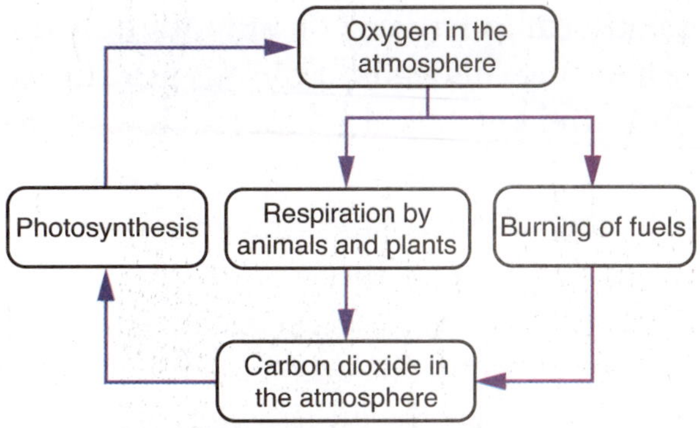


**Fig. 12.4:** Balance of carbon dioxide and oxygen in nature

As discussed in the earlier sections, all the gases in the air have a role to play in one way or the other in human activities.

Air is also useful in the following ways:

- Wind powers the windmills to generate electricity. The moving air caused by the uneven heating of the Earth by the sun is called **wind**.

  We cannot see wind or hold it, but we can feel its force. Wind can dry our clothes in summer and chill our bones in winter. It can be strong enough to carry sailing ships across the ocean and uproot huge trees from the ground.

  Wind can be used to produce clean electrical energy. The mechanism used to convert wind energy into electricity is referred to as a windmill. A windmill is a large structure with spinning blades. The blades are connected to an electromagnetic generator that generates electricity when the wind causes the blades to spin (Fig. 12.5).

**Fig. 12.5:** A windmill farm at Nagercoil

- Air provides the medium for
  - airplanes, helicopters and yachts to move.
  - birds and insects to fly.
  - dispersal of seeds, thereby helping with the growth of plants in faraway places.
  - pollination of flowers.
- Water cycle is influenced by the temperature of air and movement of wind.

## Air Pollution

**Fig. 12.6:** Causes of air pollution

Air and atmosphere are the main reasons for the life on the planet Earth. But the quality of air is decreasing due to an increase in the amount of pollutants in the air, thus causing air pollution (Fig. 12.6). The reasons for air pollution are the combustion of fuels such as petrol and diesel by the ever increasing number of vehicles in the cities. Even burning wood in the villages and smoke from the chimneys cause degradation of the quality of air we breathe. The amount of gases such as carbon dioxide, carbon monoxide, sulphur dioxide and nitrogen oxides is increasing in the air we breathe. This leads to various lung diseases such as wheezing, bronchitis and cancer. Plants and animals also face problems due to the harmful gases that are being added to the air.

Air pollution increases along with the increase in population of the human beings and their activities to meet their various demands. The control on air pollution can be brought about by stopping deforestation and planting more trees that can bring a balance in the levels of oxygen and carbon dioxide. Rules such as the emission norms for the engines in vehicles to make the air less polluted can improve the air quality in the cities. Decreasing the mining activities can reduce the amount of smoke and dust released into the air. For this, we have to recycle the items, reuse and reduce the usage of certain items.

## Revise and Recall

**State whether the following statements are true (T) or false (F).**

1. The Earth is surrounded by a layer of air called atmosphere.
2. Nitrogen is essential for the growth of plants.
3. Carbon dioxide is used by plants during photosynthesis.
4. Wind powers windmills to generate electricity.
5. Deforestation can control air pollution.

## IMPORTANCE OF WATER

Only a small percentage of water on the Earth is available for use. Therefore, water should be used judiciously and it should be conserved. Problems occur when there is:

- shortage of water to meet the demands of the population.
- usage and consumption by the population exceed the availability of the resources.

We cannot create the natural resources. The only way to provide water for the population is judicious use and conservation of the available resources.

**Conservation** is avoiding wastage or loss of the essential precious resources necessary for future use.

Providing drinking water for the population is a major challenge faced by the authorities in many towns and cities. Clean drinking water that is suitable for human consumption is known as **potable water**. Proper storage, management and distribution of water from the sources such as river and lakes should be undertaken by constructing dams, reservoirs and pipelines. A huge amount of potable water is lost during distribution due to leakage in the main water pipelines. Fixing these leakages can save a lot of water from being wasted.

## Activity 12.3

**Aim:** To estimate water usage at home per day and identify areas of water wastage

**Procedure:**

1. Talk to all the family members to know their water usage for different activities.
2. Note the number of times they perform each activity mentioned below starting from morning and note how much water they use in each activity.
3. The volume of water consumed should be recorded based on the number of mugs or bottles of water (with a capacity of 1 litre or 250 mℓ) or buckets of water (with a capacity of 15 litres) used for each activity.
4. Create a table for each family member at home to get an idea about the total volume of water used at home per day.
5. Identify activities where water is potentially wasted, such as leaving taps running or using excessive amounts of water for a task.
6. Record the instances of water wastage and suggest ways to reduce it.

| Activity | Water used (mug or bucket) | Number of times the activity is done | Amount of water used in a day for the activity | Water Wastage Observed | Suggestions to Reduce Wastage |
|---|---|---|---|---|---|
| Toilet flush | | | | | |
| Handwash | | | | | |
| Bathing | | | | | |
| Drinking | | | | | |
| Washing utensils | | | | | |

- One of the best ways to conserve water is by minimal usage of water at home. Following are the ways by which wastage of water can be avoided at home:
  - Bathe using water in a bucket and avoid the use of shower or bathtub. This will save a lot of water because using a shower and bathtub consumes huge amount of water.
  - Turn off the water tap when not in use, especially while brushing your teeth.
  - Take water in buckets and use a mug for watering plants instead of using a hose to avoid excessive use of water.
  - Instead of using a hose to wash a car, use a bucket of water and a sponge. This method significantly reduces water usage.
  - Fix the leaking taps, faucets and hoses at homes and schools.
- A lot of rainwater goes to our storm drains during rainy season. This water can be conserved for usage or to replenish the groundwater levels by the method of **rainwater harvesting**.

Rainwater (Fig. 12.7) is collected from the rooftops through pipes and allowed to flow into a tank containing sand and gravel to filter the water. This is allowed to **percolate**[1] through the soil. This will recharge the water table that is declining due to excessive usage of groundwater. Another method is collecting rainwater through pipes in the **sump**[2] and using it for washing purposes in our homes. Government policies should encourage making rainwater harvesting a mandatory requirement in houses and buildings in the urban areas.

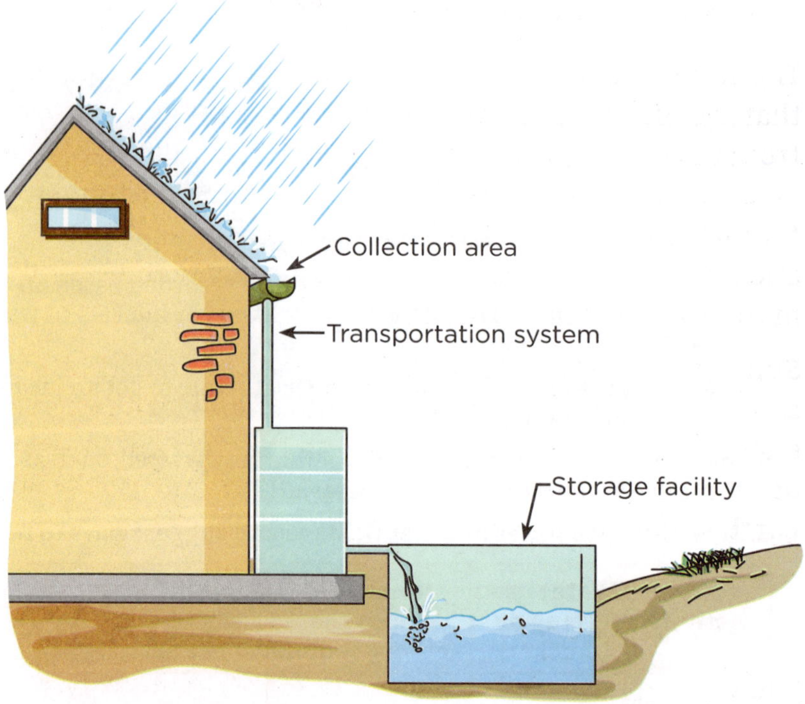


**Fig. 12.7:** Rainwater harvesting in a home

- Another simple and effective method to conserve water is recycling the treated water from the industries.
- Drip irrigation in the agricultural lands can save a lot of water. In drip irrigation method, crops and plants are given sufficient amount of water without any wastage.
- Planting trees and increasing the forest cover would lead to good rainfall and less pollution.
- Pollution of water in the rivers, lakes and ponds due to release of sewage and industrial **effluents**[3] containing harmful chemicals makes the water unsuitable for use. This polluted water can spread many diseases such as cholera, typhoid and hepatitis. Safeguarding the water bodies from pollution is an important step towards conserving water.

**Word Web**

[1]**Percolate:** move slowly through a porous surface

[2]**Sump:** a low-lying area, such as a pit

[3]**Effluents:** liquid waste generated in an industrial plant or factory

When you go to a picnic spot near a river or a pond, make sure that you do not litter the surroundings with wrappers, empty bottles, plastic plates, cups and other garbage. Keep the surroundings and the water clean.

# ENERGY FROM THE SUN

The sun is the primary source of energy for our planet. It provides both **heat** and **light** that are essential for life. Every day, we rely on the sun's energy for various activities, from drying clothes to growing food. The sun's heat helps regulate temperatures on Earth, making it possible for different environments to exist. Sunlight is vital for plants as it drives the process of photosynthesis, enabling them to produce food and oxygen. Humans and animals also depend on sunlight for warmth and for maintaining their daily activities.

Sunlight is the foundation of the food chain. Plants, which are the primary producers, capture sunlight and convert it into chemical energy through photosynthesis. This energy is then transferred through the food chain as animals consume plants or other animals. Without the Sun, plants would not be able to make food, and life on Earth would not be sustainable.

## Solar Energy

Solar energy is harnessed directly from the sun's rays, and it plays a crucial role in generating electricity, heating homes and powering devices.

*The cells that are capable of converting solar energy (energy from the sun) into electrical energy are called* ***solar cells****.*

A number of solar cells connected together can generate sufficient electric current for our applications (Fig. 12.8). When many solar cells are connected together to obtain the required current, it is called a solar panel. You might have seen solar panels for many devices such as emergency lamps, calculators, etc. They are also used for operating traffic signals, to provide electricity to artificial satellites, etc.

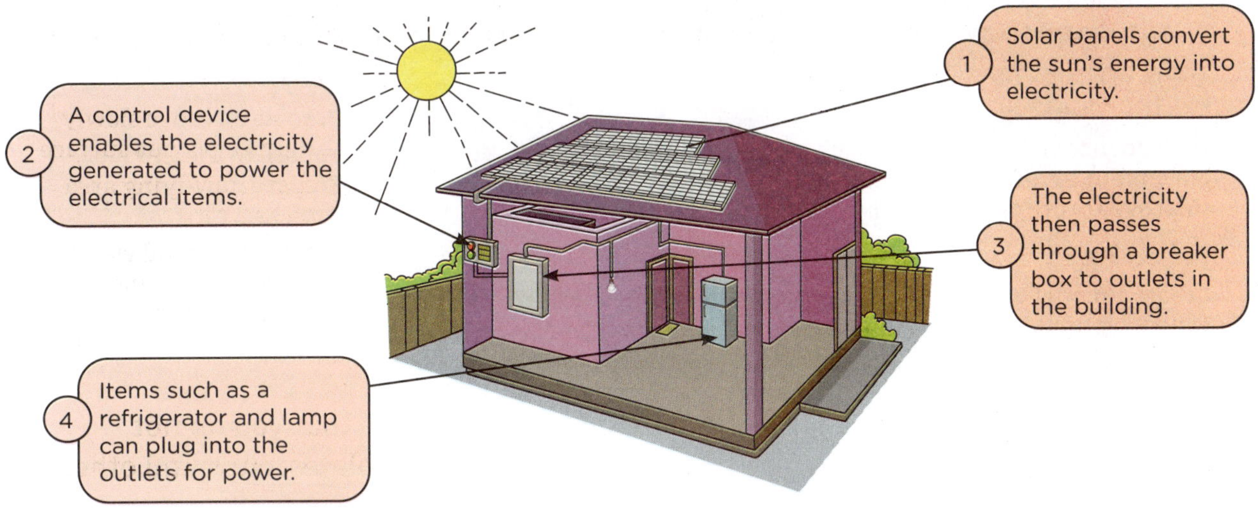


**Fig. 12.8:** Usage of solar cells for household applications

## FORESTS

Fig. 12.9: A forest

**Forests** are large areas with dense growth of various types of plants, including herbs, shrubs and trees. Forests play a crucial role in our ecosystem as they are the natural habitat for many wild animals, birds and insects. These areas provide food and shelter for numerous organisms, creating a diverse and balanced environment. Over time, however, human activities such as large-scale deforestation have significantly reduced forest cover. This reduction threatens the balance of life forms that depend on forests. To ensure the sustainability of forests, it is important to preserve and use them responsibly, allowing them enough time to regenerate (Fig. 12.9).

Forests are not just homes for wildlife but also protect the soil. The roots of trees hold the soil in place, preventing erosion, while fallen leaves decay and enrich the soil with nutrients, supporting new plant growth. This natural recycling process is vital for maintaining healthy ecosystems.

### Case Study: The Chipko Movement and Modern Efforts to Save Forests

Van Mahotsav is a weeklong festival celebrated across India in July, focusing on planting new trees and raising awareness about the importance of forests. This tradition reflects India's deep respect for forests, a value that has been upheld through various efforts to protect them. One of the most famous examples of this is the **Chipko Movement**. This movement started in the early 1970s in Uttarakhand. Local women hugged the trees to prevent them from being cut down, thereby protecting the forests from deforestation.

In recent years, movements such as the **Save Aarey Forest Movement** in Mumbai have echoed the spirit of the **Chipko Movement**. This movement, which began in 2019, saw widespread protests against the proposed cutting down of trees in the Aarey Colony for a metro car shed project. Citizens, environmentalists and activists argued that the loss of green cover would have severe ecological consequences.

**Critical Thinking**

How do modern movements such as the **Save Aarey Forest Movement** compare to the Chipko Movement in terms of strategies and outcomes? What can be learned from these movements to improve future efforts in forest conservation?

**Project Idea**

Create a model or poster depicting a forest conservation effort. Include key elements such as the causes, actions taken and the impact of the movement. Research and suggest additional strategies that could enhance the effectiveness of these conservation efforts.

# SOIL, ROCKS AND MINERALS

Soil, rocks and minerals are the components of the Earth's crust. **Soil** is formed over thousands of years through the disintegration of rocks, aided by the actions of the sun, water and living organisms. Soil is essential for supporting biodiversity, providing a medium for plant growth (Fig. 12.10), and housing many organisms such as earthworms, which help in turning and loosening the soil.

**Fig. 12.10:** Plants growing in soil

Rocks are made up of **minerals.** Rocks have been utilized by humans for thousands of years to make tools such as hand axes and arrowheads. In the modern society, these resources play a critical role in construction, manufacturing, technology and everyday life. Here are some key uses.

## Construction

- **Buildings and infrastructure**: Rocks such as granite, limestone and marble are commonly used as building materials for constructing houses, buildings, bridges and monuments.
- **Roads**: Crushed stones and gravel are essential components of asphalt and concrete, which are used in road construction.
- **Roofing**: Slate is a type of rock used for roofing materials due to its durability and water resistance.

## Manufacturing

- **Cement and concrete**: Limestone is a primary ingredient in cement production, which is then mixed with sand and gravel to produce concrete.
- **Glass production**: Silica, derived from quartz, is a key component in making glass.
- **Ceramics and pottery**: Clay minerals, such as kaolinite, are used in the production of ceramics, pottery and tiles.

## Technology and Electronics

- **Electronics**: Minerals such as copper, gold and silver are used in the manufacturing of electronic components (Fig. 12.11) such as wiring, circuits and connectors.

**Fig. 12.11:** Electronic circuit board

- **Smartphones and computers**: Minerals such as lithium (used in batteries) and silicon (used in microchips) are critical in the production of smartphones, computers and other electronic devices.

## Jewellery and Decoration

- **Gemstones**: Minerals such as diamonds, sapphires, emeralds and rubies are cut and polished to be used as gemstones in jewellery.
- **Marble and granite**: These rocks are often used for decorative purposes, including countertops, floor tiles and sculptures.

## Agriculture

- **Fertilizers**: Minerals such as phosphates and potash are used to produce fertilizers that enrich the soil and promote plant growth.
- **Soil conditioning**: Lime (calcium carbonate) is used to improve acidic soils.

## Industrial Applications

- **Steel Production**: Iron ore, a type of rock, is a primary raw material for steel production.
- **Chemicals**: Minerals such as gypsum are used in producing plaster and wallboard, while others such as barite are used in drilling fluids for oil and gas exploration.

## Environmental Applications

- **Water filtration**: Minerals such as zeolites are used in water purification and softening.
- **Pollution control**: Limestone is used in flue gas desulfurization to reduce sulphur dioxide emissions from power plants.

### Activity 12.4

**Aim:** To investigate and compare the properties of soil samples collected from different locations
**Materials required:** Small containers or bags for collecting soil samples, a magnifying lens, a notebook and pencil for recording observations, a ruler (optional for measuring soil particles) and gloves (optional for handling soil)
**Procedure:**

**1. Collect Soil Samples**

- Collect soil samples from at least four different locations around your home or school. For example, you might choose: a garden bed, playground, agricultural land and a construction site.
- Label each container with the location from which the soil was collected.

**2. Prediction:** Before observing the soil samples, predict the following for each location:

- The type of soil you expect (sandy, clayey, loamy, etc.)
- The likely colour of the soil
- The expected texture (smooth, gritty, coarse, etc.)
- Any visible materials you might expect (e.g., pebbles, plant debris)

**Observation:**

| Location | Predicted soil type | Predicted colour | Predicted texture | Predicted materials |
|---|---|---|---|---|
| Garden bed | | | | |
| Playground | | | | |
| Agricultural land | | | | |
| Construction site | | | | |

Examine each soil sample using your senses:

- **Colour:** Observe and describe the actual colour of the soil. Use magnifying glass.
- **Texture:** Feel and describe the texture of the soil (e.g., smooth, gritty, crumbly).
- **Materials:** Identify any visible materials in the soil (e.g., pebbles, roots, organic matter).

Record your observations in a table like the one below:

| Location | Actual soil type | Actual colour | Actual texture | Visible material |
|---|---|---|---|---|
| Garden bed | | | | |
| Playground | | | | |
| Agricultural land | | | | |
| Construction site | | | | |

**Analysis:**

- Compare your predictions with your actual observations.
- Discuss any discrepancies or similarities between your predictions and actual findings.
- Consider factors that might influence soil properties at each location (e.g., use of the land, plant growth, human activity).

Summarize your findings:

- How accurate were your predictions?
- What differences or similarities did you notice among the different soil samples?
- How might these properties impact the suitability of the soil for various uses?

This activity helps you understand the diversity of soil types and their properties, reinforcing the importance of soil in supporting plant life and ecosystems.

# FOSSIL FUELS

**Fossil fuels** such as coal, petroleum and natural gas are essential energy sources formed from the remains of ancient organisms buried deep within the Earth. These fuels are used for various purposes, including generating electricity and powering vehicles. However, fossil fuels are non-renewable resources. That is, they are available in limited quantities and take millions of years to form. Also, the excessive use of fossil fuels leads to air pollution and environmental degradation. Thus, it is crucial to explore and adopt alternative energy sources. See how the global primary energy consumption has changed over the years.

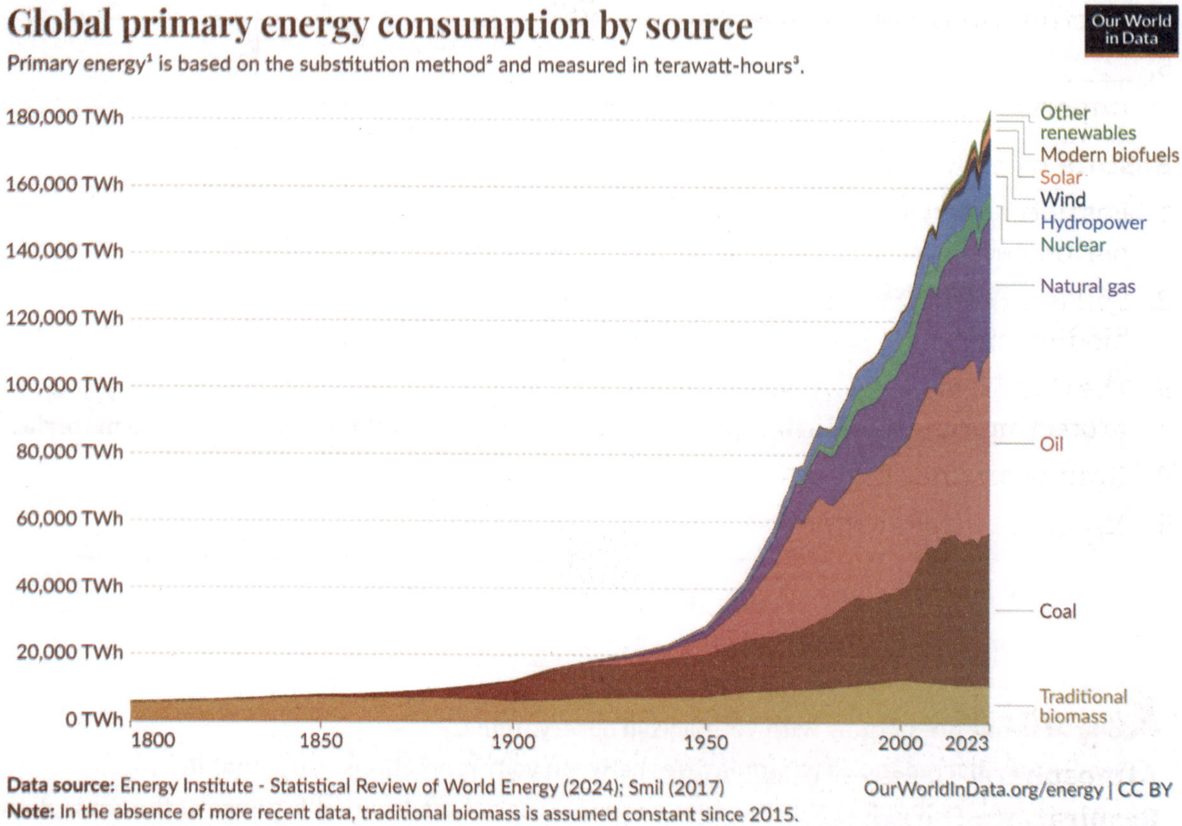


## Know the Scientist

**Saalumarada Thimmakka**

**(Born on 8 July 1911)**

Saalumarada Thimmakka, an Indian environmentalist from Karnataka, is renowned for her dedication to afforestation, notably planting and nurturing 385 banyan trees along a 45-kilometre stretch of highway. Alongside her husband, she transformed barren land into a thriving forest, planting over 8000 trees. Her efforts have significantly improved the local environment, reversing deforestation and restoring ecological balance in her region.

## Revise and Recall

**A. Fill in the blanks.**

1. Forests provide a natural habitat for many __________, __________, and __________.
2. __________ is the process by which soil is formed through the breaking apart of rocks over time.
3. __________, __________, and __________ are examples of fossil fuels.
4. Rocks are made up of __________, which are essential for manufacturing various electronic devices and vehicles.
5. __________ is a festival celebrated in India to raise awareness about the importance of forests and to plant new trees.

**B. State whether the following statements are true (T) or false (F).**

1. Fossil fuels are renewable resources that can be replenished within a short period.
2. Soil is an essential natural resource that supports plant growth and biodiversity.
3. The Chipko Movement was a significant environmental movement aimed at protecting rivers in India.
4. Granite and marble are examples of rocks commonly used in construction.
5. Minerals such as copper and gold are used in electronic circuit boards.

## Keywords

**Atmosphere:** The layer of air surrounding the Earth

**Respiration:** The process of burning digested food to release energy by using oxygen obtained through breathing

**Potable water:** Clean drinking water free from dirt, germs and fit for human consumption

**Rainwater harvesting:** The storage of rainwater collected in sumps or underground to recharge the groundwater or for domestic use

**Fossil fuels:** Essential energy sources formed from the remains of ancient organisms buried deep within the Earth

# Summary

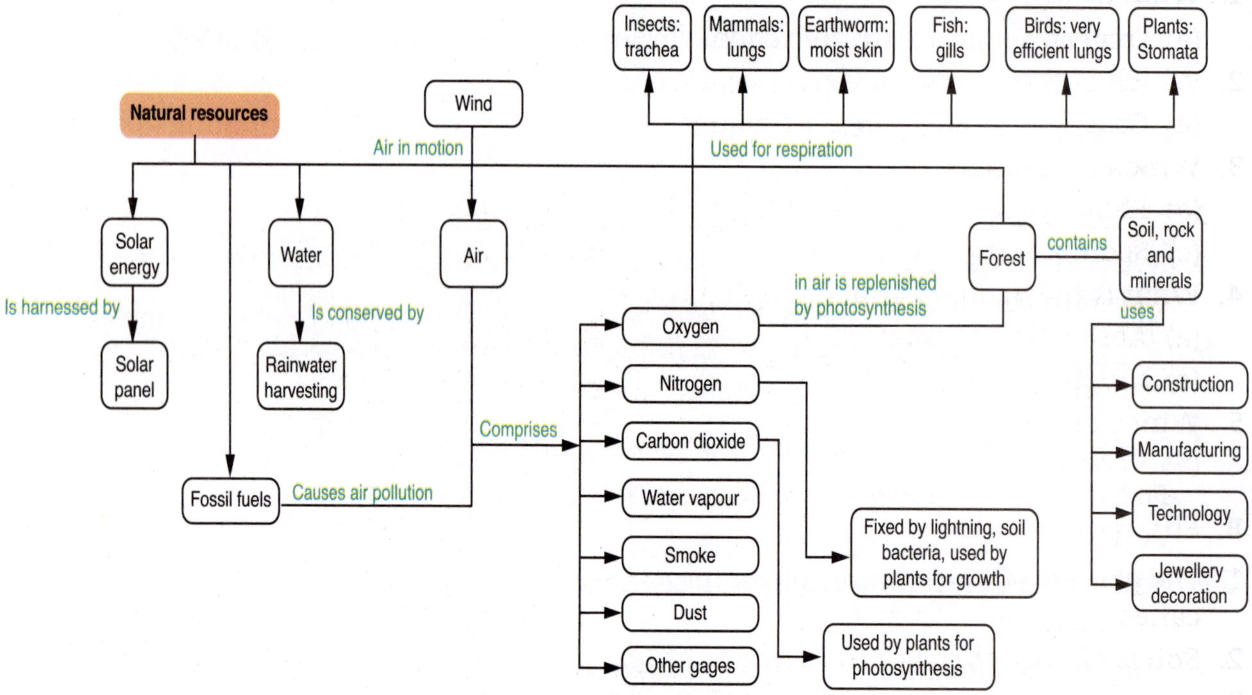
Natural resources
Wind
Air in motion
Insects: trachea
Mammals: lungs
Earthworm: moist skin
Fish: gills
Birds: very efficient lungs
Plants: Stomata
Used for respiration
Solar energy
Is harnessed by
Solar panel
Water
Is conserved by
Rainwater harvesting
Air
Forest
contains
Soil, rock and minerals
uses
in air is replenished by photosynthesis
Oxygen
Nitrogen
Carbon dioxide
Water vapour
Smoke
Dust
Other gages
Comprises
Fossil fuels
Causes air pollution
Fixed by lightning, soil bacteria, used by plants for growth
Used by plants for photosynthesis
Construction
Manufacturing
Technology
Jewellery decoration

# Exercise

**A. Choose the correct option.**

1. What is the primary gas found in Earth's atmosphere?
   (a) Oxygen (b) Nitrogen (c) Carbon dioxide (d) Argon
2. Which of the following is a renewable resource?
   (a) Coal (b) Petroleum (c) Forests (d) Natural gas
3. Which process is responsible for the formation of fossil fuels?
   (a) Photosynthesis (b) Erosion
   (c) Sedimentation (d) Decomposition of ancient organisms
4. What is the primary function of stomata in plants?
   (a) Absorption of water (b) Gas exchange
   (c) Nutrient transport (d) Photosynthesis
5. Which of the following minerals is used in the production of glass?
   (a) Kaolinite (b) Quartz (c) Gypsum (d) Hematite

**B. Fill in the blanks.**

1. The process of converting solar energy into electrical energy using solar cells is called ________.
2. Soil is formed through the disintegration of ________ over thousands of years.
3. ________ is the gas that makes up 78% of the Earth's atmosphere.
4. Plants release ________ into the atmosphere during the process of photosynthesis.
5. ________ fuels are non-renewable energy sources formed from the remains of ancient organisms.

**C. State whether the following statements are true (T) or false (F).**

1. Wind is the moving air that surrounds the Earth.
2. Nitrogen is directly absorbed by plants from the atmosphere.
3. Fossil fuels are renewable resources.
4. The roots of trees help prevent soil erosion.
5. Solar panels are used to convert electrical energy into solar energy.

**D. Give reasons for the following.**

1. It is important to conserve natural resources.
2. Fossil fuels are considered non-renewable.
3. Air pollution should be controlled.
4. Different soil samples have different properties.
5. Forests are important in preventing soil erosion.

**E. Answer the following questions briefly.**

1. What is the composition of air?
2. How is solar energy harnessed for electricity?
3. What role do stomata play in plants?
4. Why is nitrogen essential for plants?
5. What are fossil fuels, and how are they formed?
6. With the growing need for land and resources for urban development and agriculture, deforestation is increasing. Do you think this is justifiable? Discuss as a brief report.
7. List four everyday activities that depend on the presence of water. Explain how each activity relies on water.
8. A home relies on wind turbines for electricity, and a well for water. What would be the impact if there were no wind for a week?

**F. Answer the following questions.**

1. Describe the importance of air and water in supporting life on Earth.
2. Explain how soil is formed and its significance in the ecosystem.
3. Discuss the various uses of rocks and minerals in modern society.
4. How do plants contribute to maintaining the balance of oxygen and carbon dioxide in the atmosphere?
5. Why is it important to explore alternative energy sources to fossil fuels?
6. Propose a plan to reduce energy consumption in your school. What steps would you take to implement this plan, and how would it benefit the environment?

# Cognitive Corner

## Critical Thinking

1. How does deforestation impact the balance of gases in the atmosphere?
2. Why is it necessary to use water judiciously, and what measures can be taken to conserve it?
3. How can the knowledge of soil types help in agriculture?
4. What are the environmental implications of using fossil fuels for energy?

## Picture Study

**The picture shows a method of conserving water. Identify the method and label the figure.**

## Project

1. Collect information from your neighbourhood on how people commute to their workplaces and marketplaces. Then, find out whether there is an overuse of vehicles running on fuels such as petrol and diesel.
   Make a report on your findings. **(C-5.2)**
2. Based on your report in Project 1, prepare posters and handouts on measures that will reduce the burning of fuels such as carpool, using public transport, walking or cycling short distances, etc. Distribute these in your neighbourhood to create awareness. **(C-5.2)**
3. Create an awareness campaign to highlight the importance of responsible water use. Research water conservation issues, design a visual campaign on a poster board or digital presentation and create informative pamphlets or flyers. Try and include interactive components such as a pledge board and activity stations for practical water-saving tips. If possible, present to your community to educate and inspire action towards better water management. Also, gather feedback and reflect on how the campaign has helped promote the concept of water responsibility. **(C-5.1)**

## In the Library

1. Read about the noble gases, such as argon and xenon, and other gases present in the air and their uses. **(C-5.2)**
2. Read more about the ozone layer and the causes of its depletion. Also, find out the measures that have been taken to control further damage. **(C-5.2)**

## Life Skills

Air is precious. It is easy to talk about air pollution and how to reduce it. Unless each and everyone of us takes the responsibility, it is not possible to reduce air pollution. So, what can we do?

1. Can you list some ways to reduce air pollution?
2. Which is one of the major culprits for air pollution?
3. How can we reduce the use of individual vehicles?

Remind your parents to periodically get the vehicle/vehicles checked for emissions.

What are the initiatives you can take to canvas the importance of reduction of air pollution?

You can also help to reduce other forms of pollution by not using any substance that has aerosols such as hair sprays, body deodorants, air-fresheners, etc. You can instead buy those that do not use aerosols. **(C-5.2)**

# Worksheet

The quality of air has deteriorated, with harmful gases and pollutants affecting the air we breathe, leading to potential health problems. Strengthening and maintaining healthy lungs becomes crucial to cope with polluted air and promote well-being, aligning with SDG 3 (Good Health and Well-being). Traditional Indian knowledge systems, such as Yoga and Ayurveda, can offer valuable insights into natural practices for lung health and overall well-being.

Do you know that babies exercise their lungs when they cry?

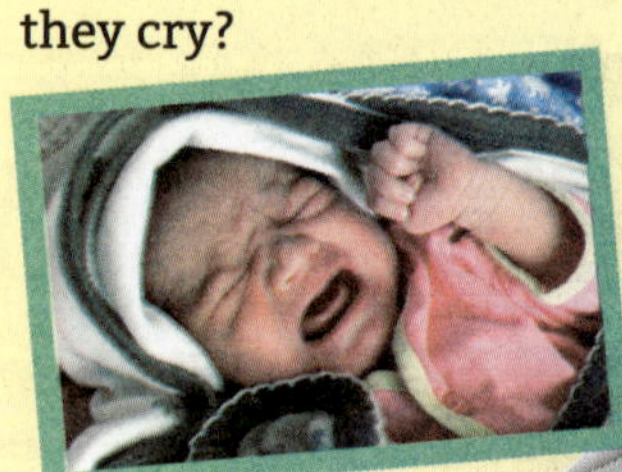

A. How can you adopt a healthier lifestyle, incorporating regular physical activity, nutritious food choices, and stress reduction techniques to support lung health and boost immunity?

______________________________________________

______________________________________________

B. Brainstorm ways to reduce air pollution in your community. List any two ways.

______________________________________________

______________________________________________

C. Investigate modern air purification technologies or natural remedies recommended in traditional Indian knowledge systems that can improve indoor air quality and reduce exposure to pollutants.

______________________________________________

______________________________________________

D. How can you become an advocate for clean air and educate others about the importance of lung health, encouraging responsible actions to protect the environment and promote well-being?

______________________________________________

______________________________________________

# 13 The Universe

## Curricular Goals

- Explore the physical world in scientific and mathematical terms **(CG-2)**
- Communicate questions, observations and conclusions related to science **(CG-7)**

## Competencies

- Observe and identify celestial objects (stars, planets, natural and artificial satellites, constellations, comets) in the night sky using a simple telescope and images/photographs, and explain their role in navigation, calendars and other phenomena (phases of the moon) **(C-2.5)**
- Use scientific vocabulary to communicate science accurately in oral and written forms, and through visual representation **(C-7.1)**

## Let's Get Started

Name the planets shown in the picture.

The sun and the eight planets that revolve around it together form the solar system. In addition to planets, the solar system also includes satellites of various planets, comets and asteroids, all of which are part of the broader universe. Let us explore more about these fascinating celestial objects and their roles in the vastness of the universe.

The universe is an incredibly vast and fascinating place that includes everything we see and even things we cannot see. It contains all the stars, planets, moons and galaxies as well as the empty space in between. Our Earth is just a tiny part of this enormous system. The universe is so big that it is hard to imagine its size, with billions of galaxies, each containing millions or even billions of stars, including our own sun. Scientists believe that the universe began with a massive explosion called the Big Bang, which created all the matter and energy we see today. As time goes on, the universe continues to expand, with galaxies moving farther apart from each other.

## STARS

Stars are huge balls of hot, glowing gas. They come in different sizes and brightness. Distance affects how bright a star looks to us. Proxima Centauri is much smaller than the sun but looks faint because it is farther away. The sun is the closest star to Earth, and Sirius and Rigil Kentaurus are two main sequence stars that are visible to the naked eye. Sirius is the brightest star visible in the night sky. We can see a star in the North which appears to be stationary all the time. This is because the position of this star is along the axis on which the Earth rotates. This star is known as the Pole Star or North Star. Stars are born in clouds of gas and dust called **nebulae**. Most of a star's life is spent in a stable phase where it converts hydrogen into helium. The sun is currently in this phase. At the beginning of the end of a star's life, they run out of hydrogen to convert into helium. Small stars like the sun become red giants and then shrink into white dwarfs. Massive stars explode in **supernovae** (singular: supernova) and can become **neutron stars** or **black holes**. Table 13.1 gives the differences between stars and planets.

**Table 13.1:** Differences between stars and planets

| Stars | Planets |
|---|---|
| Stars appear to be twinkling in the sky. | Planets do not twinkle in the sky. |
| Stars emit their own light. | Planets reflect the sunlight falling on them. |
| Stars are massive and very large in size. | Planets are much smaller in comparison. |

## Measuring Distances of Celestial Objects

Large distances between celestial objects are measured in Astronomical Unit (AU) and light year. The AU is used to measure distances within our solar system. It is the average distance from Earth to the sun, which is about 150 million kilometers (1 million = 10,00,000). For example, Jupiter is about 5.2 AU from the sun, so it is 5.2 times farther from the sun than Earth is. A **light year** is used to measure distances beyond our solar system. It is how far light travels in one year, which is about 9.5 trillion kilometers (1 trillion = 10,00,00,00,00,000). The nearest star to Earth, Proxima Centauri, is about 4.24 light years away. This means light from Proxima Centauri takes 4.24 years to reach us.

# CONSTELLATIONS

Group of stars that form recognizable shapes or figures in the night sky are called a **constellation**. They have been used for navigation and storytelling for thousands of years. They are generally named after an animal, a character from mythology or a common object. Some common constellations are discussed below.

## Orion

**Orion** (Fig. 13.1) is one of the most recognizable constellations in the night sky. It is named after a hunter from Greek mythology and is often referred to as "The Hunter." Betelgeuse, Bellatrix, Saiph and Rigel are its prominent stars which form the shoulders and legs. It consists of three closely spaced stars (Alnitak, Alnilam and Mintaka) that form a straight line across the middle of Orion which is referred as Orion's belt. It is visible in the evening during the winter months in the Northern Hemisphere. In the Southern Hemisphere, it is seen during summer.

**Fig. 13.1**: Orion

## Ursa Major

**Ursa Major** (Fig. 13.2) is the third largest constellation in the sky and the largest in the Northern Hemisphere. It is also known as the Great Bear. Its brightest stars form the Big Dipper asterism, one of the most recognizable shapes in the sky, also known as the Plough.

**Fig. 13.2**: Ursa Major

## Ursa Minor

**Ursa Minor** (Fig. 13.3), also known as the Little Bear or Little Dipper, is a constellation in the northern sky. The most famous star in Ursa Minor is Polaris, also known as the North Star or Pole Star. The significant feature is Polaris, which is located almost directly above the North Pole. It is a key navigational star because it remains almost stationary in the sky, with other stars appearing to rotate around it.

**Fig. 13.3**: Ursa Minor

## Canis Major

**Fig. 13.4**: Canis Major

**Canis Major** (Fig. 13.4) is a constellation in the southern celestial hemisphere. It is referred as the Greater Dog. Its notable star is Sirius, which is the brightest star in the night sky and often used as a reference point for stargazers.

## Taurus

**Fig. 13.5**: Taurus

**Taurus** (Fig. 13.5) is a large and prominent constellation in the Northern Hemisphere's winter sky. The constellation depicts the bull's head and horns. The Hyades is an open star cluster that forms the bull's face and includes Aldebaran. The Pleiades also known as the Seven Sisters, is a prominent and visually striking star cluster located in the shoulder area of Taurus.

# MOVEMENT OF CELESTIAL OBJECTS IN THE SKY

As we observe the night sky at various times, we notice that celestial objects seem to drift from East to West. This apparent movement is a consequence of Earth's rotation. The Earth rotates from West to East, which makes the stars and planets appear to move in the opposite direction—from East to West. Similarly, the sun rises in the East and sets in the West due to this rotation.

> **Science in Context**
>
> Calendars that we follow are based either on the movement of the sun or the moon. A solar calendar uses the year as a solar year. The time for the Earth to complete one revolution around the sun is one solar year. A lunar calendar uses the phases of the moon to measure time. The time interval between one new moon to the next new moon is considered as one month.

## The Milky Way Galaxy

Galaxies consist of stars, planets and vast clouds of gas and dust, all bound together by gravity. They are fundamental building blocks of the universe and come in various shapes and sizes. The galaxy we live in, called the Milky Way Galaxy (Fig. 13.6), is a spiral galaxy that contains our solar system.

**Fig. 13.6**: The Milky Way Galaxy

# THE SOLAR SYSTEM

The **solar system** is the gravitationally bound system of celestial objects that orbit the sun. It includes planets, moons, asteroids and comets. (Fig. 13.7).

**Fig. 13.7**: The solar system (not to scale)

## Sun

The sun is the central star of our solar system and the primary source of light and energy for Earth and the other planets. Its mass is about 3,30,000 times the mass of Earth and it is large enough to fit about 1.3 million Earths inside it. The sun consists mainly of the elements hydrogen and helium. The core is where nuclear fusion occurs, converting hydrogen into helium and releasing an immense amount of energy. This process generates the sun's energy and powers its luminosity. The temperature at its core is approximately 15 million degrees Celsius.

## Planets

The solar system comprises eight planets that orbit the sun. These planets, listed in order of their distance from the sun, are Mercury, Venus, Earth, Mars, Jupiter, Saturn, Uranus and Neptune. Pluto, previously considered the ninth planet, is now classified as a dwarf planet. The planets orbit the sun in elliptical paths, with the sun at the centre. This movement of planets around the sun is referred to as **revolution**.
The duration it takes for a planet to complete one full orbit around the sun is known as its orbital period. In addition to orbiting the sun, planets also spin on their own axes, a motion called **rotation**. The time it takes for a planet to complete one full rotation on its axis is known as its rotational period. The first four planets (Mercury, Venus, Earth and Mars) are termed the inner planets, while the remaining planets (Jupiter, Saturn, Uranus and Neptune) are known as the outer planets.

## Mercury

Mercury is the closest planet to the sun and the smallest planet in our solar system. Mercury goes around the sun faster than any other planet. It only takes about 88 days to complete one trip around the sun. It has huge temperature differences. During the day, it can get very hot, up to 800°F (430°C), but at night, it can get very cold, down to –330°F (–200°C). This is because it does not have a thick atmosphere to keep the heat in. It does not have any moons or rings.

## Venus

Venus (Fig. 13.8) is the second planet from the sun. It is the planet that shines brightly in our night sky, sometimes called the "Evening Star" or "Morning Star." It is called Earth's "sister planet" because of their similar size. Venus spins in the opposite direction to most other planets, so if you were standing on Venus, the sun would rise in the West and set in the East. It is the hottest planet because its thick atmosphere traps heat. Its surface is covered by thick clouds, so we cannot see it directly. It does not have any moons.

**Fig. 13.8**: Venus

## Earth

Earth (Fig. 13.9) is the only planet known to have life. It is bigger than Mercury and Venus but smaller than the gas giants such as Jupiter and Saturn. It spins on its axis, which is an imaginary line that goes through the North and South Poles. This spinning takes about 24 hours and gives us day and night. It orbits around the sun in an elliptical path (Fig. 13.10) and takes about 365 days and 6 hours to complete one orbit. Its axis is tilted at an angle of about 23.5 degrees which causes the different seasons as it orbits the sun. It has a diverse surface with land, water and air. Its atmosphere is made up of gases such as oxygen, nitrogen and carbon dioxide. It has one natural satellite, the moon.

**Fig. 13.9**: The Earth

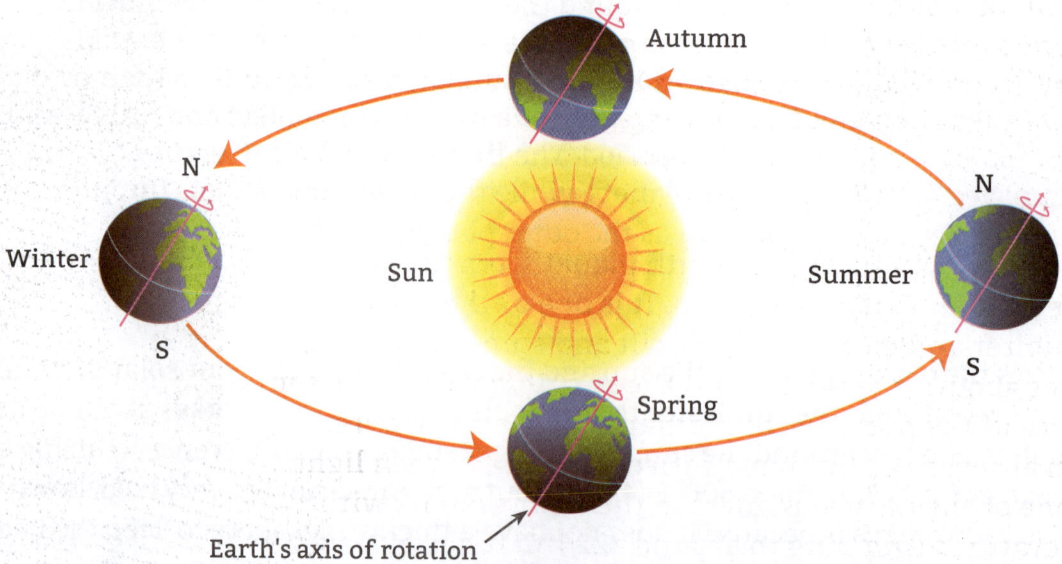


**Fig. 13.10**: Revolution of the Earth

## Mars

Mars (Fig. 13.11) is the fourth planet from the sun, coming after Earth. It is called the "Red Planet" because of its reddish appearance. It looks red because its surface is covered with iron oxide, or rust. It is about half the size of Earth. It has a very thin atmosphere, made of carbon dioxide, with very little oxygen. This atmosphere does not trap heat, so it is colder on Mars compared to Earth. It has two small moons named Phobos and Deimos. It has the largest volcano in the solar system, Olympus Mons.

**Fig. 13.11**: Mars

## Jupiter

Jupiter (Fig. 13.12) is the fifth planet from the sun and the largest planet in our solar system. It is about 11 times wider than Earth. It spins very quickly on its axis. One day on Jupiter (one full spin) lasts only about 10 hours. Because of this fast spin, it is flattened at the poles and bulging at the equator. It takes about 12 years to complete one orbit around the sun. It has bands of clouds in different colours. It has at least 95 known moons. It has a faint ring system made up of tiny particles of dust.

**Fig. 13.12**: Jupiter

## Saturn

Saturn (Fig. 13.13) is the sixth planet from the sun. It is the second largest planet in our solar system. It is about 9 times wider than Earth. It is known for its rings which are made of ice and rock particles of different sizes. These rings are divided into several main rings with smaller rings in between. It is a gas giant like Jupiter. Its atmosphere is made of hydrogen and helium, and it is very cold. It has 83 known moons and Titan is the largest moon.

**Fig. 13.13**: Saturn

## Uranus

Uranus (Fig. 13.14) is the seventh planet from the sun. It is about 4 times wider than Earth. It is one of the gas giants, like Jupiter and Saturn. It has a tilt and spins on its side. It takes about 84 years to orbit the sun. It looks blue-green because of the presence of methane in its atmosphere, which absorbs red light and reflects blue and green light. It is one of the coldest planets in the solar system, with temperatures dropping to around –224°C. It has at least 27 known moons. It has a ring system made of dark, icy particles.

**Fig. 13.14**: Uranus

## Neptune

Neptune (Fig. 13.15) is the eighth and farthest planet from the sun. It spins on its axis quickly. So, one day on Neptune lasts about 16 hours. It takes about 165 years to complete one orbit around the sun. It looks blue because of the presence of methane in its atmosphere, which absorbs red light and reflects blue light. It is very cold, with temperatures around –214°C. It has a large storm system called the Great Dark Spot and is a massive, dark area on its surface. It has 14 known moons and the largest moon is Triton.

**Fig. 13.15:** Neptune

## Natural Satellites

Natural satellites known as moons, are objects that orbit around planets. They are called "natural" because they are not human-made. Orbit is caused by the planet's gravity pulling the moon towards it while the moon is moving forward. This combination keeps the moon in a stable path around the planet.

### Science in Context

On January 19, 2006, New Horizons, a NASA space probe was launched to study the planet Pluto, its moons and one or two other Kuiper belt objects, depending on which are in a position to be explored. Pluto was earlier considered as the ninth planet of the solar system but due to its small size, it is now called a dwarf planet.

## Moon of the Earth

The moon is Earth's only natural satellite. It orbits around Earth and is the fifth largest moon in the solar system. It has a diameter of about 3474 kilometers and one-fourth the size of Earth. It takes about 27.3 days to complete one orbit around Earth, which is called a lunar month. Its surface is covered with craters, mountains and large flat plains called "maria". Moon's gravity affects Earth's oceans, creating high and low tides. This gravitational pull causes water in the oceans to bulge out on the side of Earth closest to the moon (causing high tide) and the side farthest from the moon (causing low tide).

The moon goes through different **phases** (Fig. 13.16) as it orbits the Earth. These phases include New Moon, Waxing Crescent, First Quarter, Waxing Gibbous, Full Moon, Waning Gibbous, Third Quarter and Waning Crescent.

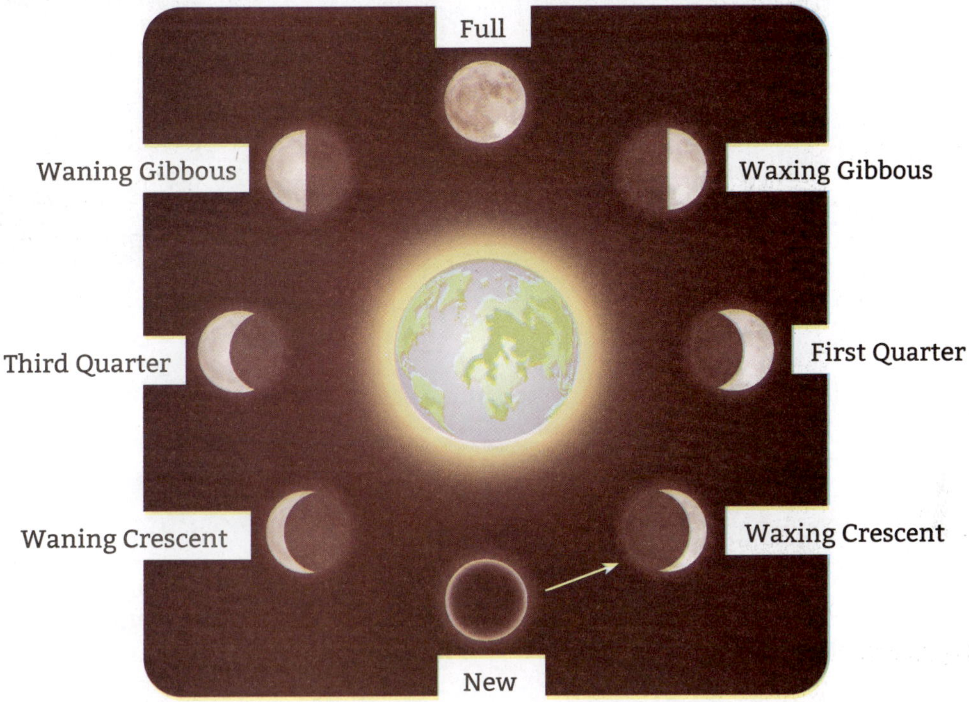


**Fig. 13.16**: Phases of the moon

## Revise and Recall

**Fill in the blanks.**

1. The brightest star visible in the night is ______________. (Sirius/Pole Star)
2. The Ursa Minor constellation is also known as ______________. (Great Bear/ Little Bear)
3. The moon takes ______________ days to complete one revolution around the Earth. (365/27.3)
4. The farthest planet from the sun in the solar system is ______________. (Mercury/Uranus)

## Case Study: Chandrayaan-3 Mission

The Indian Space Research Organisation (ISRO) launched its third lunar mission, Chandrayaan-3 on July 14 from Sriharikota, Andhra Pradesh. Chandrayaan-3 is a follow-up mission of the Chandrayaan-2 that failed to land on the moon's surface in September 2019. It is aimed to conduct a study of the lunar soil, explore the moon's surface and record moon quakes. Its propulsion module carried a lander and a rover.

The Vikram lander of Chandrayaan-3 landed on the lunar South Pole on August 23, 2023. This made India the fourth country after the United States, Russia and China to land successfully on the lunar surface. The Vikram lander is named after Dr Vikram A Sarabhai, the father of the Indian Space Programme. The Pragyan rover carried India's flag and ISRO's logo, etching the nation's identity on the lunar surface.

**Critical Thinking**

The successful landing of Chandrayaan-3 on the lunar South Pole is a significant achievement for India. How do you think this mission contributes to the global understanding of the moon? Why is it important for India to continue investing in space exploration?

**Project Idea**

Investigate the objectives, challenges and achievements of India's recent space missions, including Chandrayaan-3. How have these missions contributed to advancements in science and technology in India? Present your findings through a report or multimedia presentation.

# Other Celestial Objects Asteroids

**Asteroids** (Fig. 13.17) called "planetoids" or "minor planets", are rocky remains left over from the formation of our solar system about 4.6 billion years ago. They are found in a region called **asteroid belt** between the orbits of Mars and Jupiter. They have irregular shapes and orbit the sun in elliptical paths. When asteroids or fragments of them enter Earth's atmosphere and land on the surface, they are called meteorites.

**Fig. 13.17**: Asteroids (called Vesta)

## Comets

Fig. 13.18: A comet

Comets are icy bodies that orbit the sun. They are known as "cosmic snowballs" because they are made mostly of ice, dust and rocky material. They travel in elliptical orbits around the sun. They spend most of their time far from the sun in the outer regions of the solar system, but when they come close to the sun, they appear like a glowing ball with a long tail. Increase in the heat causes the ice within the comet to turn into a gas and release dust. Comet 12P/Pons–Brooks (Fig. 13.18) is a periodic comet with an orbital period of 71 years. It was last visible in March 2024 and will return in 2095.

### Know the Scientist

**Dr Vikram Ambalal Sarabhai**

**(12 August 1919–31 December 1971)**

Dr Vikram Ambalal Sarabhai, known as the father of the Indian space program, founded ISRO in 1969 and established India's first rocket launching facility, TERLS. He initiated projects such as the Satellite Instructional Television Experiment (SITE) and envisioned using space technology for national development. His efforts culminated in the successful launch of India's first satellite, Aryabhata, in 1975, marking the nation's entry into the space age.

### Keywords

**Celestial object**: The common name for all the objects visible in the sky

**Star**: A huge self-luminous object made up of hot gases

**Constellation**: A group of stars in the sky that form a recognizable pattern

**Galaxy**: Huge collection of stars, smoke and dust

**Astronomical Unit (AU):** The average distance from Earth to the sun

**Light year**: Distance travelled by light in one year with a speed of 3 lakh kilometres per second

**Planet**: A celestial object in the solar system that revolves around the sun

**Satellite**: A celestial object in the solar system that revolves around a planet

**Asteroids**: The rocky remains from the formation of solar system

**Comets**: Small celestial objects made up of ice, dust and rock that revolve around the sun in very long orbits

# Summary

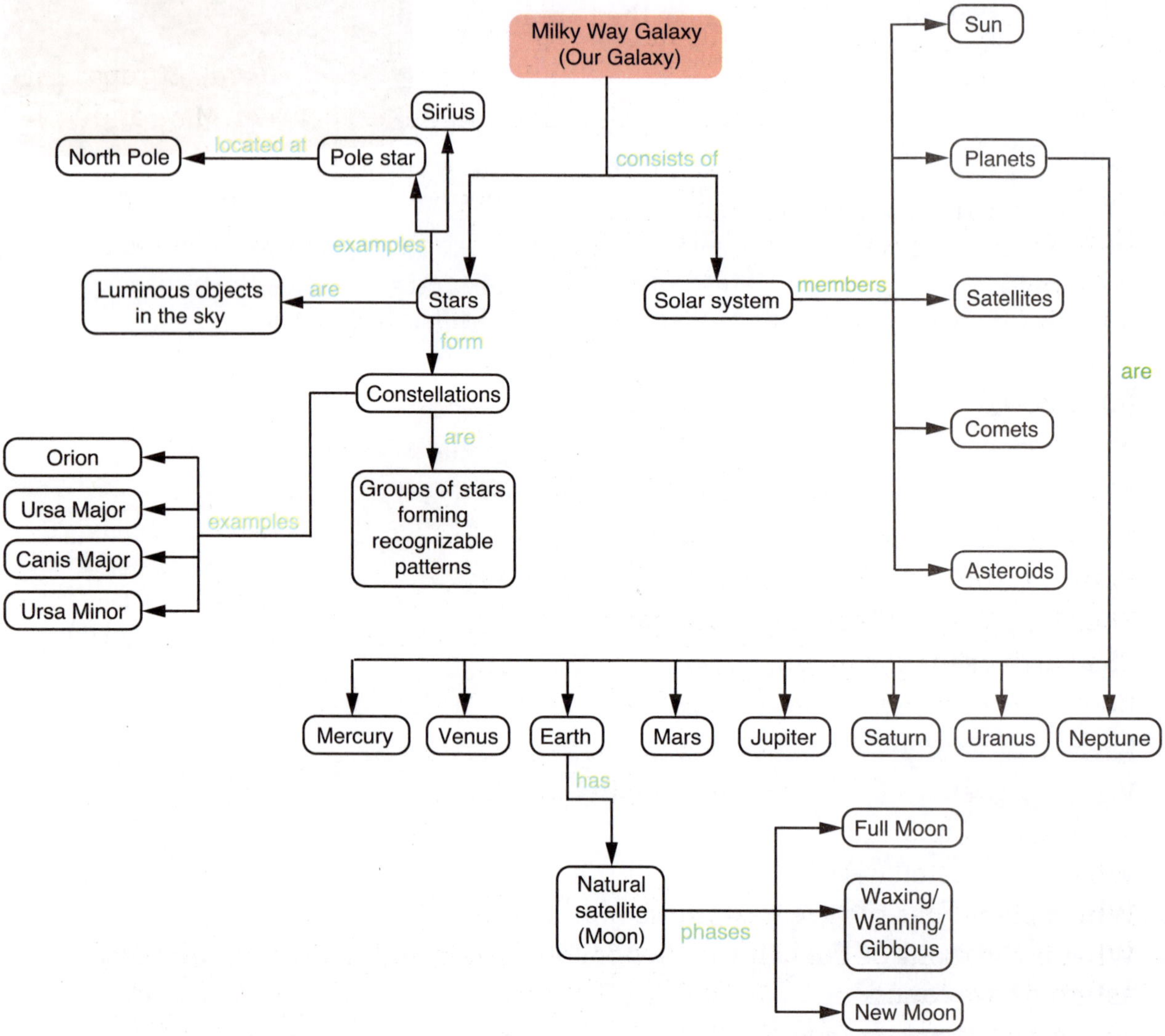

Milky Way Galaxy (Our Galaxy)
consists of
Stars
Solar system
examples
Sirius
Pole star
located at
North Pole
are
Luminous objects in the sky
form
Constellations
are
Groups of stars forming recognizable patterns
examples
Orion
Ursa Major
Canis Major
Ursa Minor
members
Sun
Planets
Satellites
Comets
Asteroids
are
Mercury
Venus
Earth
Mars
Jupiter
Saturn
Uranus
Neptune
has
Natural satellite (Moon)
phases
Full Moon
Waxing/ Wanning/ Gibbous
New Moon

# Exercise

**A. Choose the correct option.**

1. Which planet is known as the Red Planet?
   (a) Venus (b) Jupiter (c) Mars (d) Saturn
2. What is the name of Earth's only natural satellite?
   (a) Phobos (b) Titan (c) Moon (d) Europa
3. What do we call the large, rocky objects that orbit the sun between Mars and Jupiter?
   (a) Comets (b) Asteroids (c) Moon (d) Planets
4. How long does it take for the Earth to complete one orbit around the sun?
   (a) 1 year (b) 365 days
   (c) 365 days and 6 months (d) 1 and a half years
5. What is a comet made up of?
   (a) Gas and dust (b) Ice and rock
   (c) Iron and nickel (d) Water and soil

**B. State whether the following statements are true (T) or false (F).**

1. The sun is a planet in our solar system.
2. Saturn is the only planet in our solar system with rings.
3. The Milky Way is the name of our galaxy.
4. The Earth orbits the moon.
5. Comet 12P/Pons–Brooks is visible from Earth every 76 years.

**C. Answer the following questions in one sentence each.**

1. Which planet has the largest volcano in the solar system?
2. What are comets?
3. What is a constellation?
4. Which planet has the greatest number of moons?
5. What is the name of the belt that lies between Mars and Jupiter where many asteroids are found?

**D. Give reasons for the following.**

1. Venus is the hottest planet.
2. The Earth goes through different seasons.
3. Sun is also called a star.
4. Comets appear like a glowing ball with a long tail.
5. From Venus, the sun would appear to rise in the West and set in the East.

**E. Answer the following questions in brief.**

1. Define one light year.
2. Why does the pole star appear to be stationary in the sky?

3. List the different phases of the moon.
4. Define astronomical unit.
5. Differentiate between asteroids and comets.

**F. Answer the following questions in detail.**

1. What are asteroids and where can they be found in our solar system?
2. What is solar system? List the planets in order of their distance from the sun.
3. Differentiate between stars and planets.

# Cognitive Corner

## Critical Thinking

Why cannot we see the stars during the day, even though they are still present in the sky?

## Picture Study

Identify the constellation and write their name in the given space.

## Project

1. Investigate how light pollution affects astronomical observations and the study of celestial objects, and suggest a personal or community-based action to reduce light pollution's impact on astronomy. Make a detailed poster on it. **(C-6.1)**
2. Make a model of the solar system to visualize the relative sizes and positions of planets in our solar system. **(C-7.2)**
3. Create a model that demonstrates how the universe is expanding and how objects within it move apart over time.

   **Materials required:** A large balloon, a sketch pen or marker and a ruler (optional)

   **Procedure:**

   a. Start by blowing up the balloon just a little, making sure it is not too tight.
   b. Use the sketch pen to mark several dots on the surface of the balloon at almost equal distances. These dots represent galaxies in the universe.
   c. Blow up the balloon more. As you do this, observe what happens to the dots.

**Observation:** As the balloon expands, you will notice that the distance between the dots increases. This simulates how galaxies in the universe are moving away from each other as the universe expands.

How would you modify this experiment to better demonstrate the concept of the universe's expansion? If the universe is expanding, what might happen to galaxies in the far future? Can you think of any scenarios? Discuss with your classmates. **(C-6.2)**

## In the Library

1. Choose a planet (for example, Mars) and research the conditions on this celestial body and the challenges for human habitation. Make a report on it. **(C-7.1)**
2. Scientists theorize that the universe originated from a single mass approximately 13.798 ± 0.037 billion years ago. This mass suddenly exploded, causing fragments to fly outward in all directions. These fragments eventually formed stars, planets and galaxies. This explanation for the universe's formation is known as the Big Bang Theory.

   Visit a library or use reliable online sources to gather information about the Big Bang Theory. Focus on its historical context and significance in the study of cosmology.

   As you conduct your research, consider the following questions:

   a. What evidence supports the Big Bang theory?
   b. Are there alternative theories about the universe's origin?
   c. What gaps exist in our understanding of the early universe, and what questions remain unanswered by scientists today?

   Organize your research into a report or presentation. Make sure to highlight the implications of the Big Bang Theory and the challenges scientists face in understanding the universe's origins.

   Share your findings with your classmates, discussing the significance of the Big Bang Theory and any intriguing questions you uncovered during your research. **(C-9.2)**

## Life Skills

1. You and your friends are observing the night sky and notice a bright object moving slowly. Some say it is a planet, others think it is a satellite. How can you adapt your observation strategy to figure out what it is? **(C-6.2)**
2. Imagine you are part of a team planning a mission to help astronauts stay healthy in space. As the team leader, how would you take the initiative to explore the challenges they face, such as eating, exercising and sleeping in zero gravity? How would you ensure your team works efficiently and everyone contributes their best ideas? **(C-9.1)**
3. You are leading a project to design a space mission to explore another planet. How would you organize the tasks so that everyone on your team can be productive? How would you make sure the team works well together? **(C-6.1)**

# Worksheet

Artificial satellites are human-made objects placed into orbit around Earth or other celestial bodies to serve various purposes. They play a crucial role in modern technology and daily life. They are launched into space by rockets and can be positioned in various types of orbits depending on their planned function. They are equipped with sensors, cameras, antennas and other instruments required for specific functions.

A communication satellite

A. Name the first artificial satellite launched by India. What are the different types of artificial satellites?

________________________________________

________________________________________

B. List the important applications of artificial satellites.

________________________________________

________________________________________

C. Explain how artificial satellites help in communication. What role do they play in the modern communication systems used in India?

________________________________________

________________________________________

D. India's Mars Orbiter Mission (Mangalyaan) was a remarkable achievement. What made it special, and how did it contribute to our understanding of space?

________________________________________

________________________________________

E. How do weather satellites help predict natural disasters in India? Give an example of how a satellite has helped in disaster management.

________________________________________

________________________________________